Set Up/Customize menu

```
┌─────────────────────────────────────────────────┐
│ ▬▬▬▬▬▬▬▬▬▬▬▬▬▬▬▬▬▬▬▬▬▬▬▬▬▬▬▬▬▬▬            │
│              Set Up/Customize                     │
│ ─────────────────────────────────────            │
│  ▶ 1. Select/Add a Company                        │
│    2. Back Up/Restore/Copy Company Files          │
│    3. Add Company Using Data from Quicken         │
│ ─────────────────────────────────────            │
│    4. Customize Current Company                   │
│    5. Customize QuickBooks                        │
│    6. Set Up Printers                             │
│ ─────────────────────────────────────            │
│    7. Change Data Directory                       │
│ ─────────────────────────────────────            │
│  Esc-Cancel        F1-Help        ◄┘ Select       │
└─────────────────────────────────────────────────┘
```

Back Up/Restore/Copy Company Files menu

```
┌─────────────────────────────────────────┐
│ ▬▬▬▬▬▬▬▬▬▬▬▬▬▬▬▬▬▬▬▬▬▬▬           │
│  ▶ 1. Back Up Company Files               │
│    2. Copy/Shrink Company Files           │
│    3. Merge Company Files                 │
│    4. Restore Company Files               │
└─────────────────────────────────────────┘
```

Customize Current Company menu

```
┌───────────────────────────────────┐
│ ▬▬▬▬▬▬▬▬▬▬▬▬▬▬▬▬▬▬▬▬         │
│  ▶ 1. Company Information          │
│    2. Options                     │
│    3. Passwords                   │
│    4. Password Table              │
└───────────────────────────────────┘
```

Customize QuickBooks menu

```
┌───────────────────────────┐
│ ▬▬▬▬▬▬▬▬▬▬▬▬▬▬▬     │
│  ▶ 1. Options             │
│    2. Screen Colors       │
│    3. Monitor Speed       │
└───────────────────────────┘
```

Use Tutorials menu

```
┌───────────────────────────────────┐
│ ▬▬▬▬▬▬▬▬▬▬▬▬▬▬▬▬▬▬▬▬         │
│  ▶ 1. QuickBooks Overview         │
│    2. Getting Started             │
│    3. Invoicing                   │
│    4. Get Sample Company Data     │
└───────────────────────────────────┘
```

Computer users are not all alike.
Neither are SYBEX books.

We know our customers have a variety of needs. They've told us so. And because we've listened, we've developed several distinct types of books to meet the needs of each of our customers. What are you looking for in computer help?

If you're looking for the basics, try the **ABC's** series. You'll find short, unintimidating tutorials and helpful illustrations. For a more visual approach, select **Teach Yourself**, featuring screen-by-screen illustrations of how to use your latest software purchase.

Running Start books are really two books in one—a tutorial to get you off to a fast start and a reference to answer your questions when you're ready to tackle advanced tasks.

Mastering and **Understanding** titles offer you a step-by-step introduction, plus an in-depth examination of intermediate-level features, to use as you progress.

Our **Up & Running** series is designed for computer-literate consumers who want a no-nonsense overview of new programs. Just 20 basic lessons, and you're on your way.

We also publish two types of reference books. Our **Instant References** provide quick access to each of a program's commands and functions. SYBEX **Encyclopedias** and **Desktop References** provide a *comprehensive reference* and explanation of all of the commands, features, and functions of the subject software.

Our **Programming** books are specifically written for a technically sophisticated audience and provide a no-nonsense value-added approach to each topic covered, with plenty of tips, tricks, and time-saving hints.

Sometimes a subject requires a special treatment that our standard series don't provide. So you'll find we have titles like **Advanced Techniques, Handbooks, Tips & Tricks,** and others that are specifically tailored to satisfy a unique need.

We carefully select our authors for their in-depth understanding of the software they're writing about, as well as their ability to write clearly and communicate effectively. Each manuscript is thoroughly reviewed by our technical staff to ensure its complete accuracy. Our production department makes sure it's easy to use. All of this adds up to the highest quality books available, consistently appearing on best-seller charts worldwide.

You'll find SYBEX publishes a variety of books on every popular software package. Looking for computer help? Help Yourself to SYBEX.

For a brochure of our best-selling publications:

SYBEX Inc., 2021 Challenger Drive, Alameda, CA 94501
Tel: (510) 523-8233/(800) 227-2346 Telex: 336311
Fax: (510) 523-2373

SYBEX is committed to using natural resources wisely to preserve and improve our environment. As a leader in the computer book publishing industry, we are aware that over 40% of America's solid waste is paper. This is why we have been printing the text of books like this one on recycled paper since 1982.

This year our use of recycled paper will result in the saving of more than 15,300 trees. We will lower air pollution effluents by 54,000 pounds, save 6,300,000 gallons of water, and reduce landfill by 2,700 cubic yards.

In choosing a SYBEX book you are not only making a choice for the best in skills and information, you are also choosing to enhance the quality of life for all of us.

UNDERSTANDING QUICKBOOKS

UNDERSTANDING
QUICKBOOKS™

Darleen Hartley Yourzek

SYBEX®

San Francisco •Paris •Düsseldorf •Soest

ACQUISITIONS EDITOR: Dianne King
DEVELOPMENTAL EDITOR: James A. Compton
EDITOR: Marilyn Smith
PROJECT EDITORS: Michelle Nance, Kathleen Lattinville
TECHNICAL EDITOR: Cheryl Thoen
WORD PROCESSOR: Ann Dunn
BOOK DESIGNER: Based on a series design by Amparo del Rio
CHAPTER ART: Suzanne Albertson
SCREEN GRAPHICS: Aldo Bermudez
PAGE LAYOUT/TYPESETTER: Stephanie Hollier
PRODUCTION COORDINATOR/PROOFREADER: Catherine Mahoney
INDEXER: Ted Laux
COVER DESIGNER: Archer Design
PHOTOGRAPHY ART DIRECTOR: Thomas Ingalls + Associates
COVER PHOTOGRAPHER: Michael Lamotte
Screen reproductions produced with Collage Plus

Collage Plus is a trademark of Inner Media Inc.

SYBEX is a registered trademark of SYBEX Inc.

TRADEMARKS: SYBEX has attempted throughout this book to distinguish proprietary trademarks from descriptive terms by following the capitalization style used by the manufacturer.

SYBEX is not affiliated with any manufacturer.

Every effort has been made to supply complete and accurate information. However, SYBEX assumes no responsibility for its use, nor for any infringement of the intellectual property rights of third parties which would result from such use.

Library of Congress Card Number: 92-82604
ISBN: 0-7821-1164-5

Manufactured in the United States of America

10 9 8 7 6 5 4 3 2 1

To John, who clarifies my thoughts when I'm mumbling about how to explain a software program's idiosyncrasies. Thanks for keeping my hardware working and my spirits up. I can't do these books without you. And to Noah, our cat, who insists on being in the dedication because he provides moral support, distraction, and amusement, by sitting on my lap and walking across my keyboard whenever I sit down to work.

Acknowledgments

 book is always a joint effort. I would like to thank Intuit and Pam Barnett of Wilson McHenry Company for providing the QuickBooks software. I also would like to acknowledge Dianne King, always friendly, and of utmost importance, dependable; my constant savior and editor, Marilyn Smith; Cheryl Thoen, the technical reviewer who tested my examples; Michelle Nance, whose difficult task it was to pull all this together for an early deadline; Kathleen Lattinville, who assisted along the way; and the entire SYBEX team noted on the copyright page.

CONTENTS
AT A
GLANCE

TABLE OF CONTENTS

Chapter 5

SETTING UP VENDORS 71

Chapter 10
RECORDING PAYMENTS AND DEPOSITS   161

Chapter 11
MANAGING ACCOUNTS RECEIVABLE   179

Chapter 16

Chapter 17

Introduction

QuickBooks from Intuit is a bookkeeping tool for the small business owner. The software provides a method of tracking your company's financial transactions even if you don't know accounting. This book shows you how to use the software and offers tips for handling your business data.

ADVANTAGES OF QUICKBOOKS

QuickBooks is a low-priced, easy-to-use program. Here are some of its advantages:

- ◆ Minimal accounting knowledge is required because QuickBooks automates most of the bookkeeping procedures.
- ◆ The screen prompts are easy to understand.
- ◆ The on-line Help function is thorough.
- ◆ QuickBooks handles most mathematical tasks, such as extending amounts on invoices, calculating discounts and taxes, and totaling the balance in your checkbook.

◆ You can record budgets and compare your actual activity to your projections.

◆ QuickBooks provides standard reports, including a balance sheet and a profit and loss statement.

◆ By using passwords, you can restrict access to confidential financial information.

WHO SHOULD READ THIS BOOK

Understanding QuickBooks is for users who are venturing into automated bookkeeping for the first time, as well as those who want to upgrade their business procedures.

This book is written with the beginner in mind. A novice who has limited accounting experience, or whose closest contact with a computer has been a typewriter keyboard, will progress through the book and the software quickly and comfortably.

THE ACCOUNTANT'S ROLE

When you start using a computer software package, your accountant can concentrate on accounting rather than record keeping. You should seek your accountant's advice when you make the transition to an automated bookkeeping system.

From the start, an accountant can help you structure your bookkeeping data to fit your specific business needs. Don't forget to ask about federal and state regulations. Finally, look to your accountant for income tax preparation and financial counseling based on the well-organized information you can bring from your QuickBooks system.

HOW TO USE THIS BOOK

The examples used throughout this book represent real-world situations which you, as a small business owner, encounter every day. The accompanying text provides insights into procedures and concepts that will make your business easier to manage.

In *Understanding QuickBooks,* you will create a fictitious company called the Training Company. You will also set up hypothetical vendors and customers to use in the examples. The steps guide you through entering transactions, such as recording bills from vendors, writing checks, recording sales, and printing reports.

All of our activity takes place in mid-1993. The date your computer system uses affects how some data appear. QuickBooks uses the system date to determine whether transactions are current, past, or future. For example, the program may consider a check postdated when the transaction date in the tutorial is 9/6/93 and your system date is 5/20/93. However, your system date does not affect data entry.

The material is sequential; the examples will go smoothly if you start at the beginning and don't skip any exercises. Each chapter deals with a new topic that builds upon the preceding examples, building your knowledge and understanding as you go.

In the margin, you will find information related to the text:

Additional information regarding the topic under discussion is presented with this icon.

Valuable tips are presented with this icon.

Cautions and warnings are presented with this icon.

WHAT THIS BOOK COVERS

The instructions in this book cover installing the application on your computer, setting up your program, creating a company, processing your work, and printing reports. The sequence of the material follows the logical operation of a business.

Chapter 1 explains how to communicate with QuickBooks through its user interface. In Chapters 2 through 6, you will set up our sample company, including its accounts, customers, vendors, products, and services. Chapters 7 through 10 explain how to use the program for your daily work. You will learn how to record invoices from vendors, write checks, create invoices, and keep track of payments from your customers.

Chapters 11 through 15 describe how to manage your work. They include information about handling your accounts receivable, reconciling your checking and credit card accounts, working with memorized transactions, maintaining your general ledger, and generating reports. Chapter 16 guides you through entering the data for your own business into QuickBooks. Finally, in Chapter 17, you will learn how to manage your files.

The appendices contain helpful information and reference materials. Appendix A covers installing the program. Appendix B provides worksheets and information about preparing your own data for QuickBooks. Appendix C discusses using QuickBooks for recording employee payroll. Appendix D contains instructions for converting your existing data from Quicken. The glossary in Appendix E will help you understand the accounting and QuickBooks terminology used throughout the book.

CHAPTER

1

Working with QuickBooks

Working with QuickBooks involves issuing commands, entering data, and changing that data. You communicate with QuickBooks through its *user interface*, which consists of menus, keyboard commands, and mouse commands. After you become familiar with the user interface, you can begin to record information.

In this chapter, you will learn how to use the menus, keyboard, and mouse with the program. You will also learn how to enter and modify data. If you haven't already installed QuickBooks, follow the instructions in Appendix A and then return to this chapter.

A SHORT BOOKKEEPING PRIMER

Although you do not need to know accounting principles to use QuickBooks for your business finances, you should be familiar with some accounting terminology. Here's a review of some common bookkeeping terms that will be used throughout this book:

◆ A *transaction* is any financial activity, such as buying printer ribbons, selling lawn seed, or depositing money in your checking account. In a bookkeeping system, transactions are stored in accounts.

◆ An *account* is a means of classifying related transactions for grouping on reports. For example, you can print a list of all the transactions in the telephone expense account showing the money you spent on telephone bills.

◆ A *chart of accounts* is a structured list of the accounts you use to keep track of business transactions within a specific company. It contains two kinds of accounts: balance sheet accounts and profit and loss accounts.

◆ *Balance sheet accounts* are *assets* (what you own), *liabilities* (what you owe), and *equity* (the difference between your assets and liabilities, or what would remain if you paid everything that you owe). Equity applies to a business in the same sense that it applies to a home.

◆ *Profit and loss accounts* keep track of your *income* (money or value received) and your *expenses* (the costs of operation). The difference between your profit and loss accounts shows whether or not your business is successful. The profit or loss eventually affects your equity.

◆ A *general ledger* contains a summary of all your business transactions. It contains the balances in each of your accounts.

◆ A *register* is a listing of the transactions that have affected a given account. Every balance sheet account has its own unique register. For example, you will have an individual register for each checking, asset, liability, and equity account in your general ledger. Profit and loss accounts do not have registers.

Other accounting terms will be defined when they are used in the book.

STARTING QUICKBOOKS

You can turn Quick-Trainer off by selecting Set Up/Customize from the Main menu, then Customize QuickBooks, then Options. For item 1, type O and press ↵. Then press Ctrl-↵ to leave Program Options.

To start QuickBooks, at the DOS (C:\) prompt, type

    QB

The first time you start the program, a QuickTrainer window pops up. QuickTrainer is a QuickBooks Help feature. A QuickTrainer window containing helpful information appears automatically whenever you pause before taking action on a new screen. You can use the PgDn and PgUp keys to scroll through the Help text. To move to a topic and highlight it, use the Tab key. Then press ↵ to display Help text about the highlighted topic. To exit the QuickTrainer window, press Esc.

For now, read the information in the QuickTrainer window, and then press Esc. You will see the Main menu, as shown in Figure 1.1.

FIGURE 1.1:

The QuickBooks Main menu

```
              QuickBooks
              Main Menu

          1. Checkbook
          2. Invoicing/Receivables
          3. Accounts Payable
          4. Chart of Accounts
          5. Reports
          6. Company Lists
          7. Set Up/Customize
          8. Use Tutorials
       ▶  9. Register QuickBooks
          E. Exit
```

USING QUICKBOOKS MENUS

You begin your QuickBooks session at the Main menu, which is also where you should end your work with the program. Most of the options on the Main menu display a submenu of choices related to your selection. The Main menu contains the following options:

◆ **Checkbook:** Use this option to write and print checks, record activity in the check register, or reconcile your bank accounts.

◆ **Invoicing/Receivables:** Use this option to create an invoice for a sale, record payments from customers, keep track of the amount customers owe, make deposits to your bank accounts, and print invoices and customer statements.

◆ **Accounts Payable:** Use this option to record your debts to vendors and to make payments to vendors.

◆ **Chart of Accounts:** Use this option to view and maintain your general ledger accounts and to print a chart of accounts list.

◆ **Reports:** Use this option to print the financial reports provided with QuickBooks.

◆ **Company Lists:** Use this option to define customers, vendors, services, products, projects, payment terms, payment methods, and shipping methods.

◆ **Set Up/Customize:** Use this option to back up your data, set up your hardware, set up your company, and perform other setup and maintenance tasks.

◆ **Use Tutorials:** Use this option to see an overview of QuickBooks and review a sample company's transactions (provided by Intuit).

◆ **Register QuickBooks:** Use this option to register your software, as explained later in this chapter. After you register, this option will not appear on the Main menu.

◆ **Exit:** Always use this option to leave the QuickBooks program and return to DOS. If you turn off your computer before you select Exit, you could damage your files.

NOTE
NOTE
Quick-Books uses the left mouse button for most operations. The exception is that you press the right button to exit to the previous screen.

SELECTING FROM THE MAIN MENU, SUBMENUS, AND LISTS

To select an option from the Main menu or a submenu, press the number that appears next to it, such as 1 for Checkbook, or use the ↓ or ↑ key to move the cursor to the option and then press the ↵ key. If you have a mouse, you can select a menu option by positioning the mouse pointer on it and clicking the left mouse button once.

QuickBooks maintains lists of your company's records, such as the sample Customer List shown in Figure 1.2. To select from a list of items, use ↓ the or ↑ to move the cursor to the item, and then press ↵. With a mouse, point to the item and click with the mouse button to select it.

SELECTING FROM THE MENU BAR

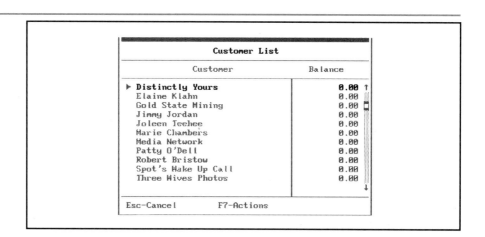 *The methods for working with memorized transactions are described in Chapter 13.*

You can press F1 from anywhere within QuickBooks to display Help text.

A menu bar appears across the top of the screen when you are writing a check, entering an invoice, or working in a register. Figure 1.3 shows the menu bar across a check-writing screen.

The menu bar contains six choices:

◆ **F1-Help:** Use this option to see Help text specific to the current screen.

◆ **F2-File/Print:** Use this option to select or set up an account, or to print checks, transactions in a register, invoices, statements, labels, or the QuickBooks supply order form.

◆ **F3-Find/Edit:** Use this option to find and edit transactions, to view transaction history, or to access the Notepad. The Notepad is a QuickBooks accessory that you can use to enter notes. It is described later in this chapter.

◆ **F4-Lists:** Use this option to view lists, to memorize and recall transactions and invoices, and to select a transaction group to process.

FIGURE 1.2:

A Customer List

```
                    Customer List

        Customer                      Balance

▶ Distinctly Yours                       0.00  ↑
  Elaine Klahn                           0.00
  Gold State Mining                      0.00
  Jimmy Jordan                           0.00
  Joleen Teehee                          0.00
  Marie Chambers                         0.00
  Media Network                          0.00
  Patty O'Dell                           0.00
  Robert Bristow                         0.00
  Spot's Wake Up Call                    0.00
  Three Wives Photos                     0.00
                                               ↓

  Esc-Cancel         F7-Actions
```

FIGURE 1.3:

The check-writing screen menu bar

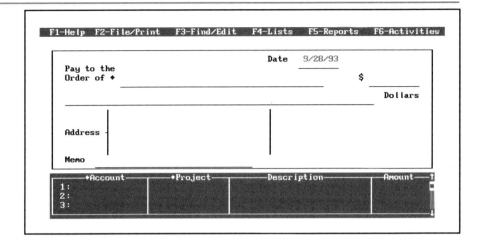

- ◆ **F5-Reports:** Use this option to select a report to process.
- ◆ **F6-Activities:** Use this option to write checks or invoices, to record receipt of payments or deposits, to reconcile check and credit card accounts, and to access the Calculator or DOS.

To select a menu bar option, press the function key listed with it or click on the option with your mouse. You can also use Ctrl-key combinations to bypass some of the pull-down menus, as explained in the next section.

USING CTRL-KEY SHORTCUTS

See the inside cover of this book for a complete list of Ctrl-key combinations and the functions they access.

Throughout the program, you can use Ctrl-key combinations to access functions quickly. QuickBooks sometimes uses the same key combinations to access different functions. For example, Ctrl-D deletes the selected transaction in a register, and it resets the options when you are choosing to print a report.

Several Ctrl-key combinations apply when the menu bar appears across the top of the screen; other combinations are listed at the bottom of the screen when they are available. In this book, the Ctrl-key combination will be noted within the discussion of the function it accesses.

GETTING HELP

You can learn more about the QuickBooks program by using its Help system. From anywhere in the program, press F1 or click on F1 (in a menu bar) with your mouse to see Help information. The Help text relates to the screen currently displayed on your monitor.

Press PgDn or PgUp to scroll through the Help window. To display Help text about a field or topic that appears in a Help window, use the ↓ or ↑ key to move the cursor to it, and then press ↵ to display the related text. You can also double-click on the topic with a mouse.

If you want to select from a list of Help topics, press Ctrl-F1 to display the Help Index. With the mouse, click on F1 (from a register, check-writing, or invoice-entry screen, for example), and then click on Index.

When you are finished reading the Help text, press Esc or click the *right* mouse button to exit the Help function.

REGISTERING YOUR SOFTWARE

The Register QuickBooks option appears until you register your software. You can use QuickBooks only a limited number of times without registering your copy. After you register, you will have access to Intuit's customer support services, and you will receive any new releases (not versions) of QuickBooks that may be issued to correct minor problems with the software.

Select the Register QuickBooks option from the Main menu by pressing the ↓ key to highlight it and then pressing the ↵ key, or by moving the mouse pointer to it and clicking with the left mouse button. The Registration screen explains how to register your software. It shows the toll-free number for the QuickBooks registration desk.

Be prepared to give your name, address, and software serial number when you call to register your software. You will be given a registration number. You should enter that number into the Customer Number field in the Registration screen and write it on your QuickBooks Customer Assistance card in your QuickBooks manual.

Whenever you call Intuit for information, you will be asked for your customer number. You can press C at the Main menu to display this number.

ENTERING YOUR DATA

You enter data in QuickBooks in much the same way as in most up-to-date software. You use the keyboard characters to type in text and numbers. You can also use the numeric keypad to enter numbers. However, if it is not a dedicated numeric keyboard (numbers only, not combined with cursor-movement keys), you must press the Num Lock key to turn on the Num Lock function before you can use the keypad to type in numbers.

MOVING THE CURSOR

To enter data in the appropriate place, you will need to move the cursor to that position. QuickBooks includes keystrokes for moving between and within fields, from screen to screen, and from line to line. Table 1.1 lists the cursor-movement keys.

You can also use a mouse to move the cursor within and among fields. Simply point to the new position and click the mouse button. To move through screens, drag the scroll box in the scroll bar along the right side of the screen, and then click where you want the cursor to appear. To exit to the previous screen, click the *right* mouse button once.

ENTERING DATA IN A FIELD

To enter data in a field, move the cursor to that field and type in the text or numbers from the keyboard. After you finish typing data into a field, press the ↵ key to record the information and move the cursor forward to the next field. You can also use the Tab key or a mouse to move to the next field.

By default, QuickBooks is in Insert mode, in which the character you type is inserted above the cursor and existing characters are moved to the right. You can change to Overtype mode, in which the character you type replaces (overwrites) the existing character above the cursor, by pressing the Insert key. To return to Insert mode, press the Insert key again.

While you are entering data, you may need to make changes to what you have typed. You can use the following methods to edit field entries:

◆ To move the cursor to the previous word in a field, press Ctrl-←.

◆ To move the cursor to the next word in a field, press Ctrl-→.

TABLE 1.1:
Cursor-Movement Keys

KEYSTROKE	DESCRIPTION
Home	Moves to beginning of current field
End	Moves to end of current field
Home Home	Moves to first field on the screen
End End	Moves to last field on the screen
Ctrl-←	Moves to previous word in a field
Ctrl-→	Moves to next word in a field
Tab	Moves forward one field
Backward Tab (Shift-Tab)	Moves backward one field
↵	Moves to next field
PgUp	Moves to previous screen
PgDn	Moves to next screen
Ctrl-PgUp	Moves to previous check or invoice
Ctrl-PgDn	Moves to next check or invoice
Ctrl-S	Moves to voucher area of check
Ctrl-↵	Moves to next area of invoice
↑	Moves up one line
↓	Moves down one line

The Insert key toggles between Insert and Overwrite mode, which means that you press the same key to change from one mode to the other.

- ◆ To erase the character above the cursor and close the space, press the Delete key.

- ◆ To erase the character to the left of the cursor but leave the space, press the Backspace key.

- ◆ To delete characters with a mouse, position the mouse pointer on the first character you want to delete, hold down the mouse button, drag the pointer through all the characters to be erased, and release the button when all the characters are highlighted.

ENTERING DATES

By default, QuickBooks uses the current (system) date for all your entries. You can change transactions to another date in two ways:

◆ Change the date in increments. To move the date forward one day at a time, press the plus (+) key. To move the date backward one day at a time, press the minus (−) key.

◆ Type in the specific date. Enter the date in *MMDDYY* format.

When you type in a date while QuickBooks is in Insert mode, or if you erased the date, you must include the slashes between the month, day, and year. When you are in Overtype mode, you don't need to type the slashes; QuickBooks will add them for you. For example, to enter February 7, 1993, while in Overtype mode, type 020793. It will appear on the screen as 02/07/93.

If QuickBooks displays the prompt

Please enter the date in MM/DD/YY format

include the slashes in your entry.

ENTERING MONETARY AMOUNTS

QuickBooks records all monetary amounts as whole dollars unless you indicate otherwise. To record cents, you must type the decimal point between the dollars and the cents. However, you should not include any dollar signs or commas in your entries.

For example, if you want to enter one thousand, two hundred, sixty-seven dollars, type 1267. To enter twelve dollars and sixty-seven cents, you would type 12.67.

SELECTING A FIELD ENTRY FROM A COMPANY LIST

When you set up your company in QuickBooks, you add records to lists of related items, such as account numbers, customers, vendors, products, services, and projects. A small diamond beside a field name indicates that you

To have Quick-Books help you find a record in a displyed list, type the first character of the entry you want to make in the field. The program will scroll to the first record that begins with that character.

can select a record that has already been defined. During data entry, you can display the related list of defined records, find the item you want to place in the field, and have QuickBooks insert it for you.

To select a field entry from a list, press Ctrl-L while the cursor is in the field. Use the PgDn or PgUp key (or the scroll bar) to scroll through the list. When you find the record, highlight it and press ↵, or click on it with the mouse. QuickBooks will insert the entry in the field that contains the cursor.

ADDING RECORDS DURING DATA ENTRY

If you are entering data and discover that you need a record that you have not already defined, you can add the new record without leaving the current function. For example, if you enter the code of a new product in the Item Code field of an invoice, QuickBooks will notify you that it cannot find that item. You can choose to select an item from the list of defined records or to add the item to the list.

When you select to add the record, QuickBooks displays a window for filling in information about the item. After you have completed the fields in that window, you can proceed with the invoice or whatever data-entry screen you were using.

SAVING YOUR ENTRIES

When the cursor moves through the last field on a screen, QuickBooks saves the data you entered. The program is set up to request confirmation before saving your entries. When you complete a check, invoice, or transaction in a register, you will see the prompt

OK to Record Transaction?

You can set the program to skip the confirmation prompt by selecting Set Up/Customize from the Main menu, then Customize QuickBooks, then Options. For item 3, type *N* and press ↵. Then press Ctrl-↵ to leave Program Options.

If you want to skip the remaining fields on a data-entry screen, you can press Ctrl-↵ or F10 to save the entries you have made. With the mouse, click on Ctrl-↵.

CHANGING OR DELETING DATA

If you simply change or delete data, you will not have a record of what went before. Instead of changing or deleting a transaction, you should enter a transaction that corrects or offsets the original one.

In QuickBooks, almost every action you take or entry you make can be changed, even after you have saved it. You can revise check amounts, account names, transactions amounts, and other entries. You can delete transactions even after they have been completed.

To change a transaction, simply type over what exists in the fields and select to save the changes. To change a record, display the appropriate list, highlight the record, and press Ctrl-E. When the record appears, change the data, and then save the changes.

For example, to change the name of a customer, select Company Lists from the Main menu, choose Customers from the submenu, highlight the customer's name, and press Ctrl-E to recall the record. Enter the new name, and then press Ctrl-↵ of F10 to save the revised record.

To delete an item, highlight it and press Ctrl-Del. Press ↵ when Quick-Books asks you to confirm the deletion.

USING QUICKBOOKS ACCESSORIES

QuickBooks provides two accessories to help you with your work in the program: the Calculator and the Notepad. You can use the Calculator for simple calculations and even insert the results in the field where the cursor is located. The Notepad provides a place to keep notes on a specific customer or vendor.

CALCULATING WITH THE CALCULATOR

The Calculator works much like a regular pocket calculator. You can enter numbers from the keyboard or from the numeric keypad (when the Num Lock function is turned on).

To pop up the Calculator, press Ctrl-C from anywhere within the program. You must enter the appropriate mathematical operator to let the program know whether to add (+), subtract (−), multiply (*), or divide (/) values; calculate percentages (%); or total the calculation (=). To use the results of an equation in your next calculation, press ↵ to make it your first entry in the next step.

To clear the entry, press the letter C. Press F9 to paste the result into the field from which you accessed the Calculator. When you are finished using the Calculator, press Esc to exit.

USING THE QUICKBOOKS NOTEPAD

You can access the Notepad from three areas in the software:

◆ From the customer or vendor list, place the cursor on the name to which you want to attach notes, press Ctrl-E to edit, and then press Ctrl-N to access the Notepad.

◆ In a register, place the cursor on a transaction containing the name of a vendor or customer, and then press Ctrl-N.

◆ From the check-writing screen, move the cursor to a transaction containing the name of a customer or vendor, and then press Ctrl-N.

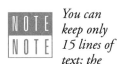 *You can keep only 15 lines of text; the top line is deleted when you begin a sixteenth line.*

From the Notepad, you can press F9 to paste the current date into your notes. The Insert key toggles text entry between Insert and Overwrite mode. Use the Delete key to delete characters, or Ctrl-Backspace to delete the line on which the cursor is located.

To record what you have written and exit the Notebook, press Ctrl-⏎. To cancel any changes you made, press Esc.

Now that you know how to give commands to QuickBooks and record your data, you are ready to use the program. Chapter 2 describes how to set up QuickBooks for your computer system and for your company records.

CHAPTER

2

Setting Up QuickBooks and Your Company

efore you begin to set up your files, you should be familiar with the QuickBooks user interface, which was described in Chapter 1. Then you can adjust the screen display, set up for printing, and set program options.

After you have set up the program, you are ready to set up your company. In this chapter, you will define a sample company, which will serve as your training ground for entering transactions, printing reports, and performing other tasks with QuickBooks.

SETTING UP YOUR MONITOR AND PRINTER

Your work in QuickBooks will be more enjoyable if you set up the screen display according to your own preferences. You can set the program to work with either a color or monochrome monitor.

The other hardware you need to set up from within QuickBooks is your printer. You can print three types of documents in QuickBooks: checks, invoices, and financial reports. You can use two separate printers or one printer with a different format set for each type of document.

ADJUSTING MONITOR SETTINGS

Intuit suggests that you choose Shades of Gray for LCD screens; select Red/Gray if you are color-blind.

QuickBooks provides color scheme choices for color and monochrome monitors. To specify the colors you want to use, select the Set Up/Customize option from the Main menu, choose Customize QuickBooks from the submenu, and then choose the Screen Colors option. You will see a list of five choices:

◆ Monochrome

◆ Navy/Azure

◆ White/Navy

◆ Red/Gray

◆ Shades of Gray

The Monochrome and Shades of Gray options are for monochrome monitors; the others are for color monitors.

Select a color scheme, and you will immediately see the results of your choice. If you have a color monitor, you may want to test each of the color choices. You can return and change the settings at any time. Press Esc three times to return to the Main menu after you have set your screen colors.

QuickBooks is set up for a fast monitor. You cannot change this monitor setting unless you have a CGA monitor. If your CGA screen looks fuzzy, changing the monitor speed to slow should help. From the Main menu, select Set Up/Customize, then Customize QuickBooks, then Monitor Speed. Choose Slow to change the quality of the image displayed on the screen.

SETTING UP FOR PRINTING

QuickBooks provides settings for many popular printers. You can select from among several predefined printer setups. Before proceeding, make sure that your printer is properly connected. Follow the steps below to set up for printing with the program. As explained in Chapter 1, you can select a menu option by using the ↑ or ↓ key to move the cursor to it and then pressing ↵, or by clicking on it with your mouse.

1. Choose Set Up/Customize from the Main menu, and then select Set Up Printers from the submenu.

2. Press ↵ to set up Printer 1.

3. In the Choose Printer Brand list, select the name of your printer. If your printer is not listed, select a compatible model. You see the Set Up Printer 1 window, with the default settings for your printer. Figure 2.1 shows the window for a Hewlett-Packard (HP) LaserJet printer.

4. For the Printer Name setting, press ↵ to accept the printer you chose as printer 1.

For Printer Port, LPT1 is selected because most printers use this port, which is parallel port 1. If your printer is not connected to LPT1, you can choose from a list of other ports. The list includes the parallel ports PRN, LPT2, and LPT3 and the serial ports AUX, COM1, and COM2.

5. For the Printer Port setting, press ↵ to accept the default of LPT1, or press Ctrl-L to select from the list of other ports and then press ↵.

The next settings are for the four types of documents that you can print: Check Style, Invoice Style, Report Style 1, and Report Style 2. You can accept the default pitch (which is the default pitch supported by the printer you chose) and orientation for each document style.

See your printer manual for information about compatible printer models and the port your printer uses. You can also check with your hardware dealer.

FIGURE 2.1:

Setting up printer 1

```
                    Set Up Printer 1

  ◆Printer name  : HP LaserJet
  ◆Printer Port  : LPT1  (parallel port #1)
  ──────────────── Styles ────────────────
  ◆Check style   : 10 cpi, Portrait
  ◆Invoice style : 10 cpi, Invoice
  ◆Report style 1: 10 cpi; Portrait
  ◆Report style 2: 17 cpi; Portrait

        Press Ctrl-L for list of printers
  Esc-Cancel          F1-Help          Ctrl↵ Done
```

The default pitch depends on the type of printer you are using.

The pitch is how many characters per inch (cpi) can be printed horizontally; 10 pitch is like Pica on a typewriter, 12 pitch is like Elite, and 17 pitch is compressed print. If you are using $8\frac{1}{2}$-inch wide paper, a setting of 10 cpi typically prints 80 characters on a line. If you use 12 cpi, the maximum is 96 characters per line; 17 cpi should result in 132 characters on a line. The orientation is how the characters will be printed across the paper. Portrait orientation prints down the length of the page, and landscape prints across the width.

6. For each document style, press ↵ to accept the default pitch and orientation, or press Ctrl-L to select from a list of document styles and then press ↵.

7. When you are finished specifying your printer settings, press Ctrl-↵ or F10.

8. Press Esc twice to return to the Main menu.

To set up another printer, follow the steps above, but choose to set up Printer 2 instead of Printer 1.

CUSTOMIZING QUICKBOOKS

You can change options and then accept the settings for the remaining ones by pressing Ctrl-↵.

You can adjust other QuickBooks settings to suit your work habits and personal preferences. To see the program options, select Set Up/Customize from the Main menu, then Customize QuickBooks from the submenu, then Options. You will see the Program Options screen, shown in Figure 2.2.

For the examples presented in this book, we will accept all but one of the default settings. For your own work with the program, you may want to make some other changes. On the Program Options screen, the settings you can enter are shown in parentheses next to each option. Here is an explanation of how the ten options affect the program:

1. You can set QuickTrainer to pop up immediately (S for Short), after a long period of no keyboard input (L for Long), or not at all (O for Off).

Program options for cus-
tomizing QuickBooks

```
                  Program Options
─────────────────────────────────────────────────
   1. QuickTrainer lag: Short/Long/Off (S/L/O): S
   2. Beep when recording and memorizing (Y/N): Y
   3. Request confirmation (for example,
         when changing the Register)     (Y/N): Y
   4. MM/DD/YY or DD/MM/YY date format    (M/D): M
   5. Days in advance to remind of scheduled
         bills, invoices, and groups   (0-30): 3
   6. Bizminder active                   (Y/N): Y
   7. 43 line register/reports (EGA,VGA) (Y/N): N
   8. On new checks/invoices, start with the
         Payee/customer or Date field    (P/D): P
   9. Double-click speed for mouse (0 turns
         mouse off)                      (0-9): 4
  10. Warn to deposit payments received  (Y/N): N
─────────────────────────────────────────────────
 Esc-Cancel          F1-Help          Ctrl◄─┘ Done
```

2. QuickBooks can beep while it is recording or memorizing so that you know an action is taking place (Y for Yes), or not beep during these activities (N for No).

3. QuickBooks can require users to confirm that they want to take the requested action, such as change or delete a transaction (Y for Yes), or not require confirmation (N for No).

4. You can print dates in *month/day/year* format, such as December 4, 1993 (M for month first), or *day/month/year* format, such as 4 Dec 93 (D for day first).

5. QuickBooks will notify you in advance of postdated checks or scheduled transaction groups according to the number of days you indicate (0 to 30).

6. If you loaded Bizminder, you can turn it off at any time (N for No), or leave it on (Y for Yes). If you did not install Bizminder initially, you can install it later from the QuickBooks installation disk.

7. If you have an EGA or VGA monitor, you can select to take advantage of the larger display and view 43 or 50 lines, respectively, of a register or report (Y for Yes), or keep the smaller display (N for No).

If you enter transactions after the fact, or are entering many old, outstanding documents when setting up your books, beginning at the Date field makes it easy to change the date to the day the transaction took place.

8. You can choose whether you want the cursor to begin in the Date field (D for Date) or the Payee/Customer field (P for Payee) when entering invoices and checks.

9. You can set the mouse to respond to slow or to fast double-clicking (1 to 9) or turn off the mouse (0).

10. QuickBooks will notify you when you have entered payments from customers and have not yet selected them for a deposit (Y for Yes), or not display a message (N for No).

We want to turn off QuickTrainer, so that we won't be interrupted by it while performing our work. Follow these steps:

1. Move the cursor to item 1.

2. Type **O** for Off and press ↵.

3. Press Ctrl-↵ to record the change and exit the Program Options screen.

4. Press Esc twice to return to the Main menu.

Now we will set up QuickBooks files to define our sample company.

SETTING UP A COMPANY

Even if you have already set up your company in QuickBooks, follow the steps here to define a new company for the exercises in this book.

To learn how to use QuickBooks, you will set up a hypothetical company, named the Training Company. You will add the company files to the default directory that QuickBooks created when you installed the software.

You do not have to set up your files in any order, and you can change the information at any time. The sequence outlined here simply ensures that your setup procedure flows smoothly and you do not overlook anything.

A diamond beside a field means you can fill the field with predefined information from a list.

ADDING A COMPANY

To begin setting up the company we will use throughout this book, follow these steps:

1. Choose Set Up/Customize from the Main menu, and then select Select/Add a Company from the submenu. You see the Add New Company window, as shown in Figure 2.3.

FIGURE 2.3:

Adding a company

```
┌─────────────────────────────────────────────────────────────────┐
│ ▓▓▓▓▓▓▓▓▓▓▓▓▓▓▓▓▓▓▓▓▓▓▓▓▓▓▓▓▓▓▓▓▓▓▓▓▓▓▓▓▓▓▓▓▓▓▓▓▓▓▓▓▓▓▓▓▓▓▓▓▓▓▓ │
│                         Add New Company                           │
│ ───────────────────────────────────────────────────────────────── │
│  Your Company's name:                                             │
│    (Enter the name of the company or person these accounts are for)│
│                                                                   │
│                                                                   │
│  ◆Preset income/expense accounts to use:                          │
│    (The "◆" symbol means you can press Ctrl-L for a List of choices)│
│ ───────────────────────────────────────────────────────────────── │
│  Esc-Cancel                 F1-Help                 Ctrl◄─┘ Done  │
└─────────────────────────────────────────────────────────────────┘
```

2. For your company's name, type **Training Company**, and then press ↵. The cursor advances to the next field, in which you indicate which accounts (chart of accounts) you want to use in your company.

You can select accounts from a predefined list, or enter None in this field and set up your own chart of accounts.

3. Press Ctrl-L to display your choices for preset Income and Expense accounts to use.

If you do not add the standard accounts at this point, you cannot return to do so later.

If you use one of the charts of accounts supplied by QuickBooks, you will probably need to add accounts and edit existing ones. You should also take the time to remove the accounts that you don't need from the sample list to conserve space on your disk. However, for our sample company, we will create our own chart of accounts instead of selecting a predefined one. You will learn how to add, edit, and delete accounts in Chapter 3.

4. Press ↵ to select the highlighted item, None.

5. Press ↵ to accept the entry, None, in the Preset Income/Expense Accounts to Use field. The Creating Company Files window appears.

QuickBooks uses the name of the company as the file name, but the name is truncated to eight characters. You can change the file name if you prefer to use another one. If you do enter a different file name when you are setting up your own files, use the DOS file-naming requirements: eight characters maximum, and without colons, slashes, periods, tildes, or square brackets. Also, do not add a three character extension.

6. Press ↵ to accept the company file name supplied by QuickBooks.

In the next field, you specify the drive, directory, and subdirectory in which to store the files for the new company. You can accept the location suggested by QuickBooks, or enter a different one. If you designate a different location when you are setting up your own files, you must enter a directory and subdirectory that already exist. QuickBooks will not create them for you.

7. Press ↵ to accept the default location. The files are created and the Chart of Accounts screen appears, as shown in Figure 2.4.

QuickBooks sets up the four accounts listed on the Chart of Accounts screen, whether or not you chose to use the preset accounts. In this chapter, we will finish supplying company information. In Chapter 3, we will add and edit accounts to complete the chart of accounts.

8. Press Esc to return to the Main menu.

FIGURE 2.4:

The initial chart of accounts

```
                    Chart Of Accounts
                 Company: Training Company

        Account            Type         Description        Balance

  ▶                    Balance Sheet                              ↑
      Receivables          A/R        A/R Account              0
      Payables             A/P        A/P Account              0
      Sales Tax            A/P        Sales Tax Payable        0
      Open Bal Equity      Equity     Opening Bal Equity       0
                       Income/Expense

                                                               ↓
                 ✳ - Account has items to act upon
  Esc-Cancel              F7-Actions                  Ctrl◄─┘ Done
```

If you have been using Quicken and want to convert your existing data into QuickBooks, read Appendix D before setting up your own company.

DEFINING A COMPANY

To complete the definition of our company, follow these steps:

1. From the Main menu, choose Set Up/Customize. From the submenu, select Customize Current Company, and then choose Company Information. The Company Information screen appears.

The company name you entered when adding the new company appears on the first line, and the cursor waits on the second line. The information you enter here will become the heading on your reports. Figure 2.5 shows the Company Information screen filled in with the data we will enter for our company.

NOTE
NOTE

Your Employer ID number is the number assigned to you by the federal government. Your company uses this number when reporting wages and paying taxes.

2. Type the street address of our company: **1 Way 2 Learn**. Then press ↵ to record your entry and move to the next line.

3. Type **Entrepreneurville, CA 95876** to complete the address.

4. Press ↵ three times to leave the last two lines for the address blank and move the cursor to the Employer ID number field.

5. Type **94-1234567** as the federal tax identification number for our company, and then press ↵.

The last two fields are for specifying shipping information. If you do not have a product-based business, you can leave them blank. However, our sample company does ship items, so we will complete these fields.

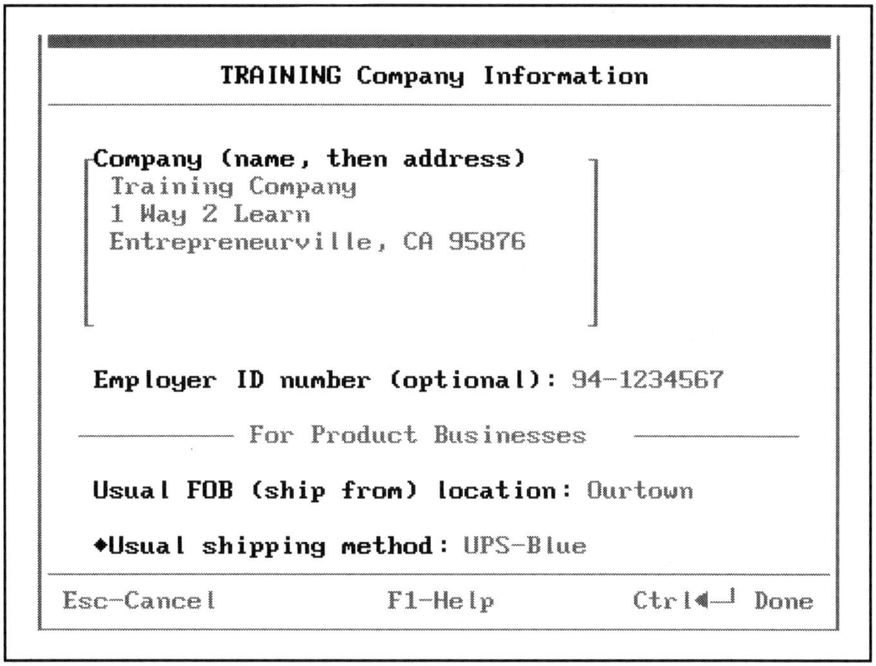

FIGURE 2.5:

Entering your company information

```
╔══════════════════════════════════════════════════╗
║          TRAINING Company Information             ║
╟──────────────────────────────────────────────────╢
║  ┌Company (name, then address)─────────┐          ║
║   Training Company                                ║
║   1 Way 2 Learn                                   ║
║   Entrepreneurville, CA 95876                     ║
║                                                   ║
║                                                   ║
║  └──────────────────────────────────┘             ║
║                                                   ║
║   Employer ID number (optional): 94-1234567       ║
║  ──────────── For Product Businesses ──────────   ║
║                                                   ║
║   Usual FOB (ship from) location: Ourtown         ║
║                                                   ║
║   ◆Usual shipping method: UPS-Blue                ║
╟──────────────────────────────────────────────────╢
║  Esc-Cancel          F1-Help          Ctrl◀┘ Done ║
╚══════════════════════════════════════════════════╝
```

6. In the Usual FOB (ship from) Location field, type **Ourtown** as the name of the place from which we assess freight charges, and then press ↵.

7. In the Usual Shipping Method field, press Ctrl-L to display a list of shipping methods.

8. Select UPS-BLUE from the list.

QuickBooks inserts your selection in the field, and because it is the last field on the screen, the program records your entries and exits the option. The Customize Current Company submenu reappears. Now we will set options for our company.

SELECTING COMPANY OPTIONS

You can adjust QuickBooks settings to designate how you want transactions handled in this company. To see the company options, select Options from the Customize Current Company submenu. You will see the Customize Options screen, as shown in Figure 2.6.

For our sample company, we will accept most of the default settings. When you set up your own company, you may want to make some other changes. On the Customize Options screen, the settings you can enter are shown in parentheses next to each option. Here is an explanation of how the 15 options affect how company transactions are handled by the program:

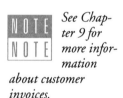

See Chapter 9 for more information about customer invoices.

1. QuickBooks provides three invoice formats: Service (S), Professional (Prof), and Product (Prod). The type you choose determines how much detail prints on a customer's invoice. Product invoices contain the most detail. Service invoices do not include item codes or shipping fields. Professional invoices have more space for a detailed description, but they do not contain the other fields that relate to billing for products.

2. When you enter a payment from a customer, QuickBooks can either apply it to every invoice, from the oldest to the most recent, until the payment is used (B for Balance Forward), or you can apply any amount to any invoice manually (O for Open Item). If you select the Balance Forward method, you can still override the payment made by QuickBooks and distribute the payment differently.

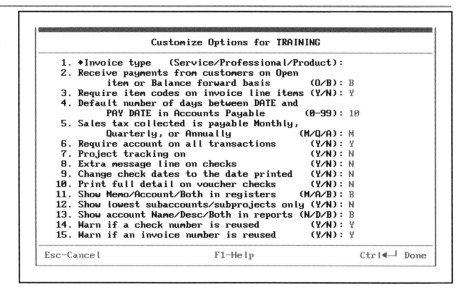

FIGURE 2.6:

Setting company options

*Requiring
item codes
ensures an
accurate
accounting of the
number of units sold
for each product and
service.*

*To
have an
accurate
picture of
all your business ac-
tivities, you should
assign each transac-
tion to an account.*

3. You can set the program so that each item on the invoice that has an amount must have a corresponding item code from your predefined list (Y for Yes), or not require an item code (N for No).

4. You can set the average number of days most vendors allow you from the invoice date before you must pay the invoice (0 to 99). Although you can establish a variety of payment terms for your customers, QuickBooks allows only one set of predefined terms for invoices you receive from vendors.

5. QuickBooks assigns a due date to the liability you incur for sales tax entered on a customer's invoice according to your choice of monthly (M), quarterly (Q), or annually (A). The time frame is set for your business by the government agency who collects the tax.

6. You can specify whether or not QuickBooks will force you to enter an account for each transaction (Y for Yes or N for No). Entries not assigned to a designated account will be assigned to system-generated default account titled Other.

7. You can turn project tracking on to assign transactions to projects (Y for Yes), or leave project tracking off (N for No). When you turn on project tracking, QuickBooks displays the Project field on accounts payable and checking transactions, but it does not require a project on every transaction.

8. You can add a message line to your checks next to the address (Y for Yes), or leave out the extra message line (N for No). The message will print with the check, but it will not be recorded in your register.

9. You can have QuickBooks use the current date on printed checks and in the related register (Y for Yes), or leave the date when the check was entered (N for No).

10. If you use the voucher check format, you can include the general ledger account on those checks (Y for Yes), or omit the information (N for No).

11. You can display only the memo (M), only the account (A), or both kinds of information (B) for each transaction in the registers.

12. QuickBooks will list all primary and all subaccounts and primary and subprojects in the account or project field on transactions (N for No), or only the subaccount or subproject to which you charged the transaction (Y for Yes). For example, when this option is set to No, you will see *Utilities:Electric*. If you set it to Yes, you will see *Electric*.

13. On reports, you can print only the account name (N), only the account description (D), or both kinds of information (B). If you use numbers to identify your accounts, the alphabetical description will be helpful.

14. QuickBooks can warn you if you are recording a duplicate check number in the register for a given account (Y for Yes), or not issue a warning (N for No).

15. QuickBooks can warn you if you are recording a duplicate invoice number from a given vendor or a duplicate of an accounts receivable invoice you issued in your company (Y for Yes), or not issue a warning (N for No).

If you have a numeric chart of accounts, you should set company option 12 to Y. See Chapter 3 for more information about subaccounts.

For our sample company, we will change the default settings for only two options, numbers 1 and 4. We will use the Service invoice format and change the vendor terms to 30 days. Follow these steps to set the options:

1. In the Invoice Type field, type **S** and press ↵ to record your entry.

2. Press the Tab key three times to move the cursor to option 4.

3. For the number of days between the invoice date and the pay date, type **30** and press ↵ to record the change.

4. Press Ctrl-↵ to skip the other fields and exit the Customize Options screen. You return to the Customize Current Company submenu.

5. Press Esc twice to return to the Main menu.

In this chapter, you set up QuickBooks for printing and to accommodate your screen color preferences and work habits. You also defined the Training Company, which is the hypothetical company we will use in the examples throughout the book. In the next chapter, you will learn how to add accounts to form our chart of accounts.

CHAPTER

3

Creating a Chart of Accounts

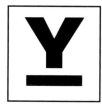**Y**ou define accounts in QuickBooks to keep track of the business transactions within your company. As explained in Chapter 1, your accounts fall into two categories: balance sheet accounts and profit and loss accounts. The accounts you set up form the chart of accounts.

In this chapter, we will add a representative set of accounts to our chart of accounts. These accounts will be used in the examples in this book.

WORKING WITH QUICKBOOKS ACCOUNTS

QuickBooks tracks your financial activity within 12 account types:

♦ **Checking Account accounts:** Identify your bank accounts such as checking, savings, and money market accounts.

♦ **Accounts Receivable accounts:** Include all the amounts owed to you by your customers.

- **Current Asset accounts:** Identify the items you own which are or can be converted quickly to cash. These include petty cash, advance payments, and deposits you have made.

- **Fixed Asset accounts:** Identify large items you own, such as your office building or automobiles. A fixed asset can depreciate or appreciate, so you will want to make entries to keep track of their decreasing or increasing value.

- **Accounts Payable accounts:** Include all the small purchases for which the vendor extended payment terms.

- **Credit Card accounts:** Identify the various charge cards you use.

- **Current Liability accounts:** Include amounts you must pay within a short period of time, such as payroll or sales taxes.

- **Long-Term Liability accounts:** Record your long-standing debts, such as the mortgage or a car loan.

- **Equity accounts:** Show what your ownership in the business is worth.

- **Income accounts:** Keep track of each type of revenue you generate.

- **Expense accounts:** Keep track of each cost of operating your business.

- **Subaccount accounts:** Divide broadly defined Income or Expense accounts into greater detail. For example, the Repairs account could be divided into Auto, Truck, and Equipment *subaccounts*. With this definition, you could report on your total maintenance expenses, then break out the amount you spent just on auto repairs. The *primary account*, Repairs, accumulates (rolls up) amounts from its lower subaccounts.

Within each account type, you can have several accounts. For example, under Checking Accounts, you might have a regular checking account, a checking account just for payroll, a savings account, and a money market account. Under Credit Cards, you might have a gasoline company credit card or a hardware supply store credit card. Under Fixed Assets, you might have the office building you own or the company car.

Transactions in each individual record increase or decrease that account's *balance*. In a bank account, typical transactions are deposits that increase your balance, checks that decrease the balance, and service charges that also decrease your balance.

ENTERING ACCOUNT BALANCES

One reason for using QuickBooks is to have accurate, up-to-date accounting information. For your balance sheet to reflect accurate data, you must record the current balance for each account when you initially define it. Thereafter, QuickBooks will update the balances automatically during routine processing. These balances, which summarize your transactions, are your general ledger.

During setup, QuickBooks uses a unique account, called the Opening Balance Equity account. At the end of setup, the balance in this account should be zero. If it is not, you have a profit or loss, resulting from your previous activity, that has not been transferred to an Equity account. The opening balances from balance sheet accounts create an offsetting entry in the Opening Balance Equity account.

You must enter current balances in all your general ledger balance sheet accounts, except for your Accounts Receivable and Accounts Payable accounts, when you define the accounts. As you enter the outstanding invoices for your customers and vendors, the program accumulates the balance for your Accounts Receivable and Accounts Payable accounts.

In QuickBooks, you do not enter opening balances directly in Income or Expense accounts. The program keeps a running balance in these accounts when you enter your customer (income) and vendor (expense) invoices.

IDENTIFYING ACCOUNTS

QuickBooks allows you to use account identifiers that are alphabetical or numeric. It is standard to use account numbers in this scheme:

    1000 - Assets
    2000 - Liabilities
    3000 - Equity
    4000 - Income
    5000 - Expense

In the examples in this book, we will use numeric account identifiers. You may choose to use words to identify your own accounts when you set up your actual company files.

DEFINING ACCOUNTING PERIODS

Chapter 15 describes how to generate QuickBooks reports.

QuickBooks, unlike other accounting packages, does not separate transactions into accounting periods, however many reports group transactions by calendar months. The date you enter for each transaction dictates where it falls in the continuum of activity.

Several reports allow you to include data for a date range you select. You do not close the period, nor the year; however, at year-end, you may want to make entries that adjust some account balances.

SETTING UP BALANCE SHEET ACCOUNTS

In the following sections, we will set up the balance sheet accounts that we will use for our sample company. These include Checking Account, Accounts Receivable, Current Asset, Fixed Asset, Accounts Payable, Credit Card, Long-Term Liability, and Equity accounts.

Note that in this chapter, and throughout the rest of the book, rather than instructing you to type something and then press ⏎, the term *enter* will be used. This means to type the information and enter it by pressing ⏎.

DEFINING A CHECKING ACCOUNT

The first account we will add is a Checking Account. Figure 3.1 shows the completed definition.

Follow these steps to enter the Checking Account information:

You can use the Ctrl-Ins key combination whenever you want to add a new record.

1. Select Chart of Accounts from the Main menu.

2. Press F7 (Actions), and then press ⏎ to select the Add New option. QuickBooks displays the Select Type of Account To Add window.

3. Under the Asset Accounts column, select Checking.

4. In the Name for this account field, enter **1000**. Our Training Company will use the traditional chart of accounts numbering scheme.

5. Enter the amount of money we have in our checking account, **25382.90**, in the Account Balance field. Remember to type the decimal point between the dollars and cents, but don't enter a comma between hundreds and thousands.

```
┌──────────────────────────────────────────────────────────────┐
│ ████████████████████████████████████████████████████████████ │
│                    Add New Checking Account                    │
│ ──────────────────────────────────────────────────────────── │
│  Name for this account: 1000                                   │
│                                                                │
│  Account balance: 25,382.90      as of:  9/ 1/93               │
│ ─────────────────── (Optional Information) ────────────────── │
│  Description: Countrywide Bank                                 │
│                                                                │
│  Notes/Account number: 1-360118                               │
│ ──────────────────────────────────────────────────────────── │
│ Esc-Cancel                F1-Help              Ctrl◄┘ Done     │
└──────────────────────────────────────────────────────────────┘
```

6. The As Of field shows the system date. Press Ctrl-Backspace to erase that date, and then enter **09/01/93**. This is the day the balance in our checkbook was $25,382.90. You should not use the bank statement balance because you could have outstanding checks or deposits the bank has not yet recorded.

7. In the Description field, enter **Countrywide Bank**, the institution where we have our checking account.

8. In the Notes/Account Number field, enter **1-360118**, the account number assigned to our checking account by the bank.

When you complete the last field, the Chart of Accounts screen reappears, with the new account listed within its type.

EDITING THE ACCOUNTS RECEIVABLE ACCOUNT

We need to change the Accounts Receivable account supplied by Quick-Books so that the account suits our company's setup. Figure 3.2 shows the edited account.

Follow these steps to modify the Accounts Receivable account:

1. Highlight the Receivables account on the Chart of Accounts screen and press Ctrl-E to edit it. The View/Edit Accounts Receivable window appears.

2. Press Ctrl-Backspace to delete the existing name.

```
┌─────────────────────────────────────────────────────┐
│ ▓▓▓▓▓▓▓▓▓▓▓▓▓▓▓▓▓▓▓▓▓▓▓▓▓▓▓▓▓▓▓▓▓▓▓▓▓▓▓▓▓▓▓▓▓▓▓▓▓▓▓▓▓ │
│       View/Edit Accounts Receivable Account           │
│ ───────────────────────────────────────────────────── │
│   Name for this account: 1100                         │
│                                                       │
│   Description (optional): Accounts Receivable         │
│ ───────────────────────────────────────────────────── │
│   Esc-Cancel          F1-Help          Ctrl◄─┘ Done   │
└─────────────────────────────────────────────────────┘
```

3. Enter **1100** as the new name for this account. This account identifier is in accordance with our numeric account identification
scheme.

4. In the Description field, type **Accounts Receivable** over the existing
characters.

5. Press Ctrl-↵ to record the changes.

You do not enter an opening balance for the Accounts Receivable account.
It will be established from the customer invoices we will enter later.

DEFINING A CURRENT ASSET ACCOUNT

Assets other than bank accounts, accounts receivable, and fixed assets are
categorized under the general heading Current Assets. We will set up three
examples of a current asset: petty cash, prepaid insurance, and beginning
inventory.

Setting Up a Petty Cash Account

Petty cash is an amount of money you keep on hand to purchase small items,
such as coffee for the lunch room or tips for a delivery person.

When you create a petty cash account, you can count the cash you have
on hand and enter that as a beginning balance, or you can write a check to
establish the account. We will use the latter method to set up the petty cash
account shown in Figure 3.3.

FIGURE 3.3:

Setting up a petty cash account

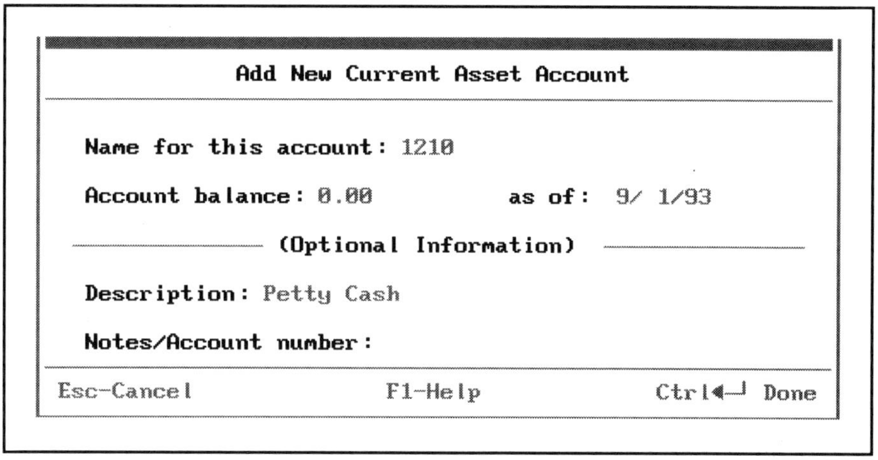

```
┌─────────────────────────────────────────────────────────┐
│  ▓▓▓▓▓▓▓▓▓▓▓▓▓▓▓▓▓▓▓▓▓▓▓▓▓▓▓▓▓▓▓▓▓▓▓▓▓▓▓▓▓▓▓▓▓▓▓▓▓▓▓▓▓   │
│              Add New Current Asset Account                │
│  ───────────────────────────────────────────────────────│
│                                                           │
│   Name for this account: 1210                            │
│                                                           │
│   Account balance: 0.00         as of:  9/ 1/93          │
│   ──────────────── (Optional Information) ─────────────   │
│   Description: Petty Cash                                 │
│                                                           │
│   Notes/Account number:                                  │
│  ───────────────────────────────────────────────────────│
│   Esc-Cancel            F1-Help          Ctrl◀┘ Done     │
└─────────────────────────────────────────────────────────┘
```

Follow these steps to set up the petty cash account for our sample company:

1. Press Ctrl-Ins to add a new account. In the Select Type of Account To Add window, under the Asset Accounts column, select Current Asset.

2. In the Name for this Account field, enter **1210**.

3. Press ↵ in the Account Balance field, leaving it at zero. Later, we will establish the petty cash fund from money already in our checking account.

4. Enter **090193** in the As Of field.

5. In the Description field, enter **Petty Cash**.

6. Press ↵ in the Notes/Account Number field to leave it blank.

Entering Prepaid Insurance

Payments you give in advance of incurring the expense are called *prepaid expenses*. In our example, we paid our vehicle insurance a year in advance. Other examples of advance payments are prepaid rent and utility deposits.

Follow these steps to define the prepaid insurance account for our sample company:

1. Press Ctrl-Ins, and then select to add a Current Asset account.

2. In the Name for this Account field, enter **1220**.

3. Enter **544** in the Account Balance field. QuickBooks makes the entry whole dollars. This is the amount of the advance payment that remains unused.

4. Enter **090193** in the As Of field.

5. In the Description field, enter **Prepaid Insurance**.

6. Enter **P20854**, our insurance policy number, in the Notes/Account Number field.

Recording Beginning Inventory

Inventory is the merchandise you have on hand to sell. It is also an asset. QuickBooks does not maintain a count of the number of the items on hand, nor track inventory's increasing and decreasing value as you purchase and resell merchandise. You should calculate and enter the value of your merchandise at the time you begin QuickBooks, then periodically adjust the amount. We will discuss adjustments later in the book. For now, we will enter the beginning value. Follow these steps:

1. Press Ctrl-Ins and select to add a Current Asset account.

2. In the Name for this Account field, enter **1230**.

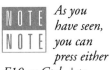
As you have seen, you can press either F10 or Ctrl-↵ to record a transaction. Use the method you prefer.

3. Enter **8600** in the Account Balance field. This is the amount that we have determined our current stock is worth.

4. Enter **090193** in the As Of field.

5. In the Description field, enter **Inventory**.

6. Press F10 to skip the Notes/Account Number field and record the account definition.

CREATING A FIXED ASSET ACCOUNT

Our business owns a new delivery truck, some farm machinery, and acreage. We could set up a separate account for each asset, but for our sample company, we will lump everything into one Fixed Asset account. Your accountant may advise you to keep track of each asset separately, rather than combining them into one account.

Follow these steps to set up the account with its opening balance:

If you press ↵ in the last field, QuickBooks records the entry.

1. Press Ctrl-Ins and select to add a Fixed Asset account.

2. In the Name for this Account field, enter **1310**.

3. Enter **58600** in the Account Balance field. This is the combined purchase price of our fixed assets.

4. Enter **090193** in the As Of field.

5. In the Description field, enter **Land & Equipment**.

6. Press ↵ in the Notes/Account Number field to leave it blank. If we were setting up separate accounts, we would enter the license plate of the truck, the model number for the machinery, or the address of our property.

ENTERING ACCUMULATED DEPRECIATION

Accumulated depreciation is an account that tracks the reduction in value of an asset due to normal wear and tear. It is called a *contra asset account* because its balance is deducted from another asset account, Fixed Assets. Together, the two accounts provide a picture of the asset's true value. In our example, we record all our fixed assets in one account, and lump the accumulated depreciation for all those assets in another single account. The completed information is shown in Figure 3.4.

Follow these steps to set up the contra asset account for our sample company:

The IRS determines how you can depreciate each asset. Consult your tax accountant before recording depreciation for your own assets.

1. Press Ctrl-Ins and select to add a Fixed Asset account.

2. In the Name for this Account field, enter **1315**.

FIGURE 3.4:

Setting up an accumulated depreciation account

```
╔═══════════════════════════════════════════════════════╗
║              Add New Fixed Asset Account              ║
╟───────────────────────────────────────────────────────╢
║                                                       ║
║   Name for this account: 1315                         ║
║                                                       ║
║   Account balance: -4,580.00     as of:  9/ 1/93      ║
║                                                       ║
║ ───────────────── (Optional Information) ───────────  ║
║                                                       ║
║   Description: Accum. Depreciation                    ║
║                                                       ║
║   Notes/Account number:                               ║
║ ───────────────────────────────────────────────────  ║
║  Esc-Cancel            F1-Help           Ctrl◄─┘ Done ║
╚═══════════════════════════════════════════════════════╝
```

3. Enter − (minus sign) **4580** in the Account Balance field. The account balance is *subtracted* from the total of the Fixed Assets account type.

4. Enter **090193** in the As Of field.

5. In the Description field, enter **Accum. Depreciation**.

6. Press ⏎ in the Notes/Account Number field.

EDITING THE ACCOUNTS PAYABLE ACCOUNT

Just as we changed the QuickBooks-supplied Accounts Receivable account to suit our company setup, we also need to edit the Accounts Payable account provided by the program. Follow these steps to change the name and description of the account:

1. On the Chart of Accounts screen, highlight Payables and press Ctrl-E to edit the account.

2. Press Ctrl-Backspace to delete the existing name.

3. Enter **2000** as the new name for this account.

4. In the Description field, type **Accounts Payable** over the existing characters.

5. Press Ctrl-⏎ to record your entries.

The opening balance for this account will be established from the unpaid vendor invoices we will enter later.

EDITING THE SALES TAX PAYABLE ACCOUNT

If you collect sales tax for several districts, you cannot record each district in separate liability accounts. However, you will have a record of the transaction history (charges and payments) in the individual vendor records.

A sales tax payable account is created for you by QuickBooks. If your business operations do not require that you collect sales tax on your sales, you can delete this account.

For our sample company, we will use the supplied sales tax payable account. We just need to change its name to fit into our numeric scheme. Follow these steps:

1. On the Chart of Accounts screen, highlight Sales Tax and press Ctrl-E to edit the account.

2. Press Ctrl-Backspace to delete the existing name.

3. Enter **2010** as the new name for this account.

4. Press F10 to skip the remaining field and record the change.

Entries you make for sales tax on customer invoices will be recorded in this one liability account.

CREATING A CREDIT CARD ACCOUNT

Using plastic can be a real convenience, especially if you travel and don't want to carry cash. However, many of us tend to look upon items and services obtained with plastic as free. Your QuickBooks Credit Card accounts remind you that your charges are debts you must eventually pay.

Credit Card accounts keep track of the purchases, payments, and finance charges on your charge cards. The amount you owe on your credit cards qualifies as a liability. You can set up as many accounts as you have cards. Each account has its own register, which you can use to reconcile against your monthly bill from the credit card company.

For our sample company, we will set up one Credit Card account for a gasoline credit card. Figure 3.5 shows the completed information.

FIGURE 3.5:

Setting up a credit card account

```
┌─────────────────────────────────────────────────────────────┐
│ ▬▬▬▬▬▬▬▬▬▬▬▬▬▬▬▬▬▬▬▬▬▬▬▬▬▬▬▬▬▬▬▬▬▬▬▬▬▬▬▬▬▬▬▬▬▬▬▬▬▬▬▬▬▬▬▬ │
│              Add New Credit Card Account                     │
│ ─────────────────────────────────────────────────────────── │
│                                                              │
│  Name for this account: 2110                                 │
│                                                              │
│  Account balance: 15.80          as of:  9/ 1/93             │
│                                                              │
│  ───────────────── (Optional Information) ───────────────    │
│                                                              │
│  Description: Dutch Oil                                       │
│                                                              │
│  Credit limit: 1,000.00                                      │
│                                                              │
│  Notes/Account number: 450-69112                             │
│                                                              │
│  ◆Vendor:                                                    │
│     (Press F1 for an explanation of the Vendor field)        │
│ ─────────────────────────────────────────────────────────── │
│  Esc-Cancel              F1-Help            Ctrl◄─┘ Done      │
└─────────────────────────────────────────────────────────────┘
```

Follow these steps to set up the Credit Card account:

1. Press Ctrl-Ins and, under the Liability Accounts column in the Select Type of Account To Add window, select Credit Card.

2. In the Name for this Account field, enter **2110**.

3. Enter **15.80** in the Account Balance field. This is the amount outstanding on our charge card.

4. Enter **090193** in the As Of field.

5. In the Description field, enter **Dutch Oil**.

6. In the Credit Limit field, enter **1000**, the most the gasoline company lets us charge. The register calculates and displays the amount of credit remaining after each transaction you enter.

7. Enter the credit card number, **450-69112**, in the Notes/Account Number field.

Notice the Vendor field has a diamond, indicating that QuickBooks expects an entry from a predefined list. We could display the vendor list (which is currently empty) and add a vendor to use for this Credit Card account. Instead, we will leave the Vendor field blank for now and return to complete this record after setting up all our vendors.

8. Press F10 to skip the Vendor field and record the account.

CREATING CURRENT AND LONG-TERM LIABILITY ACCOUNTS

When we bought the delivery truck, we got a five-year loan from the bank. The loan amount is recorded in a Long-Term Liability account. Follow these steps to set up the account:

1. Press Ctrl-Ins and select to add a Long-Term Liability account.

2. In the Name for this Account field, enter **2310**.

3. Enter **13748** in the Account Balance field. This is the amount that remains unpaid on the loan.

4. Enter **090193** in the As Of field.

5. In the Description field, enter **Truck Loan**.

6. Enter **28032-4**, the number assigned to our loan by the bank, in the Notes/Account Number field.

Our sample company does not have any short-term, or current, liabilities right now. If we did, we would set up a Current Liability account, using the same procedure as we did for the Long-Term Liability account. The only difference is the account type you select in the Select Type of Account To Add window.

CREATING AN EQUITY ACCOUNT

Equity, or ownership in the business, can be divided into several separate accounts. In a small business, the following three accounts are usually sufficient:

◆ A *capital account* reflects one owner's portion.

◆ A *drawing account* reflects what an owner has taken out of the business. Each partner should have both a capital and a drawing account.

◆ A *retained earnings* account shows the amount of profits the owners have set aside for future company growth.

Currently, the Training Company is a sole proprietorship, but negotiations are underway to add a partner. We will set up the present owner's accounts.

Adding a Capital Account

Follow these steps to add a capital account for our sample company:

1. From the Chart of Accounts screen, press Ctrl-Ins and select to add an Equity account. Equity is under the Liability Accounts column, because what is owed to the owner is a liability to the business as a whole after all other liabilities are paid.

2. In the Name for this Account field, enter **3010**.

3. Enter **48200** in the Account Balance field. This amount reflects the value of the land (25,000) the owner brought into the business, the cash (10,000) the owner used to start the business, and some of the profits (13,200) from last year.

4. Enter **090193** in the As Of field.

5. In the Description field, enter **Owner's Capital**.

6. Enter **Phyllis**, the name of the owner, in the Notes/Account Number field.

Adding a Drawing Account

Follow these steps to add a drawing account:

1. Press Ctrl-Ins and select to add an Equity account.

2. In the Name for this Account field, enter **3015**.

3. Enter – (minus) **12000** in the Account Balance field. This is the total amount of cash the owner has taken out of the business this year. QuickBooks will subtract this amount from the total of our Equity account types.

4. Enter **090193** in the As Of field.

5. In the Description field, enter **Owner's Draw**.

6. Enter **Phyllis** in the Notes/Account Number field.

Adding a Retained Earnings Account

Follow these steps to add a retained earnings account:

1. Press Ctrl-Ins and select to add an Equity account.

2. In the Name for this Account field, enter **3500**.

3. Enter **36800** in the Account Balance field. This is the amount of profit that is being set aside in the company as a financial "cushion." It is actually part of the owner's equity, but it is maintained in a separate account earmarked as reserve.

4. Enter **090193** in the As Of field.

5. In the Description field, enter **Retained Earnings**.

6. Press F10 to leave the Notes/Account Number field blank and record the account information.

Printing the Chart of Accounts

Now that all our balance sheet accounts are entered, let's print a report to verify our entries. Follow the steps below:

1. Be sure the printer cable is connected to the computer and the printer is turned on.

2. Press F7 (Actions) and select Print. The Print Chart of Accounts window appears, with the name of your printer in the Print To field.

3. Press ↵ to accept that printer. The report is sent to the printer.

You can use the Ctrl-P key combination to print a report without displaying the Actions pull-down menu.

Compare your report to the one shown in Figure 3.6. If they do not match, read the following section.

The chart of accounts with its balance sheet accounts

```
                        Chart Of Accounts|Company: Training Company
Training Company                                                    Page 1
9/ 1/93

       Account              Type            Description            Balance
    --------------      --------------   ------------------------  ----------

                        Balance Sheet
       1000             Checking         Countrywide Bank          25,382.90
       1100             A/R              Accounts Receivable            0.00
       1210             Cur Asset        Petty Cash                     0.00
       1220             Cur Asset        Prepaid Insurance            544.00
       1230             Cur Asset        Inventory                  8,600.00
       1310             Fxd Asset        Land & Equipment          58,600.00
       1315             Fxd Asset        Accum. Depreciation       -4,580.00
       2000             A/P              Accounts Payable               0.00
       2010             A/P              Sales Tax Payable              0.00
       2110             Cred Card        Dutch Oil                    -15.80
       2310             L-T Liab         Truck Loan               -13,748.00
       3010             Equity           Owner's Capital          -48,200.00
       3015             Equity           Owner's Draw              12,000.00
       3500             Equity           Retained Earnings        -36,800.00
   Open Bal Equity      Equity           Opening Bal Equity        -1,783.10

                        Income/Expense
```

EDITING AND DELETING ACCOUNTS

You can edit any field in the original account definition except the Balance field. To edit the account name or description, highlight the account on the Chart of Accounts screen and press Ctrl-E to display the View/Edit window. When the account appears, make the necessary changes to the data already in the field, and then press F10.

If you made a mistake in the balance, the easiest way to correct it is to delete the account and reenter the account information. You cannot change an account balance by editing the account definition. The Balance field is no longer available after the initial opening balance entry, regardless of whether or not you delete the transaction from the register.

Note that you cannot delete an account that has transactions linked to another balance sheet account (called *transfers*). Therefore, you must delete the transaction that opened the account (because a transfer entry was made in the offsetting Opening Balance Equity account for each opening balance we entered), before you can delete the account itself.

Follow these general steps to remove an account with an incorrect balance:

1. Highlight the account on the Chart of Accounts screen, and then press ↵ to display the account register.
2. Press the ↑ key to highlight the Opening Balance entry.
3. Press Ctrl-Del to delete the transaction. QuickBooks asks you to confirm the deletion.
4. Select Delete Transaction.
5. Press Esc to exit the register.
6. Select Chart of Accounts from the Main menu.
7. Highlight the account that was in error and press Ctrl-Del to delete the account definition. Read the warning that appears.
8. Enter **Yes** to confirm that you want to delete the account.
9. Reenter the account following the instructions given earlier in this chapter.

 After all your beginning account balances are correct and you have started entering daily transactions, you should not delete a general ledger account.

When you set up your own company, you might choose to use one of the account lists supplied by QuickBooks. Before you begin using QuickBooks on a daily basis, you should delete any of those accounts that are not applicable to your business.

SETTING UP INCOME AND EXPENSE ACCOUNTS

Income and expense accounts are collectively called the profit and loss accounts. Income accounts show how you generate revenue. Most of the revenue in a business comes from selling products or services; some comes from interest you earn on loans to others, money in a savings account, or dividends on investments.

QuickBooks starts keeping track of how much you sold or how much you incurred in expenses as you begin entering new invoices to your customers or from your vendors.

CREATING INCOME ACCOUNTS

The Training Company separates income into two accounts: pet products and equine products. Pet products include dog, cat, and bird items. The company records horse-related revenue, rental of pastureland, and sale of hay under equine products. Figure 3.7 shows the completed information for the pet products account.

Another type of Income account is for sales returns. When someone returns a product, you should note the amount as a reduction in the amount of your sales. The sales returns account is a *contra revenue account*. It reduces the related Income account to arrive at your net sales. You keep the account separate so you can judge how many items are being returned and take steps to eliminate the cause of the lost sales.

FIGURE 3.7:

*Setting up an
Income account*

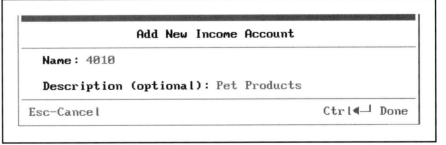

```
                    Add New Income Account

    Name: 4010

    Description (optional): Pet Products

  Esc-Cancel                              Ctrl◄┘ Done
```

Follow these steps to create the Income accounts for our sample company:

1. Select Chart of Accounts from the Main menu.
2. Press Ctrl-Ins to add an account and select Income.
3. In the Name field, enter **4000**. This account number will appear on the Chart of Accounts screen as part of the Income/Expense category title.
4. In the Description field, enter **Title**. QuickBooks records the title.
5. To add our first account, press Ctrl-Ins and select Income.
6. In the Name field, enter **4010**.
7. In the Description field, enter **Pet Products**. Notice we do not enter an opening balance for an Income account.

When you press ↵ in the Description field, the account is added to the Chart of Accounts screen under the Income/Expense heading. Now let's continue and add the equine products and sales return accounts.

8. At the Chart of Accounts screen, select to add another Income account.
9. Enter **4020** for the Name and **Equine Products** for the Description.
10. At the Chart of Accounts screen, select to add another Income account.
11. Enter **4055** for the Name and **Sales Returns** for the Description.

CREATING EXPENSE ACCOUNTS

The Training Company separates expenses into many different accounts. One of the Expense accounts, Merchandise Purchases, relates directly to sales; it records how much we pay for the products we resell. Merchandise purchased for resale usually falls into the category *cost of goods*.

Expense accounts, like Income accounts, do not include an opening balance in the definition. Follow these steps to add our first Expense account:

1. At the Chart of Accounts screen, press Ctrl-Ins and select to add an Expense account.
2. In the Name field, enter **5000**.
3. In the Description field, enter **Merchandise Purchases**.

When you press ↵ in the Description field, the account is added to the Chart of Accounts screen under the Income/Expense accounts.

The other Expense accounts we will use for our sample company are listed below. Add each account as an Expense account type following the instructions above. Be sure to highlight Expense in the Select Type of Account To Add window.

NAME	DESCRIPTION
5110	Auto/Truck Expense
5120	Crop Maintenance
5130	Depreciation Expense
5140	Insurance Expense
5150	Miscellaneous Expense
5160	Office Supplies
5170	Subscriptions
5180	Travel Expense

Creating Subaccounts

You can create subaccounts only for Income or Expense accounts. We will place two subaccounts beneath our primary expense, travel. The completed information for the first subaccount is shown in Figure 3.8.

FIGURE 3.8:

Adding a subaccount

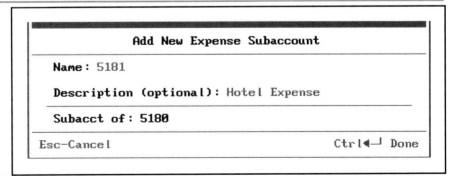

Add New Expense Subaccount

Name: 5181

Description (optional): Hotel Expense

Subacct of: 5180

Esc-Cancel   Ctrl◀↵ Done

NOTE NOTE *When you have sub-accounts, you must record transactions in the subaccounts, not in the primary account.*

Follow the steps below to set up the Expense subaccount for our sample company:

1. Highlight Travel Expense on the Chart of Accounts screen and press Ctrl-Ins.

2. Exp Subaccount, under the Income/Expense column, should already be highlighted. Press ↵ to select it.

3. Enter **5181** in the Name field.

4. Enter **Hotel Expense** in the Description field.

We will add another subaccount for meals directly under the primary account. We will keep meal expenses separate because of IRS regulations, which currently do not allow businesses to take the full amount paid for meals as a deduction.

5. Highlight Travel Expense again on the Chart of Accounts screen, press Ctrl-Ins, and select to add an Exp Subaccount.

6. Enter **5182** in the Name field.

7. Enter **Meals Expense** in the Description field.

The new subaccounts appear on the Chart of Accounts screen, indented under their primary account.

REVIEWING THE PROFIT AND LOSS ACCOUNTS

Print a new Chart of Accounts report, as explained earlier in this chapter, to review your Income and Expense account entries. Then press Esc to return to the Main menu.

The report does not include a balance for Income or Expense accounts, even after you enter transactions. Instead, you can determine the total activity for a specified time period by printing the Profit and Loss report (see Chapter 15).

If you discover an error in the Chart of Accounts report, edit the Income or Expense account to make changes to the account definition, as explained earlier in this chapter.

In this chapter, you learned how to set up each type of QuickBooks account. These accounts form your chart of accounts, and their balances are entries in your general ledger. Now that you have created the general ledger accounts for our sample company, you are ready to set up other company records. In the next chapter, you will enter information about customers.

CHAPTER

4

Setting Up Customers

n Chapter 2, we set up QuickBooks and company parameters, the foundation of your system. In Chapter 3, we
set up a chart of accounts, which forms the foundation
of financial books. Now you will learn how to set up
and maintain your customer records.

You can add, edit, or delete records from your files at any time and in
any order. However, for efficiency, we will set up the records that will be used
in our customer file before we define a customer record.

SETTING UP CUSTOMER TYPES

QuickBooks classifies customers by type. It provides a list of predefined customer types, which you can edit to suit your company setup. For our sample
company, we will delete three types and add two new ones.

REMOVING CUSTOMER TYPES

The Dealer, Distributor, and Manufacturer customer types are not applicable to the Training Company. Follow these steps to delete them from the list:

1. Select Company Lists from the Main menu. The Select List submenu appears, as shown in Figure 4.1.

2. Choose Customer Types from the submenu. You see the list of predefined types. The cursor waits on the first type, Dealer.

3. Press Ctrl-Del to delete the Dealer type, and then press ↵ to confirm the deletion.

4. Highlight the next type, Distributor.

5. Press Ctrl-Del and confirm that you want to delete this type.

6. Highlight Manufacturer, press Ctrl-Del, and then press ↵ to delete it.

FIGURE 4.1:

The Select List submenu

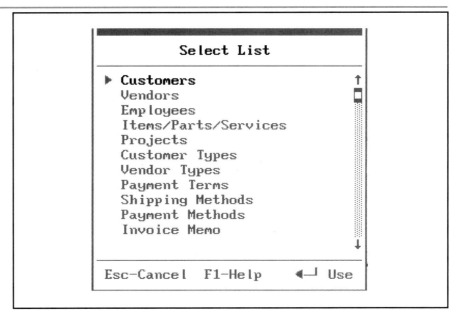

ADDING CUSTOMER TYPES

Our company wants to be able to review how much we sell to individuals, to other businesses who use our products and services, and to wholesale companies who resell products we provide to them. This information will help direct our marketing efforts. QuickBooks has already supplied the Wholesaler customer type, so we need to add only the Individual and Business types.

Follow these steps to add customer types to the list:

1. From the Customer Type List, press Ctrl-Ins to add a type. The Add New Customer Type window appears.

2. Enter **Individual** in the Customer Type field. The new type is added to the list.

3. Press Ctrl-Ins again and enter **Business** in the Customer Type field. You should now see Business, Individual, and Wholesaler on your list of customer types.

4. Press Esc to return to the Select List menu.

DEFINING CUSTOMER PAYMENT TERMS AND METHODS

QuickBooks uses terms codes to define the time in which a customer's invoice is due, the discount percentage (if any), and the number of days the discount can be taken. *Net* means when the balance on an invoice is due. One of the most common payment terms is Net 30, which means that the entire invoice, with no discount allowed, is due 30 days from the invoice date. The predefined terms supplied by QuickBooks appear on the Terms List.

Payment methods show how your customers pay their invoices. The predefined methods appear on the Payment Methods menu.

DELETING A TERMS CODE

The Training Company will not offer a 1 percent discount if the customer pays an invoice within 10 days of the invoice date. Follow these steps to delete that code from the list:

1. Choose Payment Terms from the Select List menu.

2. Highlight the terms code 1% 10 Net 30.

3. Press Ctrl-Del, and then press ↵ to confirm the deletion.

ADDING A TERMS CODE

Now we will add a typical terms definition: 3%, 15 days, Net 45. This means that customers can take a 3 percent discount if they pay within 15 days after the invoice date; otherwise, the total invoice is due in 45 days. The completed information for the new terms code is shown in Figure 4.2.

FIGURE 4.2:

Entering a terms code

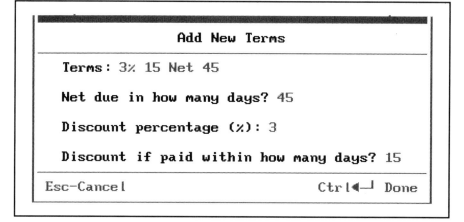

Follow these steps to add the terms code to the list:

1. From the Terms List, press Ctrl-Ins to add a code.

2. In the Terms field, enter **3% 15 Net 45**.

3. For the Net Due in How Many Days? field, enter **45**.

4. Enter **3** for Discount Percentage. QuickBooks automatically converts the number to a percent; don't type a decimal point or percent sign.

5. For the Discount If Paid Within How Many Days? field, enter **15**.

6. Press Esc to return to the Select List menu. The new terms code appears on the Terms List.

REVIEWING PAYMENT METHODS

The QuickBooks predefined customer payment methods include cash, check, and some major credit cards. These methods are suitable for our sample company, but for your own company, you might want to add some other credit cards that you accept.

You can use the categories to group payments for deposits and to verify the accuracy of your deposit slip. Keeping a separate record for each credit card you accept allows you to analyze the value versus the cost of accepting the charge card, as well as to confirm the amount you should deposit to your account with the credit card institution.

To see the list of payment methods, select Payment Methods from the Select List menu. When you are finished reviewing the list, press Esc to return to the Select List menu.

SETTING UP EMPLOYEE RECORDS

 You can override the employee assigned to a customer only on product format invoices. See Chapter 9 for details.

Your employee records can help you keep track of the sales made by each employee, as well as the expenses charged to each one. You can assign an employee (or sales representative) to a customer, and that employee will receive credit for all invoices entered for that customer. However, you are not required to assign a sales representative to each customer. For example, our company assigns representatives only to business customers, not to individuals who purchase items from the retail floor.

You can print reports that total sales by employee, so you can use QuickBooks as a basis for calculating commissions. The reports can also list all the expenses charged to each employee.

When you write checks to an employee, usually for wages, the address in the employee record appears on the check. Using QuickBooks for payroll is discussed in Appendix C.

We will add one employee record to our company files. Follow these steps to enter the employee information:

1. Select Employees from the Select List menu. The Employee List appears.

2. Press Ctrl-Ins to add an employee.

3. Enter **KMW** in the Initials field.

4. Enter the following employee name and address:

> **Kenneth M. Wade**
> **14 Gogetum Lane**
> **Quotaville, CA 95679**

5. Press F10 to save the record.

6. Press Esc to return to the Select List menu.

DEFINING YOUR SHIPPING METHOD

If you are using product format invoices (for a product-based business), your invoice form includes a field for the method to be used to deliver the merchandise to the customer. You enter the method that you will usually use as part of your company setup, as described in Chapter 2. However, you can override that method when you are entering an invoice.

QuickBooks provides a list of predefined shipping methods. As with the other lists, you can add or delete choices as necessary. To see the predefined methods, select Shipping Methods from the Select List menu. When you are finished reviewing the list, press Esc to return to the menu.

CREATING INVOICE MEMOS

Instead of handwriting messages on your customer invoices, you can have QuickBooks print them for you neatly. Figure 4.3 shows the predefined messages on the Invoice Memo List.

You can use the messages supplied by QuickBooks as they are or edit them to suit your needs. You can also define your own memos. For example, you could use an invoice memo to entice inactive customers to start buying again by enclosing a coupon and printing the message

Save 20% on your next purchase—use the enclosed coupon soon!

on their invoices.

Your invoice memos can be as long as two 40-character lines.

ADDING AN INVOICE MEMO

The Training Company wants to remind customers gently when their accounts are past due. Follow these steps to add a new invoice memo to the list:

1. Select Invoice Memo from the Select List menu.

Predefined messages for customer invoices

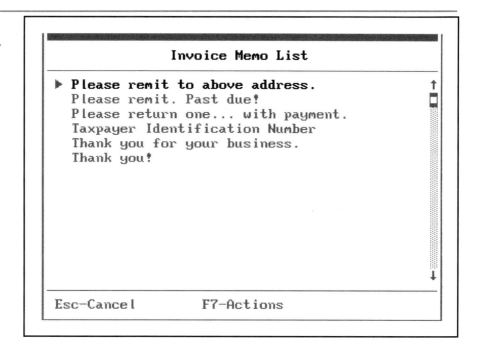

```
                    Invoice Memo List
▶ Please remit to above address.                    ↑
  Please remit. Past due!                            ▯
  Please return one... with payment.
  Taxpayer Identification Number
  Thank you for your business.
  Thank you!




                                                    ↓

  Esc-Cancel          F7-Actions
```

2. Press Ctrl-Ins to add a new memo.

3. Type the following message:

Oops. Did you forget to mail this month's payment?

You can edit the text by moving the cursor and deleting and inserting characters, as described in Chapter 1. Let's make a few changes to improve our memo.

4. Press the Home key to move the cursor to the beginning of the line.

5. Use the → key to move the cursor to the period.

6. Press the Delete key to remove the period. Notice the remaining characters move over to fill in the deleted character's space.

7. Type ! in place of the period.

8. Press the Insert key (to switch to Insert mode), and then press the spacebar to put a space back in the sentence after the punctuation mark.

9. Press Ctrl-↵ to record the new memo.

Our memo is added to the list in alphabetical order. The dots in the message indicate that the text is too long to fit on the list. However, the entire message will print on the invoice.

10. Press Esc to return to the Select List menu.

11. Press the Insert key to change back to Overtype mode.

Editing Invoice Memos

You can edit the QuickBooks predefined invoice memos, as well as any memos that you created. To change a memo, select Company Lists from the Main menu, and then choose Invoice Memo from the submenu. Highlight the message and press Ctrl-E to edit it.

In the View/Edit Invoice Memo window, you can revise the memo as necessary. Change an existing message simply by typing over it or by using the text-editing techniques, as we did to correct the memo new invoice we added in the previous section.

MAINTAINING YOUR CUSTOMER FILE

When customers don't pay you immediately, the amounts they owe become your accounts receivable. You need to set up customer records to keep track of your customers' purchases and payments. QuickBooks updates the customer balance during daily processing.

Adding Customers

We will now create records for the customers that we will use in the examples throughout the book. We will add one wholesale customer, one business customer, and three individual customers.

Adding a Wholesaler

The first record we will add is for a customer who purchases bulk bird seed from the Training Company and packages it in small containers to sell in an aviary shop. The completed customer information is shown in Figure 4.4.

Adding a customer

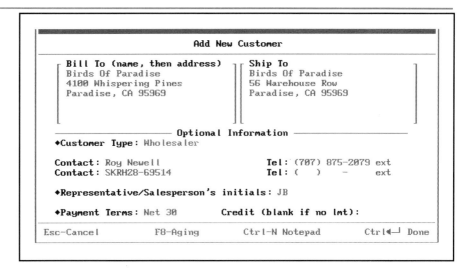

Follow these steps to set up the customer record:

1. If the Select List menu isn't on your screen, select Company Lists from Main menu, and then choose Customers from the submenu.

2. Press Ctrl-Ins to add a new customer. The Add New Customer window appears. Notice that the list of functions at the bottom of the screen differs from the one you see when you are adding an account to the chart of accounts.

3. In the Bill To field, enter the following name and mailing address for invoices and statements:

Birds Of Paradise

4100 Whispering Pines

Paradise, CA 95969

4. Press the Tab key twice to move to the Ship To field.

5. Press the " (quotation mark) key to duplicate the information from the Bill To field. QuickBooks fills in the Ship To field and moves the cursor to the Customer Type field.

6. Press the Back Tab key four times to return to the street address in the Ship To field.

7. Press Ctrl-Backspace to erase the street address.

When you print the Customer List, include the shipping address. Place the printed address on 3-by-5-inch cards for your shipping department's reference.

8. Enter **56 Warehouse Row** as the Ship To address. This is the storage facility where the customer receives shipments and packages the seed before taking it to the shop.

9. Use the Tab key to return the cursor to the Customer Type field.

10. Press Ctrl-L to choose from the predefined list of types.

11. Select Wholesaler from the list. QuickBooks enters your selection in the field.

12. In the Contact field, enter **Roy Newell**. He is the business office manager at the bird shop.

13. Enter **707 875 2079** in the Tel field. The cursor advances from the area code and jumps across the hyphen in the phone number.

14. Skip the phone extension field and press ↵ to move to the second Contact field.

You can use the second Tel field for the customer's other phone number or for a fax machine number. The second Contact field does not have to contain a name. If you do not have another contact person for a customer, you can use this field for miscellaneous information. In our example, we will use this field for the customer's resale number, which we must keep on file because we do not charge sales tax on purchases made for resale.

15. Enter **SKRH28-69514**, the customer's resale number, in the second Contact field.

16. Press Tab to skip the second Tel field.

17. In the Representative/Salesperson's Initials field, enter **JB**, the initials of the salesman who services this account. Because this employee isn't defined yet (and doesn't appear on the list of employees), you see the prompt

    Employee Not Found

18. Choose the Add to Employee List option.

19. Enter the employee's name, **Jim Bartlett**. Press Ctrl-↵ to record just the name. We can add his address later.

20. In the Payment Terms field, press Ctrl-L and select Net 30 from the list.

You can leave the Payment Terms field blank, but making an entry can make invoice entry more efficient. For every invoice you enter for this customer, QuickBooks will automatically place the payment terms you specified here in the Terms field. You can accept the terms or override them with different ones.

You can leave the Credit field blank if you do not want to set a limit on the amount of purchases this customer can charge. If you do enter a limit, QuickBooks will display a warning when you enter an invoice that goes over that amount, but you can override the warning and record the invoice anyway. This warning is useful if you are entering invoices as each sale is made. However, if you gather and enter invoices at the end of the day, the warning will occur after the fact. But you can give your cashiers a list of the customers who are over their limit and should not be allowed to charge their purchases.

If you enter a zero in the Credit field, you are indicating that the customer cannot charge at all (for a cash-only customer). Since our company doesn't set a credit limit on our customers unless we have problems collecting from them, we will leave the Credit field blank.

21. Press F10 to record the customer.

Our first customer now appears on the Customer List. Notice the Balance field contains zeros. QuickBooks updates the customer balance each time you enter an invoice or a payment. After you define each customer, you should enter the customer's outstanding invoices, as described later in this chapter.

Adding a Business Customer

We ship organically grown hay to our second customer. Follow these steps to add the next customer record:

1. From the Customer List, press Ctrl-Ins to add a customer.

2. In the Bill To field, enter the following name and address:

Pony Pen
56 Country Road
Paniolo Town, HI 96768

3. Press Tab to reach the Ship To field, and then press ".

4. Press Ctrl-L in the Customer Type field and select Business to categorize this customer.

5. Enter **Jon Karcey** in the Contact field.

6. In the Tel field, enter **808 245 7788**.

7. Skip the second Contact and Tel fields, and enter **jb** for the salesperson who handles this business account. Notice QuickBooks converts the letters to uppercase.

8. Press Ctrl-L in the Payment Terms field and select 3% 15 Net 45 from the Terms List.

9. Press F10 to record your entries.

Adding Individual Customers

Our next three customers are individuals who can charge their purchases. They don't have a shipping address nor a sales representative assigned to their account. Add each record as follows:

1. In the Bill To field enter the following name and address.

   Grannie Jones
   103 Morningside Park
   Benicia, CA 94591

2. Select Individual from the Customer Type List.

3. Enter **Net 30** in the Payment Terms field.

4. Press F10 to record the account.

5. Press Ctrl-Ins to add a new customer, and enter this billing address:

   Carol Hendrickson
   76 Rodgers Street
   Vallejo, CA 94590

6. Press Ctrl-L and select Individual from the Customer Type List.

7. Enter **Net 30** in the Payment Terms field.

8. Press F10 to record the account.

9. Press Ctrl-Ins to add a new customer and enter this billing address:

   Ted Costa
   #1 Flakey Jake Road
   Sacramento, CA 95814

10. Press Ctrl-L and select Individual from the Customer Type List.

11. Enter **Net 30** in the Payment Terms field.

12. In the Credit Limit field, enter **0** (zero). This customer is past due on his payments, and we don't want to extend further credit to him. QuickBooks records the account.

13. Press Esc twice to return to the Main menu.

CHANGING AND DELETING CUSTOMER RECORDS

Deleting recorded transactions is not accepted accounting pactice, because it alters your data after the fact, thereby falsifying your audit trail.

To delete or edit an existing customer record, select Company Lists from the Main menu, and then choose Customers from the submenu. Highlight the customer name and press Ctrl-E to recall the record. If you need to edit the record, just make the changes in the appropriate fields.

You cannot delete a customer for whom you have recorded an invoice or a payment. You must first delete all transactions involving the customer from the Accounts Receivable register.

If you have not recorded any transactions involving this customer, you can delete the customer record by highlighting the customer on the Customer List and pressing Ctrl-Del. The program displays the warning

Permanently deleting this customer.

Press ↵ to delete the customer record. If you did not mean to delete the customer record, press Esc to cancel the request.

ENTERING OUTSTANDING BALANCES
FOR CUSTOMERS

The Balance Forward item is used only during system setup.

An *open invoice* is one that is not yet paid. Entering the invoices that are open at the time you convert to QuickBooks is the same as entering daily invoices after your records are set up. The only differences are that you charge the amount due to Balance Forward rather than to an Income account, and you don't enter the detail of what was purchased. That information should be in your old records.

ENTERING OPEN CUSTOMER INVOICES

Three of the customers we just set up have outstanding invoices. We bill one of our customers in advance for the pastureland she rents from us. Figure 4.5 shows the completed entry for the outstanding balance.

Follow these steps to record the information about the open invoice:

1. Select Invoicing/Receivables, and then choose Write/Print Invoices from the submenu.

2. Press Back Tab twice to move the cursor to the Invoice Number field.

3. Enter the number of the original unpaid invoice, **33182**.

4. In the Date field, enter **080193** over the supplied date. We want to record the date this bill was incurred so that our *aging* of the customer's account, a breakdown of how old each invoice is, will be correct.

5. In the Bill To field, press Ctrl-L and select Carol Hendrickson from the list.

6. Press Tab to move the cursor to the Description field and press Ctrl-L.

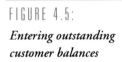

FIGURE 4.5:

Entering outstanding customer balances

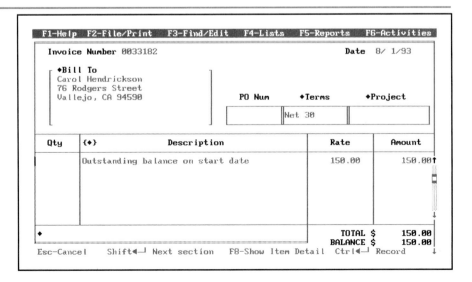

The list displays the item QuickBooks provides for entering outstanding invoices, Bal Forwd. Press ↵ to select it.

7. In the Rate field, enter **150**, the amount this customer owes us.

8. Press ↵ to accept the program-calculated total.

9. Press F10 to record your entries. The invoice is recorded, and the screen clears for your next invoice entry.

The amount on the invoice will update the balance in the customer's record. This amount will be charged to the Accounts Receivable account, with an offset to the Opening Balance Equity account in your general ledger.

Our next customer buys a month's supply of pet food at a time for the stray cats and dogs she takes in.

10. Press Back Tab twice to move the cursor to the Invoice Number field.

11. Enter the number of the original invoice, **33601**.

12. In the Date field, enter **082893**, the original date of the outstanding invoice.

13. In the Bill To field, press Ctrl-L and select Grannie Jones from the list.

14. Press Tab to move the cursor to the Description field, press Ctrl-L, and select Bal Forwd from the list.

15. In the Rate field, enter **62.10**, the amount this customer still owes.

16. Press ↵ to accept the program-calculated total.

17. Press F10 to record your entries.

The last customer has an old account that we have been trying to collect.

18. In the Invoice Number field, enter **1000000**.

NOTE NOTE *Quick-Books does not allow alphabet characters in the invoice number.*

The balance on this account consists of several invoices from last year. Rather than enter each one individually, we are assigning this arbitrary indicator to the group. Our old records contain the detail. You can do something similar when you set up your own company.

If you cannot identify the individual invoices that make up what the customer owes you, you can make a single entry of the entire balance. Enter a slightly different number, such as 100000, 100001, and so on, for each customer you set up. As payments come in, apply them to this "invoice" until it is paid in full.

19. Enter **113092** as the date this account was last active.

20. In the Bill To field, press Ctrl-L and select Ted Costa.

21. In the Description field, select Bal Forwd from the list.

22. In the Rate field, enter **456.12**, the amount that is still owed to us.

23. Press F10 to record your entries. The warning message associated with the credit limit we established for this customer appears.

24. In this case, we want to record the invoice to get it into our new books, so enter **Y** to record this invoice anyway. The invoice is recorded, and the screen clears.

ENTERING OPEN CREDITS

Think of credit memos as negative invoices.

A *credit memo* is a document that reduces the balance due. The screen for invoices is also used for recording *open credits*, those that have not yet been applied toward paying an invoice. For example, the customer may have returned a dog leash that broke. You issued a credit memo for the invoice that was already paid in full. The customer has not yet purchased anything else, so an open credit remains on his account.

You enter an open credit in the same way that you enter an open invoice, except that you must precede the amount in the Rate field with a minus sign (–). The customer's balance will also appear with a minus sign, and the credit will be available to use on a future invoice.

VERIFYING AND CORRECTING CUSTOMER RECORDS

When you have set up all your customers and recorded their outstanding amounts, you should verify that you entered all your data correctly. You can check the balances and print the Customer List.

REVIEWING CUSTOMER BALANCES

The Customer List shows the balances resulting from your invoice entries. When you enter payments later, they will be included in the balance amount.

To see the list, press Esc twice to return to the Main menu, select Company Lists, and then choose Customers. Figure 4.6 shows the list with our company's five customers and their balance amounts. If you notice any errors as you review the balances, you can correct them, as described shortly.

FIGURE 4.6:

Viewing customer balances

```
┌─────────────────────────────────────────────────────┐
│  ▓▓▓▓▓▓▓▓▓▓▓▓▓▓▓▓▓▓▓▓▓▓▓▓▓▓▓▓▓▓▓▓▓▓▓▓▓▓▓▓▓▓▓▓▓▓      │
│                    Customer  List                    │
│  ─────────────────────────────────────────────────  │
│            Customer              │    Balance         │
│  ─────────────────────────────────────────────────  │
│  ▶ Birds Of Paradise            │        0.00   ↑    │
│    Carol Hendrickson            │      150.00   ▯    │
│    Grannie Jones                │       62.10        │
│    Pony Pen                     │        0.00        │
│    Ted Costa                    │      456.12        │
│                                 │                    │
│                                 │                    │
│                                 │                    │
│                                 │               ↓    │
│  ─────────────────────────────────────────────────  │
│   Esc-Cancel          F7-Actions                     │
└─────────────────────────────────────────────────────┘
```

PRINTING THE CUSTOMER LIST

You can print the Customer List at any time to review the customer information. Follow these steps to print the list:

1. Display the Customer List and press Ctrl-P.

2. At the prompt

   Select specific customers to include?

   press ↵ to accept N for No.

We want to print all the customer records. When you want to print information for only certain customers, enter Y at the prompt, and the Customer List will reappear. Then, to mark each customer you want to include, highlight the name and press the spacebar. To mark all the customers, press Ctrl-spacebar.

3. At the prompt

Print name and balance only?

enter N for No to list the entire customer definition.

When you set up your own company, you could print a report of just the names and balances to keep as a record of the balances with which you began your books.

4. At the prompt

Include customer transaction history?

enter Y to include a listing of each invoice and credit memo you entered.

5. Press ↵ to accept the default printer, or press Ctrl-L and select the printer to which you want to send the report.

6. At the final prompt

Print transaction history from: through:

enter **113092** and **083193**, the dates of the oldest invoice and the most recent invoice we want to show on the transaction history portion of the listing.

7. Press Esc twice to return to the Main menu.

CORRECTING CUSTOMER INVOICE ERRORS

After you record the customer's invoices or balance, if you discover an error, you can make an adjustment directly on the invoice. Alternatively, you can select that transaction in the Accounts Receivable register and correct it there.

To make changes to the invoice itself, select Invoicing/Receivables from the Main menu, and then choose Write/Print Invoices. From the invoice-entry screen, press Ctrl-PgUp to scroll through the invoices. Press Tab to move the cursor to the field that contains a mistake, press Ctrl-Backspace to erase the existing entry, and then enter the correct information. Press F10 to record your changes.

In this chapter, you learned how to set up the records you need to handle your customers. You worked with the Customer Type, Employee, Payment Terms, Payment Method, Shipping Method, Invoice Memo, and Customer lists. In the next chapter, we will set up the records for our vendors.

5

Setting Up Vendors

endors provide you with merchandise for resale and services or items to use in operating your business. The bank that lends you money becomes a vendor to whom you make monthly payments. The telephone company is also a vendor.

In this chapter, we will set up the vendors that we will use in the examples throughout this book. First we will establish the vendor types we will use. Then we will create vendor records and enter the amounts we owe on vendor invoices.

SETTING UP VENDOR TYPES

Like customers, vendors are classified by type. You can use the vendor types supplied by QuickBooks or create your own. For our sample company, we will delete three of the predefined types and add two new types.

REMOVING VENDOR TYPES

The Design, Materials, and Supplies vendor types are not appropriate for the Training Company. Follow these steps to remove those predefined vendor types:

 Remember, you can press Esc to return to the previous screen or to get back to a menu.

1. Select Company Lists from the Main menu.

2. Choose Vendor Types from the Select List menu. The cursor waits on the first type, Design.

3. Press Ctrl-Del, then ↵ to delete this type.

4. Delete the next two types, Materials and Supplies.

ADDING VENDOR TYPES

Our company wants to be able to review how much merchandise we buy from vendors to resell in our business. We also want to mark the vendors who require a 1099 form. Follow these steps to add the Merchandise and 1099 vendor types to the list:

1. From the Vendor Type List, press Ctrl-Ins to add a record. The Add New Vendor Type window appears.

2. Enter **Merchandise**. The new type is added to the list.

3. Press Ctrl-Ins again and enter **1099** in the Add Vendor Type window. Your Vendor Type List should now contain Merchandise, 1099, and Tax Collector.

4. Press Esc to return to the Select List menu.

MAINTAINING YOUR VENDOR FILE

If you do not pay for a product or service in full when you incur the obligation, the unpaid amount becomes an account payable. Even if you pay the vendor with a credit card, you still owe the credit card company. You should include your credit card accounts, such as Visa and American Express, in your vendor file.

ADDING VENDORS

We will now create records for the vendors we will use in the examples in this book. We will add two merchandise vendors, a finance company, and an independent contractor.

Adding a Merchandise Vendor

Our first vendor provides us with pet products, which we resell to our customers. The completed information is shown in Figure 5.1.

Follow these steps to set up the vendor record:

1. Select Vendors from the Select List menu.

2. From the Vendor List, press Ctrl-Ins to add a new vendor.

3. In the Pay To field, enter the following name and mailing address for payments:

   Four Paws Pet Center

   3001 Amherst Avenue

   Hartford, CT 06114

   When you write checks to the vendor, this information will appear automatically.

4. Move the cursor to the Vendor Type field.

FIGURE 5.1:

Adding a vendor

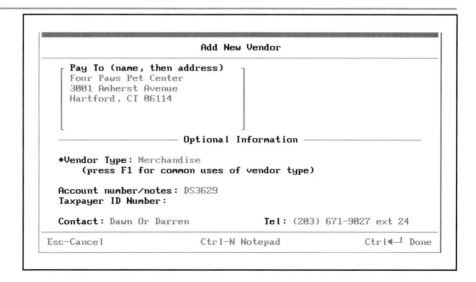

5. Type the first few characters of the vendor type, **Mer**, and press ↵. QuickBooks fills in the vendor type (Merchandise) that matches your entry.

6. In the Account Number/Notes field, enter **DS3629**, the number this vendor assigned to our account. This information will print on the memo line of your accounts payable checks. You can use the memo line for other notes that you want to appear on your checks.

7. Press ↵ to leave the Taxpayer ID Number field blank. We do not need to report payments made for resale merchandise.

8. In the Contact field, enter **Dawn or Darren**, the two people who handle our account at the Pet Center.

9. Enter **203 671 9027** in the Tel field, and **24** for the extension.

> NOTE *Quick-Books uppercases the first character in each word, no matter how you type it.*

When you complete the last field, the Vendor List appears. Our new vendor is on the list, and the Balance field contains zeros. QuickBooks updates the vendor balance whenever you enter an invoice or make a payment. After you define all your vendors, you should enter their outstanding invoices, as described later in this chapter.

Adding a Second Merchandise Vendor

Follow the steps below to add the second vendor who provides us with products for resale:

1. Select to add a new vendor.

2. In the Pay To field, enter the following name and mailing address:

   Kat Kastle
   22 Garfield Lane
   Denver, CO 80011

3. Press Ctrl-L in the Vendor Type field and select Merchandise from the list.

4. Enter **TTC4069** in the Account Number/Notes field.

5. In the Contact field, enter **Gloria Weiss**.

6. Enter **303 920 2200** in the Tel field.

Adding a Finance Company

Our next vendor is the finance company that loaned us money for our delivery truck. Follow these steps to set up the vendor record:

1. From the Vendor List, press Ctrl-Ins to add a new vendor.

2. In the Pay To field, enter the following name and address:

   Countrywide Loans
   1404 State Street
   Sacramento, CA 95842

3. Press ↵ to skip the Vendor Type field. Our company assigns types only to vendors who provide merchandise for resale, tax collectors, and those requiring 1099 forms.

4. In the Account Number/Notes field, enter **28032-4**, the loan identification given to us by the vendor. We made the same notation in the Long-Term Liability account we established to keep track of our loan balance in the chart of accounts (in Chapter 3).

5. In the Contact field, enter **Carmen Moreno**.

6. In the Tel field, enter **916 332 9620**, extension **4**.

Adding a 1099 Vendor

CAUTION The IRS regulations determine who should be classified as a 1099 vendor.

The last vendor we will add is the man who maintains our pastureland and crops. Follow these steps:

1. From the Vendor List, press Ctrl-Ins to add a vendor.

2. In the Pay To field, enter his name and address:

   Sam Spade
   501 Gardeners Row
   Orangevale, CA 95662

3. Select 1099 as the Vendor Type. Sam is an independent contractor, and we must report how much we pay him to the IRS.

4. Press ↵ to skip the Account number field.

5. In the Taxpayer ID Number field, enter **554-56-3593**, the vendor's federal tax identification number for 1099 reporting. We need this number to identify the vendor when we prepare 1099 forms.

6. In the Tel field, enter **916 989 2920**.

QuickBooks provides a report that lists the taxpayer ID number and payments made to vendors in the current year, but it does not prepare the 1099 forms for you. You must select the vendors that require 1099 forms and fill in the forms yourself.

ADDING VENDOR INFORMATION TO AN ACCOUNT RECORD

When we set up our company's chart of accounts (in Chapter 2), we didn't supply the vendor information for our gasoline Credit Card account. Now we will return and complete that record, and we will define a new vendor at the same time. Follow these steps:

1. Press Esc until you return to the Main menu.

2. Select Chart of Accounts.

3. Highlight the Dutch Oil Credit Card account (2110) and press Ctrl-E to edit it.

> **NOTE** *In a field that requires a predefined entry (one with a diamond), if you type characters that don't match anything on the list, Quick-Books will ask if you want to add the new item to the list or select a valid entry from the list.*

4. Press the End key twice to move to the end of the first field, then to the last field in the record, Vendor.

5. Type **Dutch Oil** and press ↵. QuickBooks notifies you that it cannot find the vendor.

6. Select to add a vendor to the list. The Add New Vendor window appears.

7. Complete the record with the following address:

   44 Middenweg
   Holland, PA 18966

8. Press Ctrl-↵ to record the information. QuickBooks adds the vendor to the Vendor List and to the Credit Card account, and then redisplays the Chart of Accounts screen.

9. Press Esc to return to the Main Menu.

Entering a vendor in the Credit Card account record is optional, but it can facilitate your check writing. When you pay the bill (during credit card reconciliation), the program will supply the vendor address.

CHANGING AND DELETING VENDOR RECORDS

You can change vendor information at any time. However, as with customers, you cannot delete vendors who have an outstanding balance or transaction records.

To edit or delete a vendor record, select Vendors from the Select List menu and highlight the vendor's name. Then press Ctrl-E to recall the record for editing, or press Ctrl-Del to delete the record.

ENTERING OUTSTANDING BALANCES FOR INVOICES

 The Open Balance Equity account is a special account that is used only during setup.

You enter amounts that you still owe to vendors when you set up your records in the same way that you will enter invoices during routine processing, except that you charge the amount to the Open Balance Equity account. The detail of what you purchased from the vendor is already in your old records, so you don't need to duplicate that information here.

ENTERING OPEN VENDOR INVOICES

You enter outstanding vendor invoices through the Accounts Payable register (not an invoice-entry screen, as for customers). Two of the vendors we defined have invoices that we have not yet paid. Follow these steps to enter the open invoice information:

1. Select Accounts Payable from the Main menu.

2. Select A/P Register from the submenu.

3. In the Date field, enter **080793**, the date on the original outstanding invoice.

4. In the Inv Num field, enter **53629k**, the number on the vendor's invoice.

5. Press Ctrl-L in the next field, Vendor, to select from the Vendor List, and choose Kat Kastle, the vendor from whom we received this invoice.

6. Press ↵ in the Pay Date field to accept the date supplied by QuickBooks.

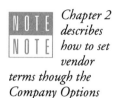

Chapter 2 describes how to set vendor terms though the Company Options function.

The program calculates the vendor invoice pay date from the invoice date and the number of days you specified when setting up your company (our default is 30 days). If the terms on a particular invoice are different, you can override the pay date with the day the invoice must be paid.

7. In the Owed column, enter **1271.32**, the amount we have not yet paid on this invoice.

8. Press ↵ in the Memo field to leave it blank. For your actual records, you can use this field for miscellaneous notes regarding the transaction.

9. In the Account field, press Ctrl-L to display the Chart of Accounts screen.

You can set the program options to bypass this verification prompt. Choose Set Up/Customize from the Main menu, then Customize QuickBooks, then Options. See Chapter 2 for details.

When we originally received the invoice, we charged the appropriate Expense account. Now, to record the outstanding balance on the vendor account in QuickBooks, we will use the offsetting account provided by the program.

10. Press PgDn, highlight Open Bal Equity, and press ↵. The account appears in the Account field, and you see the prompt

   OK to Record Transaction?

11. Press ↵ to accept the default to record the transaction. The transaction is recorded, and the cursor moves to the next line.

We have two outstanding invoices from Four Paws Pet Center. We could record only one transaction with the combined total, but to keep more complete information, we will enter them individually.

12. In the Date field, enter **080493**, the invoice date.

13. Enter **4P-781**, the invoice number, in the Inv Num field.

14. In the Vendor field, press Ctrl-L and select Four Paws Pet Center from the list.

15. In the Owed column, enter **250**, the amount of the invoice.

16. In the Account field, press Ctrl-L and select Open Bal Equity from the Chart of Accounts screen.

17. Press ↵ to record the transaction.

18. For the final outstanding invoice, enter **081693** in the Date field.

19. Enter **4P-932** in the Inv Num field.

20. In the Vendor field, press Ctrl-L and select Four Paws Pet Center.

21. Enter **930** in the Owed field.

22. In the Account field, press Ctrl-L and select Open Bal Equity.

23. Press ↵ to record the transaction. Your register should look like the one shown in Figure 5.2.

FIGURE 5.2:

Entering outstanding vendor invoices

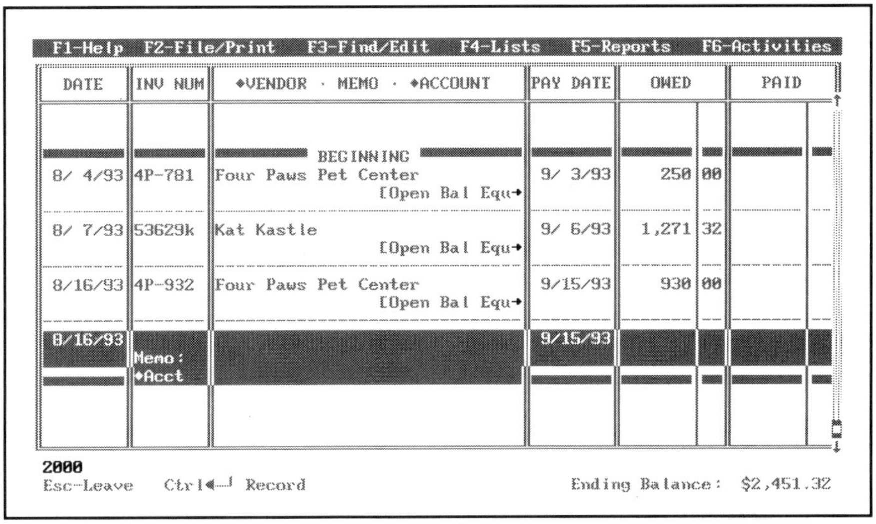

HANDLING OPEN VENDOR CREDITS

In QuickBooks, you cannot enter open credit memos for vendors. If you receive a credit from a vendor, you must subtract it from a future invoice before entering the invoice.

The problem with deducting a credit from an invoice before entering the invoice is that the recorded invoice amount is not correct. However, you can record the credit and full invoice amount in the general ledger accounts. In Chapter 7, you will learn how to enter a credit memo from a vendor.

REVIEWING AND CORRECTING VENDOR RECORDS

After you have entered all your vendors and their outstanding amounts, you should verify that you recorded all your data correctly. You can check the balances and print the Vendor List.

REVIEWING VENDOR BALANCES

The Vendor List shows the balances resulting from the outstanding invoices. When you make payments to vendors, the payment amounts will be included in the balance amount.

To see the vendor balances, select Company Lists from the Main menu, and then choose Vendors. Your Vendors List should look like this:

Countrywide Loans	0.00
Dutch Oil	0.00
Four Paws Pet Center	1,180.00
Kat Kastle	1,271.32
Sam Spade	0.00

If your balances don't match these amounts, you can correct them, as explained shortly.

PRINTING THE VENDOR LIST

The prompts you see when printing the Vendor List are the same as the ones that appear when you choose to print the Customer List. See Chapter 4 for descriptions.

You can print the Vendor List at any time to review the vendor information, as well as vendor transaction history. Follow these steps to print the list:

1. From the Vendor List, press Ctrl-P.

2. When you are asked if you want to select specific vendors, press ↵ to accept No.

3. Choose not to print just the name and balance; we want to print all the vendor information.

4. Choose to include the transaction history.

5. Accept the default printer, or select another printer from the list.

6. For the transaction history dates print, specify from **080493** through **081693**.

CORRECTING VENDOR INVOICE ERRORS

After you record a vendor's invoice or balance, you can correct transaction errors in the Accounts Payable register. To display the register, select Accounts Payable from the Main menu, and then choose A/P Register from the submenu.

In the Accounts Payable register, use the ↑ or ↓ key to highlight the transaction you want to edit. Then press Tab to reach the field that contains the mistake, press Ctrl-Backspace to erase the existing data, and enter the correct information. Press F10 to record your changes.

REVIEWING YOUR ACCOUNTS RECEIVABLE AND ACCOUNTS PAYABLE BALANCES

Chapter 14 describes the Quick-Books Balance Sheet report.

Now that we have entered all the customer and vendor invoice amounts that were outstanding as of the date we set up our company, let's print a report to review our work. Follow these steps:

1. From the Main menu, select Reports, and then choose Balance Sheet from the submenu.

2. Press ↵ in the Report Title field.

3. Enter **9/1/93** in the Show Balances As Of Field. The Balance Sheet Report appears on your screen.

4. Press Ctrl-P to print the report and select the printer you want to use.

The Balance Sheet report, shown in Figure 5.3, lists the balances for our Asset, Liability, and Equity accounts. You should see that the Accounts Receivable account balance is 668.22, and the Accounts Payable account balance is 2451.32. The Opening Balance Equity account should now have a balance of 0.00.

FIGURE 5.3:

The Training Company Balance Sheet

```
                            BALANCE SHEET
                           As of 9/ 1/93
Training Company  -All Accounts                              Page 1
9/ 1/93
                                             9/ 1/93
                     Account                 Balance
-------------------------------------------- -----------  .
ASSETS
   CURRENT ASSETS
     1000-Countrywide Bank                    25,382.90
     1100-Accounts Receivable                    668.22
     1220-Prepaid Insurance                      544.00
     1230-Inventory                            8,600.00
                                             -----------
     TOTAL CURRENT ASSETS                     35,195.12

   FIXED ASSETS
     1310-Land & Equipment                    58,600.00
     1315-Accum. Depreciation                 -4,580.00
                                             -----------
     TOTAL FIXED ASSETS                       54,020.00

                                             -----------
   TOTAL ASSETS                               89,215.12
                                             ===========


LIABILITIES
   CURRENT LIABILITIES
     2000-Accounts Payable                     2,451.32
     2110-Dutch Oil                               15.80
                                             -----------
     TOTAL CURRENT LIABILITIES                 2,467.12

   LONG TERM LIABILITIES
     2310-Truck Loan                          13,748.00
                                             -----------
     TOTAL LONG TERM LIABILITIES              13,748.00

                                             -----------
   TOTAL LIABILITIES                          16,215.12

EQUITY
   EQUITY ACCOUNTS
     3010-Owner's Capital                     48,200.00
     3015-Owner's Draw                       -12,000.00
     3500-Retained Earnings                   36,800.00
     Open Bal Equity-Opening Bal Equity            0.00
                                             -----------
     TOTAL EQUITY ACCOUNTS                    73,000.00

   CURRENT EARNINGS                                0.00
                                             -----------
   TOTAL EQUITY                               73,000.00

                                             -----------
   TOTAL LIABILITIES AND EQUITY              89,215.12
                                             ===========
```

In this chapter, you learned how to set up the records you need to handle your vendors. You worked with the Vendor Type and Vendor lists, as well as the Accounts Payable register. In the next chapter, we will set up the records for our company's products and services.

6

Defining Products, Services, and Items

**P**roducts and services are things you provide to or do for your customers to generate income. In addition to products and service records, you can set up other invoice-related records, including those for other charges, price discounts, subtotals, payment codes, sales tax, and refunds.

In this chapter, we will set up records for products, services, delivery charges, and miscellaneous invoice-related items. We will use these items in the examples throughout this book.

SETTING UP PRODUCT RECORDS

NOTE NOTE You do not need product records for items that are not resale merchandise, such as used vehicles or other fixed assets.

The product file should contain a record of every item in your inventory. Our company sells products for pets and horses. Some of the merchandise we purchase and resell; others, like hay and bird seed, we grow and harvest on our own property. We will set up records for a few of those products to use in our examples.

We currently have only two general ledger accounts to record income from products and services. We accumulate sales from pet products in one account and income from horse (equine) products in the second account. However, we maintain separate item codes for each product we sell. The codes allow us to list each item individually on a customer's invoice, as well as keep track of the number of units of each item we have sold.

Adding Products Charged to the Same Account

We will add records for four *parts* (the QuickBooks terminology for tangible products): dog leashes, flea shampoo, cat food, and bird seed. We want to record the sales of these products in the same Income account, the one for pet products. The completed information for the first product is shown in Figure 6.1.

Follow these steps to add the pet product records:

1. Select Company Lists from the Main menu.

2. Select Items/Parts/Services from the Select List menu. The Item List appears.

3. Press Ctrl-Ins to add a record. You see the item type selections, as shown in Figure 6.2.

4. Select Part. The Add New Part Item window appears.

5. In the Code field, enter **D4112**, our stockkeeping number for dog leashes.

FIGURE 6.1:

Adding a product record

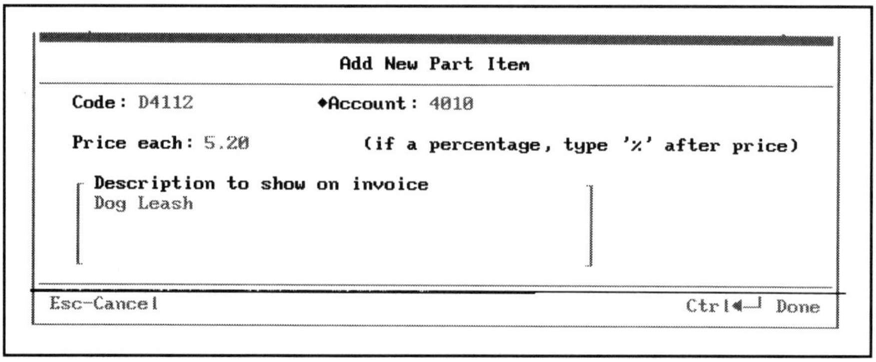

```
                    Add New Part Item

   Code: D4112              ◆Account: 4010

   Price each: 5.20         (if a percentage, type '%' after price)

   Description to show on invoice
   Dog Leash


   Esc-Cancel                                Ctrl◄┘ Done
```

FIGURE 6.2:

QuickBooks item types

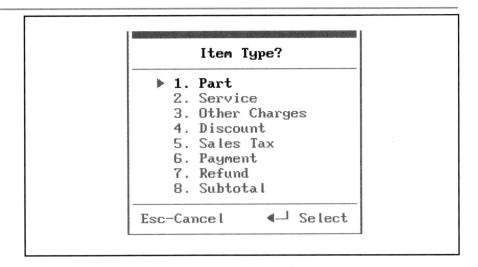

QuickBooks lists items by type, then by code within type. To keep similar products together on the list, we begin product codes for dogs with D, cat product codes with C, bird product codes with B, and horse product codes with H.

 Our sample company requires accounts on all transactions, and your actual company should also have this requirement. You indicate whether or not accounts are required on transactions through the company options. See Chapter 2 for details.

6. In the Account field, press Ctrl-L and select 4010, Pet Products, from the Chart of Accounts screen.

7. Enter **5.20** in the Price Each field. This is the amount we charge for one leash.

You can define a price with up to three decimal places. When you sell a product or service, or bill for other charges, QuickBooks enters the price from this field on the invoice. You can override the price during invoice entry.

8. In the Description to Show on Invoice field, enter **Dog Leash**.

You can enter up to three lines if you need more room to describe the product. This information prints on the customer's invoice.

9. Press Ctrl-↵ to record the definition. The part appears on the Item List.

10. To add the next pet product, press Ctrl-Ins and select to add a Part.

11. In the Code field, enter **D4165**, our stockkeeping number for canine flea shampoo.

12. In the Account field, press Ctrl-L and select Pet Products, 4010.

13. Enter **6.55**, the amount we charge for one bottle, in the Price Each field.

14. Enter **Flea Shampoo** as the description.

15. Press F10 to record the product definition.

16. From the Item List, press Ctrl-Ins and select to add a Part.

17. In the Code field, enter **C7341**, our code for canned cat food.

18. In the Account field, enter **4010**.

19. Enter **8.40** in the Price Each field. This is our price for one case of cat food.

20. Enter **Diet Specific Cat Food** as the description.

21. Press F10 to record the product definition.

22. From the Item List, press Ctrl-Ins and select to add a Part.

23. In the Code field, enter **B2159**, our code for bird seed.

24. In the Account field, enter **4010**.

25. Enter **4** in the Price Each field. We charge $4.00 a pound for the seed.

26. For the description, enter **Sunflower Seed Mix**.

27. Press F10 to record the new product.

ADDING A PRODUCT CHARGED TO ANOTHER ACCOUNT

Our final product is charged to a different general ledger account than the four we just added. We keep track of the income from hay in our account for equine products. Follow these steps to add the horse-related product:

1. From the Item List, press Ctrl-Ins and select to add a Part.

2. In the Code field, enter **H1000**, the number we use for hay.

3. In the Account field, press Ctrl-L and select Equine Products, 4020.

4. Enter **165** in the Price Each field. This is our price per ton of hay.

5. For the description, enter **Alfalfa Hay.**

6. Press F10 to record your entries.

ADDING A RECORD FOR SPECIAL ORDERS

When you set up the product records for your own company, you might also want to add a record for special orders. You can use this record to keep track of items you buy and sell but do not intend to stock.

You can specify the account in which you want to record the income from special orders and enter Special Orders in the Description to Show on Invoice field. You do not need to assign a product code or price.

SETTING UP SERVICE RECORDS

Services are usually labor-related activities your customers pay you to perform. The services you offer can be related to the products you sell. For example, gardening is a service, and the tree you plant is a product. Repairing a flat tire is a service, but the inner tube you replace is a product.

ADDING A RENTAL SERVICE

The first service we will add is renting pastureland for horses. The completed service information is shown in Figure 6.3.

FIGURE 6.3:

Adding a service record

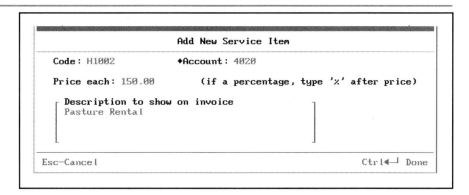

Follow these steps to add the service record:

1. From the Item List, press Ctrl-Ins to add an item.

2. Select Service as the item type.

3. In the Code field, enter **H1002**, the number we use when we rent pastureland.

4. In the Account field, press Ctrl-L and select Equine Products, 4020.

5. Enter **150** in the Price Each field. This is how much we charge per month for each acre the customer uses.

6. For the description, enter **Pasture Rental**.

7. Press F10 to record your entries. The code is added to the Item List, under the Service type.

ADDING A GROOMING SERVICE

The Training Company just started offering dog grooming. We want to separate income from this service from income for pet-related merchandise so that we can compare product sales with the associated cost of goods. In order to keep the income separate, we need to create a new general ledger account for service income. We will add this account while we are setting up the service record.

Follow these steps to add the dog-grooming service:

1. From the Item List, press Ctrl-Ins and select to add a Service.

2. In the Code field, enter **D4100**, the number we assigned to dog grooming.

3. In the Account field, enter **4030**. QuickBooks informs you that it cannot find this account.

4. Select Add to Chart of Accounts List.

5. Choose Income as the account type.

6. Enter **Pet Services** in the Description field. The program adds the new general ledger account and returns to the Add New Service Item window.

7. Enter **28** in the Price Each field. This is our price for bathing and clipping a dog.

You should consult the appropriate government agency to learn which of your products and services are taxable and which are not.

Bows are extra. We sell them as a taxable product. Note that if you purchase items for resale but use them yourself (or give them away) instead of reselling them, you must pay tax, called a *use tax*, on what you used. You report the personal use of the resale items on your sales tax return. In some tax districts, you could pay tax on the items yourself when you buy them, and then include them as part of a service at no charge.

8. For the description, enter **Dog Grooming**.

9. Press F10 to record your entries.

SETTING UP RECORDS FOR OTHER CHARGES

Some items don't fit the product or service definition. For example, you may charge your customers for freight, insurance on shipments, charges for a rush order, or a restocking fee. QuickBooks categorizes such items as Other Charges.

Our company charges customers extra if we must deliver hay to them. Follow these steps to create a record for delivery fees:

1. From the Item List, press Ctrl-Ins to add an item.

2. Select Other Charges as the item type.

3. In the Code field, enter **Deliver**.

4. In the Account field, press Ctrl-L and select Equine Products, 4020. We want to record income from hay and the fees to deliver it in the same account.

5. Press Tab to leave the Price Each field blank. Delivery fees are determined at the time of the sale according to the distance we must travel.

6. In the Description to Show on Invoice field, enter **Delivery Charge**.

7. Press F10 to record your entries. The code is added to the Item List, under the Charge type.

SETTING UP MISCELLANEOUS INVOICING ITEMS

You can set up records for miscellaneous entries you need to complete an invoice, such as sales tax, or to note subtotals, calculate price discounts, or enter payments received at the time of sale.

ADDING PRICE DISCOUNT CODES

A *price discount* is a reduction in the sales price of an item. You should not confuse it with an early *payment discount*, which discounts the entire bill when the customer pays early.

Selling an item for less than full value can be considered an expense, as can discounts you give for early payment. It is like a promotional cost. For example, you can use a price discount to reduce prices when you have a holiday sale. Price discounts allow you to avoid changing the prices in your product records.

Our company reduces our sales price by 20 percent when people buy large quantities. Figure 6.4 shows the completed discount information.

Follow these steps to define a price discount for Training Company items:

1. From the Item List, press Ctrl-Ins to add an item.

2. Select Discount as the item type.

3. In the Code field, enter **Price Disc**.

FIGURE 6.4:

Creating a price discount record

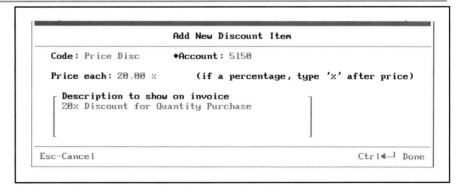

```
                        Add New Discount Item

Code: Price Disc       ◆Account: 5150

Price each: 20.00 %        (if a percentage, type '%' after price)

  Description to show on invoice
  20% Discount for Quantity Purchase



Esc-Cancel                                          Ctrl◀─┘ Done
```

4. In the Account field, press Ctrl-L and select Miscellaneous Expense, 5150.

5. In the Price Each field, enter **20%** (20 followed by a percent sign).

The Price Each field can be used for flat dollar amounts or for percentages. The percent sign changes the field from a dollar discount into a percentage.

6. For the description, enter **20% Discount for Quantity Purchase**.

7. Press F10 to record your entries. The code is added to the Item List, under the Discount type.

You'll see how the price discount works in Chapter 9, when we enter sales.

CREATING SUBTOTAL CODES

Subtotal codes subtotal all the preceding lines on an invoice (up to the last subtotal). If you want to enter a grand total on the invoice, ignoring previous subtotals, put one subtotal code immediately after another subtotal code.

Our company uses subtotal codes to add up all the taxable items so QuickBooks can compute the sales tax. Follow these steps to create the code:

1. From the Item List, press Ctrl-Ins to add an item, and then select Subtotal as the item type.

2. In the Code field, enter **SubTot**.

3. For the description, enter **Taxable Item Subtotal**. The code appears on the Item List, under the Subtotal type.

CREATING SALES TAX CODES

Although we did not create a tax agency vendor record for our sample company, you should set up such a vendor for your own company.

When you use sales tax codes, QuickBooks can calculate the sales tax and enter it on the customer invoice. The amount calculated is recorded automatically in the sales tax payable account created by QuickBooks when you set up your company. If you set up the agency to whom you pay taxes as a vendor, QuickBooks will keep the transaction history in the vendor file and print the vendor address on checks.

Follow these steps to create a sales tax code for our company:

1. From the Item List, press Ctrl-Ins and select Sales Tax as the item type.

2. In the Code field, enter **Tax**.

3. In the Tax Rate field, enter **6.50**. You do not include the percent sign here because QuickBooks automatically calculates it as a percentage. Our entry will become .0650 when the code is used in calculations.

4. In the Tax District Name field, enter **California**. This field is for the name of the state, county, or city for which you must collect sales tax.

5. Leave the Vendor field blank, and enter **California Sales Tax** as the description. The code is added to the Item List, under the Tax type.

If you assess and pay local taxes separately, you should create a sales tax code for each taxing district.

CREATING PAYMENT CODES FOR INVOICE ENTRY

NOTE
NOTE

You select whether or not to require item codes on invoices through the company options, as described in Chapter 2.

Payment codes are used in combination with payment methods to record payments that are received at the time of the sale. If you require item codes on invoice items, every entry you make, including payments, must be initiated by a predefined code. You should set up a payment code for each payment method. For our company, we will define a code for checks, cash, and credit card payments.

Follow these steps to define the payment codes:

1. From the Item List, press Ctrl-Ins and select Payment as the item type.

2. In the Code field, enter **1**, the code we will assign for payments made in cash at the time of sale.

3. In the Payment Method field, press Ctrl-L and select Cash from the Payment Method List.

4. Enter **Received Cash** as the description. This will print on the customer's invoice to identify the amount received.

5. Press F10 to record the code and return to the Item List.

6. Press Ctrl-Ins and choose to add a Payment.

7. Enter **2** in the Code field.

8. For Payment Method, Press Ctrl-L and select Check from the list.

9. Enter **Paid by Check** as the description.

10. Press F10 to record the code.

11. Press Ctrl-Ins to enter one more Payment code.

12. Enter **3** in the Code field.

13. Select VISA as the Payment Method.

14. Enter **Payment put on VISA** as the description.

15. Press F10 to record the code.

When you view a summary of payments (on the Deposit Summary screen), the payments are identified by the payment method, not by the payment code. Using the Deposit Summary screen is described in Chapter 10.

CREATING REFUND CODES

When customers return merchandise or overpay a bill, they may want the credit applied to a future purchase, or they may prefer a refund check. To give a customer a refund, you must use a refund code.

You can set up different refund codes with designated amounts, or codes that calculate the refund based on a percentage of the previous line on the invoice. For example, if a wholesaler returns merchandise, you may refund only 90 percent of the original invoice, retaining 10 percent as a restocking charge.

Follow these steps to create a refund code for our company:

1. From the Item List, press Ctrl-Ins to add an item.

2. For the item type, select Refund.

3. In the Code field, enter **Refund**.

4. In the Account field, press Ctrl-L and select 1000 (Countrywide Bank). This is the checking account from which the refund is issued, and the only account type you can use with a Refund item type.

We will leave the Refund Amt field blank, because the amount of the refund will vary depending on the circumstances. For your own company, you can specify an amount or percentage for each refund code. To define the refund as a percentage rather than a flat dollar amount, follow the entry in the Refund Amt field with a % sign.

5. In the Description to Show on Invoice field, enter **Refund to Customer.** You can use this field to explain the reason for the refund.

6. Press F10 to record the code.

When you enter a refund code and amount on an invoice, QuickBooks automatically writes a check in the Checkbook for the amount. Chapter 8 describes how to view, create, and print checks in the QuickBooks Checkbook.

PRINTING THE ITEM LIST

To ensure that you entered all your products and services accurately, review a printed copy of the Item List. To print the list, press Ctrl-P from the Item List, select the printer you want to use, and then press ↵.

The list includes the code, type, description, and price (if any) of each item. Compare the list with the one shown in Figure 6.5. If they do not match, edit, delete, or add items as necessary, following the instructions in the next section.

FIGURE 6.5:

The Item List printout

```
                              Item List
                                                              Page 1
  9/ 1/93


    Code        Type        Description                   Price Each
  ----------  -------   ------------------------------   -----------
  SubTot      Subt      Taxable Item Subtotal               0.000
  B2159       Part      Sunflower Seed Mix                  4.000
  C7341       Part      Diet Specific Cat Food              8.400
  D4112       Part      Dog Leash                           5.200
  D4165       Part      Flea Shampoo                        6.550
  H1000       Part      Alfalfa Hay                       165.000
  D4100       Service   Dog Grooming                       28.000
  H1002       Service   Pasture Rental                    150.000
  bal forwd   Charge    Outstanding balance on start date   0.000
  Deliver     Charge    Delivery Charge                     0.000
  Price Disc  Disc      20% Discount for Quantity Purchase -20.000%
  1           Paymt     Received Cash                       0.000
  2           Paymt     Paid by Check                       0.000
  3           Paymt     Payment put on VISA                 0.000
  Refund      Refund    Refund to Customer                  0.000
  Tax         Tax       California Sales Tax                6.500%
                        Dist: California
```

EDITING AND DELETING ITEM RECORDS

After your product, service, and other invoice-related records are defined, you may want to delete a record you no longer use, or change the sales price for a product or service. You can edit and delete these records even after using the information in transactions.

To edit an item on the Item List, highlight the item and press Ctrl-E to display the record. Modify the information as necessary, and then record your changes. The changes you make are not retroactive; they affect only future invoices.

You can delete records for products, services, and other items at any time. For example, you may no longer carry a certain product or offer a specific service.

Now that our customer account balances are accurate and the balance sheet is correct, we can delete the Balance Forward item, which is used only during setup. Follow these steps to delete the item:

 *Delete the Balance Forward item only after you are certain your customers' opening balances and the balance sheet are correct.*

1. On the Item List, highlight Bal Forwd.
2. Press Ctrl-Del to delete the item.
3. When the warning appears, press ↵ to confirm that you want to remove the item.

This completes the setup of our company, chart of accounts, customer, employee, vendor, and item records. The following chapters explain how to use QuickBooks in your daily work. Next, you will learn how to record and pay invoices from your vendors.

CHAPTER

7

Managing Vendor Invoices

**V**endor invoices are bills for resale products or operating expenses. Usually, you do not pay the full invoice amount immediately. Therefore, you record vendor invoices as a liability (an account payable). An invoice from a vendor increases what you owe that vendor, and thereby increases the balance in the Accounts Payable account in the general ledger.

HANDLING ACCOUNTS PAYABLE

The QuickBooks Accounts Payable function has several limitations:

◆ Although your vendors may offer different payment terms, QuickBooks allows only one definition for assigning due dates to vendor invoices. You can override the due date when entering an invoice, but you must calculate the date from the terms on the invoice yourself.

◆ QuickBooks does not allow you to take discounts when you pay your vendors. If your vendor offers an early payment discount, you must calculate it yourself and deduct it from the invoice total before you record the invoice in your system.

◆ You cannot enter an open credit memo (one that is not applied to an invoice). You must hold a credit memo until you have a new invoice to enter, and then subtract the credit from that invoice's total. Recording the credit this way incorrectly states your liabilities. Another disadvantage is that it's easy to forget or lose the document and never get a refund from the vendor.

You will learn how to handle vendor discounts and credit memos later in this chapter.

If you want to be able to review how much you owe, print vendor history (previous invoices and payments), and report payments to 1099 vendors, you must use QuickBooks as follows:

◆ Set up the vendor in your company lists (see Chapter 5).

◆ Record invoices when you incur the expense (*accrual basis accounting*), rather than when you pay the invoice (*cash-basis accounting*).

◆ Enter invoices in the Accounts Payable register.

◆ Create checks through the Pay Bills option on the Accounts Payable submenu. If you write checks using the Checkbook option on the Main menu, QuickBooks will not reduce the balance on the vendor's account, nor record the payments in the Accounts Payable register.

ENTERING VENDOR INVOICES

NOTE NOTE *Enter a vendor debit memo, such as a fee for re-stocking returned merchandise, in the same way that you record a vendor invoice.*

You record invoices from your vendors in the QuickBooks Accounts Payable register. Vendor invoice amounts are automatically recorded in the Accounts Payable account. When you are recording a vendor invoice, you must select which account indicates the reason for the invoice. You can use this information to evaluate your business activities. For example, to calculate profit on resale merchandise (and see if your overall markup is sufficient), you can compare the Expense account for merchandise purchases with the Income accounts for product sales.

RECORDING INVOICES FOR MERCHANDISE

The items you buy to resell to your customers are referred to as *merchandise*. We will enter a vendor invoice for dog houses purchased by the Training Company. The completed entry is shown in Figure 7.1.

Follow these steps to enter the invoice:

1. Choose Accounts Payable from the Main menu, then A/P Register from the submenu. The Accounts Payable register appears. You can see the account number in the bottom-left corner of the screen.

2. Override the current date in the Date field by typing **090493**, the date on the vendor's invoice. QuickBooks uses the date in this field to determine the date by which the invoice must be paid.

3. Enter **4P-1137** in the Inv Num field. This is the number on the invoice we received from the vendor.

4. In the Vendor field, press Ctrl-L and select Four Paws Pet Center from the Vendor List.

The Pay Date field entry, supplied by QuickBooks, is based on the vendor terms you set through the company options. In Chapter 2, we specified that the payment terms for our company's vendor invoices are 30 days after the invoice date. If a particular invoice should be paid sooner or later than those terms, you can override the program-supplied pay date and enter a different due date.

5. Press ↵ to accept the entry in the Pay Date field.

6. In the Owed field, enter **428.35**, the total amount of the invoice.

QuickBooks skips the Paid field. You cannot make an entry in this field. The program fills it in when you write a check through the Pay Bills option.

NOTE NOTE
NOTE
If you have installed Biz-minder, it will check the Pay Date field and remind you of payments you need to make.

FIGURE 7.1:

Entering a vendor invoice

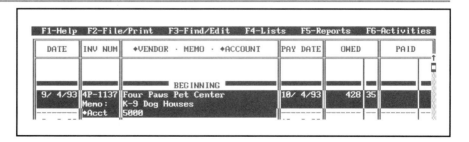

7. Enter **K-9 Dog Houses** in the Memo field. This is extra information to identify the invoice. You can use the Memo field to include transactions on reports.

8. In the Account field, press Ctrl-L and select the Expense account for merchandise purchases, 5000. By charging this account, we indicate that we are buying merchandise to resell.

 Ask your accountant how to record merchandise and related costs in your company.

If you want to record vendor charges for freight or shipping insurance separately, you can set up individual Expense accounts for them in the chart of accounts. Our company combines these types of incidental costs into the cost of goods.

9. When QuickBooks asks for confirmation before recording the transaction, press ↵. QuickBooks updates the balances in the vendor record and in the Accounts Payable account. The register remains open, ready for entry of the next invoice.

If you chose to keep track of projects when you set up your company (see Chapter 2), a Project field also appears in the Accounts Payable register. You could enter the predefined project that was responsible for the expense (or select it from your Project List).

RECORDING INVOICES FOR OPERATING EXPENSES

Operating expenses are costs that are not directly related to the merchandise you buy to resell. They include expenses such as utility bills, rent, office supplies, and repairs. Follow these steps to enter a sample invoice for vendor services:

1. In the Accounts Payable register, enter **090593** in the Date field.

2. In the Inv Num field, enter **746**.

3. Press Ctrl-L in the Vendor field and select Sam Spade from the list.

4. Enter **092593** in the Pay Date field. This vendor wants payment 20 days after the invoice date, so we need to override the program-supplied date.

5. In the Owed field, enter **1000**. This is the amount the vendor charged to plant hay in one of our fields.

6. In the Memo field, enter **Hay, East 40** to indicate what he did and which field was planted.

7. In the Account field, press Ctrl-L and select the Expense account for crop maintenance, 5120.

8. Press ↵ at the prompt to record the transaction.

DEDUCTING A CREDIT MEMO FROM AN INVOICE

A credit memo from a vendor is a reduction of the amount you owe.

The next invoice we will enter is for a shipment of cat condos we just received. Last week, this same vendor sent us a credit memo for some defective cat toys we returned after we paid for them. To use our credit, we will adjust the total invoice amount. Follow these steps to record the next invoice:

1. In the Accounts Payable register, press + in the Date field to increase the date by one day. The date on the invoice is 9/6/93.

2. In the Inv Num field, enter **43758-K**, the invoice number.

3. In the Vendor field, type **K** and press ↵. QuickBooks searches through the Vendor List, finds the only record that begins with K (Kat Kastle), and places it in the register.

4. Press ↵ to accept the entry in the Pay Date field.

If you are not sure how much the amount owed should be, enter the vendor, then press Ctrl-S (leave the Amount field blank). As you enter each account amount, QuickBooks increases the amount owed. When you are finished, the result appears in the Owed field.

5. In the Owed field, enter **81.50**. This is the amount of the current invoice, $98.50, less the amount of the credit memo, $17.00.

6. Enter **Cat Condos & CM66592** in the Memo field. This notation indicates what the invoice is for and also references the number of the credit memo we used against it.

7. In the Account field, press Ctrl-S to display the Split Transaction window.

Split transactions divide the total amount of a transaction between two or more general ledger accounts. We will enter two lines to show the original invoice amount and the credit memo amount.

8. Press Ctrl-L in the Account field and select the Expense account for merchandise purchases, 5000.

9. Enter **Total of Invoice # 43758-K** in the Description field for this line.

10. In the Amount field, enter **98.50**, the full amount of the invoice.

11. In the Account field, type " (a quotation mark) to copy the account, 5000, from the previous line.

The credit memo relates to an invoice for toys, which was originally charged to the Merchandise Purchases account. Therefore, we used the " data-entry shortcut to repeat the same account number.

12. In the Description field, enter **Credit for Inv # 43644-K** to describe the reason for this line.

Because our first entry was $17.00 more than the original invoice amount, QuickBooks has entered -**17.00** in the Amount field, as shown in Figure 7.2. The minus sign preceding the entry causes the amount to be subtracted from the account balance.

13. Press Ctrl-↵ to record your entries and return to the register. The first account appears in the Acct column, but the word *SPLIT* under the date shows that other entries exist for this invoice.

14. Press ↵ to accept the entry in the Account field.

15. Press ↵ when QuickBooks asks if it can record the transaction.

16. Press Esc to return to the Main menu.

RECORDING INVOICE PAYMENT DISCOUNTS

If a vendor allows you an early payment discount, subtract the amount of the discount from the invoice total and enter the result in the Owed column.

FIGURE 7.2:

Splitting a transaction to record a credit memo

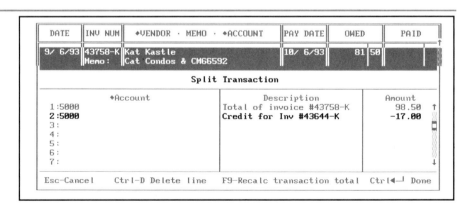

Then split the transaction (press Ctrl-S in the Account field), as we did to record a credit memo in the previous example.

Discounts you take are money you "earned" because of your timely payment.

Record the original amount of the invoice in the Expense account for merchandise purchases. Your accountant may suggest that you record vendor discounts in an Income account. Change the due date to the discount allowed date to ensure the vendor will allow the reduced payment. Your entries in the Split Transaction window would reflect this information:

Invoice amount owed	45.00
Merchandise Expense account	50.00
Discounts Earned (Income) account	−5.00

When you are making vendor payments, the invoice amount will be the total invoice less the discount you created. The voucher detail on the check stub shows only the net payment; it will not indicate the original amount of the invoice nor your early payment discount.

RECORDING A LOAN

You record your loans in Current Liability (for short-term loans) or Long-Term Liability accounts. Our company got a loan in order to purchase a laser printer. The loan must be repaid in six months. Before we enter the loan, we must set up the vendor and a liability account.

SETTING UP THE VENDOR

We need to add a new vendor record so that we can make payments on the loan. Follow these steps to enter the vendor information:

1. From the Main menu, select Company Lists, choose Vendors from the Select List menu, and press Ctrl-Ins to add a new vendor.

2. In the Pay To field, enter the following name and address:

   Loans-R-Us
   49 Silver Dollar Road
   Elko, NV 89801

3. Press ↵ twice to skip the Vendor Type and Taxpayer ID No. fields.

4. Enter **31-7921**, the loan identification given us by the vendor, for the Account Number/Notes field.

5. In the Contact field, enter **LuAnn Sharke**.

6. Enter **702 985 6138** in the Tel field.

7. Press ↵ to record your entries, and then press Esc to return to the Main menu.

Setting Up the Liability Account

Now we will add a Current Liability account to keep track of what we owe. You can record all your short-term liabilities in one account, but we prefer to set up separate accounts for each loan. Follow these steps to add the account:

 *You estab-lish an opening balance for an account only when you are setting up QuickBooks and adding an existing account.*

1. From the Main menu, select Chart of Accounts, press Ctrl-Ins, and choose to add a Current Liability.

2. In the Name for this Account field, enter **2200**.

3. Press ↵ to leave the zero in the Account Balance field.

4. In the As Of field, enter the date we are establishing this account, **090793**.

5. Enter **Computer Loan** in the Description field.

6. Enter the number on our loan, **559207**, in the Notes/Account Number field. QuickBooks records the account and places it in the chart of accounts.

Entering the Loan

After setting up the vendor and the liability account, we are ready to enter the loan amount. The completed information is shown in Figure 7.3. Follow these steps to record the short-term loan:

1. The new Current Liability account, 2200, should be highlighted on the Chart of Accounts screen. Press ↵ to display its register.

2. In the Date field, enter **090793**, the date we got the loan.

3. In the Payee field, press Ctrl-L and select Loans-R-Us from the list.

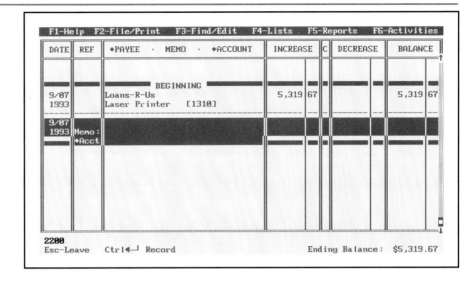

Recording a loan for a fixed asset

 Don't forget to have your accountant set up a depreciation schedule for each asset you get. You should enter depreciation into the depreciation expense account monthly or yearly, as your accountant advises.

4. Enter **5319.67** in the Increase column to record the amount by which we are increasing our liabilities.

5. Skip to the Memo field and enter **Laser Printer**.

6. In the Account field, press Ctrl-L and select account 1310 (Land and Equipment) to record the laser printer as a fixed asset. This entry simultaneously increases your outstanding debts and your assets.

7. Press ↵ at the prompt to record the transaction.

The account to which we charged this transaction is another balance sheet account. QuickBooks calls it a *transfer* when two balance sheet accounts are affected by the same transaction. To call your attention to the transfer, the account affected is enclosed in brackets: [1310]. The account in which you are working, 2200, is noted in the lower-left corner of the screen.

RECORDING CREDIT CARD CHARGES

To keep on top of your charge accounts, you should enter the charges and payments in your Credit Card register as they occur, rather than after your statement arrives. This allows you to see what you owe at any time.

We just used our credit card to charge a lube, oil, and filter for the delivery truck. The completed entry in the Credit Card register is shown in Figure 7.4.

Follow these steps to record the credit card transaction in the register:

1. From the Main menu, select Chart of Accounts.

2. On the Chart of Accounts screen, move the cursor to account 2110, Dutch Oil, and press ⏎ to display its register. The opening balance from when we set up the account appears.

3. In the Date field, enter **091293**, the date on the charge slip.

4. Press ⏎ to move past the Ref field. We do not want to make a special notation about this charge.

5. Enter **Hans' Auto Service** in the Payee field. We don't need to set this company up as a vendor because we neither owe them, nor write checks to them. We owe, and will make payments to, the credit card company.

6. Enter **19.95**, the cost of the service, in the Charge column.

7. Move to the Memo field and enter **1DWE846**. This is the license plate number on the truck we had serviced.

FIGURE 7.4:

Entering charges in a Credit Card register

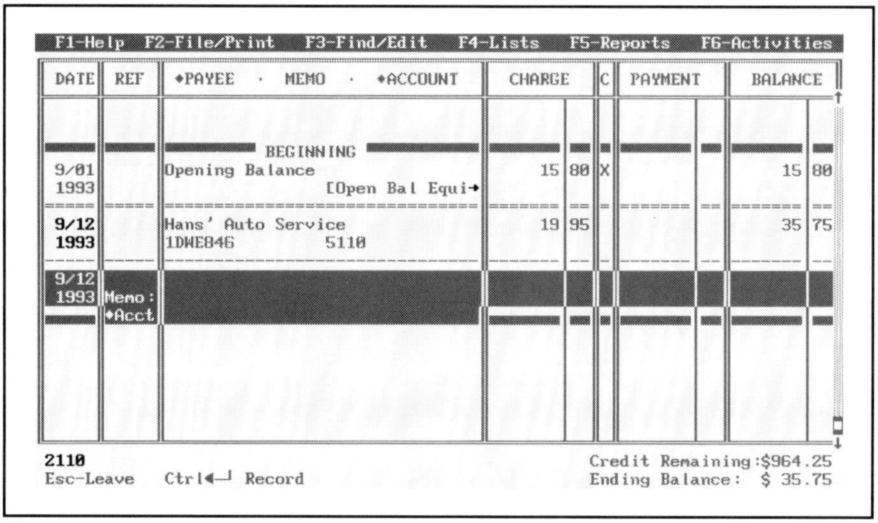

8. In the Account field, press Ctrl-L and select account 5110 (Auto/Truck Expense) to indicate how we want to categorize the charge.

9. At the prompt, select to record the transaction.

The Credit Remaining field in the lower-right corner of the register shows how much we can still charge on this card, according to the limit we entered in the account record. The Ending Balance field indicates what we currently owe on the account.

PAYING VENDOR BILLS

Before you create checks to pay Accounts Payable invoices, you should determine which invoices are due. In general, you should not pay invoices before their due date. If you are not being charged interest or finance charges, you can gain by holding the money in an interest-bearing account until the invoice must be paid.

PRINTING THE ACCOUNTS PAYABLE AGING REPORT

The Cash Flow Forecast report contains combined information from the Accounts Payable and Accounts Receivable Aging reports. Use it to determine when you can expect money to come in from your customers and when money is due to go out.

You can use the Accounts Payable Aging report to determine which accounts are coming due and prepare to make payments. This report separates your vendor balances into the time periods you designate. The aging periods can be manipulated so that the listing becomes a *cash-requirements report*. For example, if you specify periods that are only one week long, you can predict how much money you will need for bills due this week, next week, and the following week.

The Accounts Payable Aging report shows the vendor name, the total due, and the amounts due each aging period. It includes a grand total of all outstanding bills and a grand total for each period.

Follow these steps to print the report:

1. From the Main menu, select Reports, choose A/P Reports, and then select Aging Report.

2. Press ↵ in the Report Title field to accept the QuickBooks report name as the heading printed on the report.

3. In the Create Report As Of field, enter **092093**, the day we will be writing checks.

4. In the Show Aging at Intervals Of field, override the existing entry by entering **14**. We want to see how much we owe separated into two-week increments.

5. In the Through field, enter **28**. We want the report to have columns representing 28 days past 9/20/93, for two columns of 14 days each.

6. Press ↵ to accept No in the Select Vendors to Include field. We want the report to include all the vendors who meet the criteria we are entering.

7. Press ↵ to accept A, for All, in the Use All/Selected A/P Accounts field. We want to print all the Accounts Payable accounts in the chart of accounts.

When you move the cursor through the last field, QuickBooks generates the report and displays it on the screen, as shown in Figure 7.5.

8. To print the report, press Ctrl-P and select the printer to which you want the report sent.

9. After the report prints, press Esc to return to the Main menu.

For the report, QuickBooks compares the invoice due dates with the as of date, 9/20/93. Invoices that are due *after* 9/20/93 are listed as current. Invoices due *before* 9/20/93 are past due and listed according to how late they are. The Four

FIGURE 7.5:

Viewing the Accounts Payable Aging report

```
                              A/P AGING REPORT

                                As of 9/20/93
Training Company-All A/P Accounts
9/20/93
                                                                     OVERALL
          Vendor            Current    1 - 14    15 - 28     > 28     TOTAL

Four Paws Pet Center         428.35    930.00    250.00      0.00   1,608.35
Kat Kastle                    81.50  1,271.32      0.00      0.00   1,352.82
Sam Spade                  1,000.00      0.00      0.00      0.00   1,000.00

OVERALL TOTAL              1,509.85  2,201.32    250.00      0.00   3,961.17
```

Paws Pet Center invoice for $930 was due 9/15/93, 5 days ago, so it falls in the 1 to 14 days past due (1 - 14) column. The Kat Kastle invoice was due 9/6/93, exactly 14 days ago, and is also in the 1 to 14 days past due category. The oldest invoice from Four Paws, for $250, was due 17 days ago, on 9/3/93, and it is in the 15 to 28 days past-due category.

SELECTING INVOICES TO PAY

NOTE *You make payments to individuals or companies who are not defined as Accounts Payable vendors through the QuickBooks Checkbook, as described in Chapter 8.*

After recording vendor's invoices, and reviewing the aging report, you select the ones you want to pay. We will pay both past-due invoices to Four Paws and make a partial payment on the older Kat Kastle invoice.

Follow these steps to choose invoices for payment:

1. From the Main menu, select Accounts Payable, and then choose Pay Bills. The Pay Vendors screen appears.

2. Enter **092093** in the Pay Bills with Pay Dates Through field. This field indicates how much earlier than the due date you want to pay your bills. For example, you can select bills that are due through today or through next Friday. We want to select invoices that are due up to and including today, September 20.

3. In the Checking Account to Use field, press Ctrl-L and select 1000 (Countrywide Bank). Hereafter, QuickBooks will automatically enter the last account you used in this field. If you have more than one checking account, you can select which one to use each time you process bills to pay.

4. In the Pay All/Selected Bills field, press ↵ to accept A (for All). Either choice lists all invoices that meet the due-date criteria. However, when All is selected, they all are marked to be paid in full; otherwise, no payment amount appears.

5. On the Choose Bills to Pay screen, press ↵ to accept the payments that appear for both Four Paws invoices. We will pay both of these invoices in full.

6. In the Payment field for the Kat Kastle invoice, press F9 to place zeros in the field. This is a *toggle* key that switches back and forth between payment in full and no payment.

7. Enter the amount of the partial payment we want to make, **1000**, in the Payment field.

The completed Choose Bills to Pay screen is shown in Figure 7.6. At the bottom of the screen, you see the bank account number, the current balance in that account, and the total amount of the checks we are about to write. Beneath that information, in the bottom-left corner, the name of our company and the number of the Accounts Payable account in which we are working appear.

8. Press Ctrl-⏎ to record your entries.

9. On the next screen, select to print a payment summary (for your reference) and choose the printer. After the report prints, the Preparing to Record Checks window appears.

To reduce the balance of invoices entered in the Accounts Payable register, you must use the Pay Bills option. Any check initiated from the Checkbook will not affect the vendor records.

10. Enter **092093** as the date to record the checks in our check register and the date that will print on the checks. (You can change the printed date when you generate the checks.)

When you have QuickBooks record the Checks in the Check register, the vendor balance is reduced, even though you have not printed or distributed the checks. Remember, after the checks are created, you still have to print the physical checks. You will learn how to print checks in the next chapter.

FIGURE 7.6:

Selecting vendor invoices to pay

```
                        Choose Bills to Pay

            Vendor          Invoice  Pay Date   Balance    Payment

     Four Paws Pet Center   4P-781    9/ 3/93     250.00     250.00    ↑
     Four Paws Pet Center   4P-932    9/15/93     930.00     930.00
     Kat Kastle             53629k    9/ 6/93   1,271.32   1,000.00

                                                                       ⬜
                                                                       ↓

     1000 Balance $25,382.90                       TOTAL   2,180.00

     Esc-Cancel            F9-Pay in full/Don't pay          Ctrl◀⏎ Done


     Training Company (2000)
```

VERIFYING AND DELETING INVOICE PAYMENTS

Before you print checks, you should review the Payment Summary report that you printed after selecting invoices to pay. This report shows each invoice and the amount to be paid. It also totals the amount of cash you will need to pay those invoices.

Review the list to make sure each vendor will be paid as you intended and the total is what you expected. You can remove a payment before actually printing checks.

To delete a payment, choose Accounts Payable from the Main menu, and then select A/P Register from the submenu. Highlight the payment entry and press Ctrl-Del to delete the transaction. The invoice is returned to open invoices. If you want to pay a different amount on the invoice, after deleting the current payment, return to the Pay Bills option. Select that invoice for payment and specify the amount you want to pay.

In this chapter, you have learned how to record vendor invoices, loans, and credit card charges. You also learned how to pay your Accounts Payable vendors. When you want to write checks to other businesses or individuals, you use the Checkbook, which is the subject of the next chapter.

CHAPTER

8

Using the Checkbook

uickBooks handles two types of checks: those that the computer generates and prints and those that you write manually and enter as a transaction in the Check register. You can write checks in the QuickBooks Checkbook and have the program print them for you. Checks you write manually should be recorded in the Check register.

In this chapter, you will learn how to view the checks to your vendors (created through the Accounts Payable function), write checks in the Checkbook, and print all your checks. You will also learn how to work with the Check register.

VIEWING ACCOUNTS PAYABLE CHECKS

When you use QuickBooks to pay your vendors (through the Pay Bills option on the Accounts Payable submenu), the program creates the checks for you. The checks remain on the check-writing screen, in chronological order, until you print them.

Do not write a check to an Accounts Payable vendor from the Checkbook. Chapter 7 describes how to write Accounts Payable checks.

In the Check register, postdated checks appear under a double line, and their date is highlighted.

Note that you cannot edit an Accounts Payable check (one created through the Pay Bills option) on the check-writing screen. If you need to change the bank account, you can edit this information in the Accounts Payable register. If you make any other type of error, such as entering the wrong payee, date, or amount, you must delete the payment transaction in the Accounts Payable register, and then reenter the payment through the Pay Bills option.

To view the checks QuickBooks created for us when we selected to pay vendors (in the previous chapter), select Checkbook from the Main menu, and then choose Write/Print Checks from the submenu. Press Ctrl-PgUp to see the checks. The check to Kat Kastle is shown in Figure 8.1.

Information about the status of your checks appears at the bottom of the screen. The checking account number is in the lower-left corner. The Checks to Print field, in the lower-right corner, shows the total amount of the checks that are ready to print. Below this is the Ending Balance field, which includes all recorded checks, even those that are *postdated* (dated after today's date). You may also see the Current Balance field, which notes the balance as of your system date. The check number does not appear anywhere on the screen because it will be added when you print the checks.

You can print your Accounts Payable checks at the same time as you print the checks you write in the Checkbook.

FIGURE 8.1:

A check ready to print

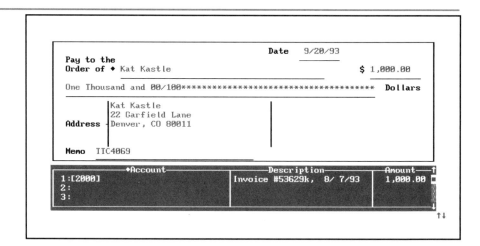

WRITING CHECKS IN THE CHECKBOOK

When you write checks from the Checkbook, you are recording the expense at the same time you make the payment. If you don't need to keep information about the payee, you can enter the check directly in the Checkbook. For example, you might create checks to pay obligations as soon as you receive the invoice, such as reimbursement of employee expenses. Other common business transactions that would originate in the Checkbook include reimbursing a petty cash fund and paying the paper boy.

SETTING UP A PETTY CASH FUND

Cash has a way of "slipping through your fingers" if you don't keep good records. Save the receipts when you pay in cash. Carry a small envelope, put the receipts and the change in it, and return them to the cash box at the office.

1. If you are not already in the Checkbook, from the Main menu, select Checkbook, and then choose Write/Print Checks.

2. Press Ctrl-End to move past the last check.

3. Press Back Tab to reach the Date field, and then override the system date by entering **091593**, the date we are setting up our petty cash fund. This is the date the transaction is recorded in the Check register, as well as the date that will print on the check.

4. In the Pay to the Order Of field, type **CASH**. We are taking money from our checking account to put in the petty cash box.

5. In the field marked with a dollar sign ($), enter **200** as the amount of the check. This is the money we want to keep on hand at the office. QuickBooks spells out the amount on the line below the payee.

6. Press ↵ to skip the Address field and move to the Memo field.

You can add a second message line to appear on your checks through the company options. See Chapter 2 for details.

7. In the Memo field, enter **Set Up Petty Cash Fund** to explain the reason for the transaction. This memo will appear on the printed check and in the Check register. It is also included on some reports.

The account-distribution window below the check area contains fields for specifying how check amounts will be recorded. In the Account field, you enter the general ledger account (or accounts) in which this transaction is to be recorded. Any entry you make in the Description field will print on the stub of a voucher check. You can use this field to enter more information than will fit in the Memo field. The Amount field indicates the amount that will be charged to the account you specified in the Account field. You can split the amount between several accounts, as we will do for our next check.

If, through the company options, you chose to keep track of projects, the check-writing screen would also include a field for specifying the project to which this check relates. You could enter one of your predefined projects, or press Ctrl-L and select from your Project List.

8. In the Account field, press Ctrl-L and select 1210 (Petty Cash) from the list. We are transferring the money to the petty cash account we defined when we set up our chart of accounts. Because we are writing a check, QuickBooks will reduce the balance in our checking account automatically.

9. Press ↵ to leave the Description field blank. QuickBooks places the check amount in the Amount field.

10. Press Ctrl-↵ to record this check.

Periodically, you will need to replace the petty cash you have spent and record where the money went. You will learn how to replenish the petty cash fund later in this chapter.

REIMBURSING AN EMPLOYEE'S EXPENSES

The next check we will write is to reimburse employee expenses. One of our sales representatives paid for a hotel room and also had to buy a tire for his car while he was using it for business. Follow these steps to write the check:

1. In the Pay to the Order Of field, press Ctrl-L to select from the Payee List.

The Payee List includes your vendors, employees, and customers. You cannot add, delete, or edit payees directly from this list. Its contents originate from the other company lists. If you type a payee name into the Pay to the Order Of field, QuickBooks won't look in the payee record for the payee's address. However, when you select the payee from the list, the program will insert the address on the check.

2. Select Kenneth M. Wade as the payee.

3. In the $ field, enter **152.90**, the amount of the check.

4. Press Shift-↵ to skip the completed Address field.

5. Enter **9/14 Expense Report** in the Memo field.

6. In the first Account field, press Ctrl-L and select 5110 (Auto/Truck Expense).

7. Enter **Radial Tire for Car** in the Description field.

8. Press Ctrl-Backspace to erase the entry in the Amount field (the full amount of the check). We are going to split the amount of the check between two expense accounts.

9. Enter **57.10** as the amount spent on a new tire. This entry increases the balance in the Auto/Truck Expense account.

10. In the second Account field, press Ctrl-L and select 5181 (Hotel Expense), a subaccount under Travel Expense.

Notice that the primary account number precedes the subaccount number in the Account field. If, through the company options, you chose to show lowest subaccounts/subprojects only, you would not see the primary account here.

You cannot charge transactions directly to a primary account that has subaccounts; they must be charged to one of its subaccounts. If you don't designate which subaccount to use, QuickBooks creates an account called Other beneath the primary account and enters the transaction in it.

11. Enter **Home-When-Away Hotel** in the Description field. The remainder of the check amount appears in the Amount field. Figure 8.2 shows the completed check.

FIGURE 8.2:

Recording various expenses on a check

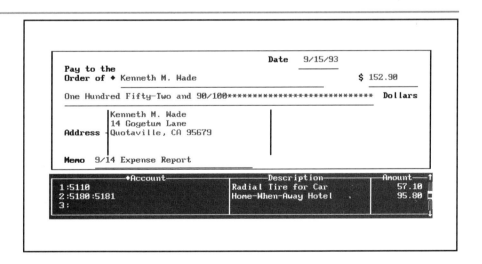

12. Press ↵ to accept the amount in the Amount field. Notice that the account-distribution window rolls up to allow you to divide the check among other accounts.

13. Press F10 to record the check.

MAKING A LOAN PAYMENT

When you get a loan, you record it as a current or long-term liability, not as an account payable. You enter the entire liability amount at once, then you reduce the balance with each payment. You do not enter an invoice for these kinds of debts.

 If you want a payment to appear in the liability account and you also want to split the transaction, charging it to both principal and tax-deductible interest, you must make a separate entry in the liability account register to record the reduction in your balance.

When you write a check to make a payment on a liability or a credit card, enter the name of the Current Liability or Long-Term Liability account in the Account field on the check. QuickBooks will automatically make an entry in the liability account to note the payment and reduce the amount in the Balance field of the register.

Follow these steps to write a check for our loan payment:

1. Press Back Tab to move to the Date field and enter **092293**, the date we want printed on the check.

2. In the Pay to the Order of field, press Ctrl-L and select Loans-R-Us from the Payee List.

3. In the $ field, enter **886.50**, the amount of our monthly payment.

4. Press Shift-↵ to skip to the Memo field.

5. Enter **31-7921**, our loan number, in the Memo field.

6. In the Account field, press Ctrl-L and select 2200 (Computer Loan).

7. Enter **Monthly Payment** in the Description field.

8. Press ↵ to accept the amount in the Amount field. The entire amount is recorded in the Current Liability account, reducing the amount we owe. Do *not* record the check yet.

Before we record the check, we will save it so we can use the format again. In the next section, we will have QuickBooks memorize the check.

Memorizing a Check

Many of your financial activities are repetitive. Instead of reentering these transactions each time you need them, you can use the QuickBooks function for memorizing transactions. This function allows you to save the transaction and later recall it. The recurring transaction can be a check, customer invoice, or transaction in an account register.

Now we will memorize our loan-payment check. This way, instead of writing the check each month, we can copy the stored check. Follow these steps:

1. After completing the fields in the account-distribution window, press Ctrl-M to memorize the check. (Ctrl-M is the shortcut for the Memorize Transaction option on the F4 menu.) The program highlights the fields in the check that will be memorized and prompts you to verify that you want to memorize the transaction, as shown in Figure 8.3.

2. Press ↵ to memorize the highlighted fields.

3. After Quicken memorizes the check, press F10 to record the current check.

If you didn't want to process the check (or another transaction) after Quick-Books memorized it, you could delete it. The check itself would be removed, but the memorized copy would remain.

FIGURE 8.3:

Memorizing a check

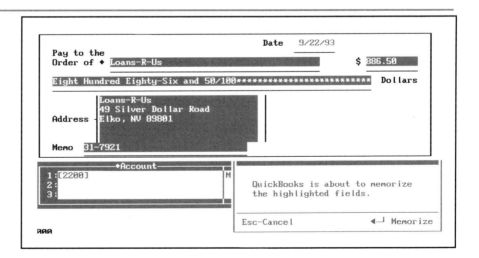

PRINTING CHECKS

 You can order checks from Intuit that are designed for continuous feed or laser and inkjet printers.

All the checks you created in QuickBooks—through the Accounts Payable Pay Bills option and through the Checkbook--are waiting to be printed. You can choose to print all the checks dated through a specific date or to print only selected checks. We will print all of the checks we wrote in this and the previous chapter, with one exception. We will not print the postdated check, which is the one to Loans-R-Us.

Load blank paper (not check forms) into your printer, and then follow these steps to print our checks:

1. From the check-writing screen, press F2 (File/Print) and select the Print Checks option. You see the Print Checks window, as shown Figure 8.4.

The number of checks to print (all the checks ready for printing) is noted at the top of the window, followed by the number of postdated checks. In our examples, the system date is 9/20/93. Therefore, the loan payment we recorded with a 9/22/93 date is a postdated check. The information on your screen will reflect your actual system date.

You can include all checks through a specific future date by entering that date in the Print Checks Dated Through field. To select specific checks to print, enter S in the Print All/Selected Checks field.

FIGURE 8.4:

Printing checks

```
                          Print Checks

                   There are 5 checks to print.
                   (There is 1 postdated check.)
         Print checks dated through:  9/20/93

         Print All/Selected checks (A/S): A

         ◆Print to: HP LaserJet, 10 cpi, Portrait, LPT1

         ◆Type of check:          Additional copies (0-9): 0

         To print a sample check to help with alignment, press F9.

                         F9-Print sample
         Esc-Cancel          F1-Help              Ctrl◄─┘ Print
```

2. Override the system date in the Print Checks Dated Through field by entering **092093**.

3. In the Print All/Selected Checks field, enter **S** to review and select the checks that will be printed.

4. Choose the printer that you want to use to print the checks.

5. In the Type of Check field, press Ctrl-L and select either the Voucher or Standard check style. Standard is an $8^{1}/_{2}$-by-$3^{1}/_{2}$-inch check. Voucher is an $8^{1}/_{2}$-by-7-inch form, with a $3^{1}/_{2}$-inch high check and a $3^{1}/_{2}$-inch detachable stub on the bottom.

6. Press F9 to print a sample check to test the check alignment. QuickBooks uses the first check to verify the alignment of the forms in your printer. It prints *VOID CHECK* on the body of the check and voids the first check number.

If you are using a laser printer, an alignment test is not necessary, as long as you have placed the check forms in the paper tray facing the right direction. If letterhead goes in face up, the highest check number should be on top. If letterhead goes in the tray face down, put the lowest check number on top.

If you have continuous feed checks, the alignment test prints a pointer line, corresponding to the line numbers on the continuous feed strip on the check forms, and displays the Automatic Form Alignment window. If the test shows the checks are not aligned properly, enter the line number of the pointer line in the Position number field. QuickBooks will immediately print a second test. Each check used in the test is voided. When the checks are properly aligned, leave the Position Number field blank and press ↵.

7. After the alignment test, press ↵ in the Additional Copies field to accept 0 (zero). If you are using a laser printer, you can print additional copies (as a duplicate for your records) by entering the number of copies you want. The Select Checks to Print screen appears, as shown in Figure 8.5.

In the bottom-right corner, the Checks to Print field shows the total amount of all the checks that have been written, regardless of their date. The Current Balance field shows what your checking account balance is as of the current

Remember, you can set up two printers. You might keep checks loaded in one and use the other for reports.

FIGURE 8.5:

Selecting specific checks to print

```
 F1-Help      File/Print       Find/Edit       Lists      Reports      Activities

                            Select Checks to Print

      Date           Payee                    Memo              Amount       Print

  ▶  9/15/93  CASH                     Set Up Petty Cash Fun    200.00      Print↑
     9/15/93  Kenneth M. Wade          9/14 Expense Report      152.90      Print▯
     9/20/93  Four Paws Pet Center     DS3629                 1,180.00      Print
     9/20/93  Kat Kastle              TTC4069                 1,000.00      Print
     9/22/93  Loans-R-Us              31-7921                   886.50

                                                                             ↓

              Spacebar-Select/Deselect      Ctrl-Spacebar All/None
    Esc-Cancel                         F1-Help                       Ctrl◄┘ Done
                                                                              ↑
    1000                              Checks to Print: $ 3,419.40
                                      Current Balance: $22,850.00
                                      Ending Balance:  $21,963.50
```

date, including checks and deposits made with dates up to and including your system date (which is 9/20/93 in our sample). The Ending Balance field shows the balance, including any future-dated transactions in the Check register.

In the list of checks, all but the one to Loans-R-Us (the postdated one) are marked to print. To mark a check to print, highlight it and then press the spacebar. Use the Ctrl-spacebar combination to toggle between marking all the checks to print or not to print. The spacebar alone marks or unmarks one check at a time.

8. Press Ctrl-↵ to accept printing all but the postdated check and exit the Select Checks to Print screen. The Set Check Number window appears. It shows the number of the first check to be printed in the Next Check Number field.

9. If the Next Check Number field does not contain 1001, enter **1001** in that field. The checks print immediately.

10. After the checks print, QuickBooks displays a prompt asking if the checks printed correctly. Press ↵ at the prompt, and then press Esc to return to the Checkbook submenu.

REPRINTING CHECKS

To get on-line help about printing from QuickBooks, press F1 from any Print window.

If your first printing is incorrect because your printer mangled the checks or you ran them on plain paper by mistake, you can print them a second time. QuickBooks will ignore the record of the original checks and print new ones starting with the number you indicate. You must physically nullify the original checks.

To reprint the checks, enter the number of the first check in the series you want to cancel at the prompt:

First incorrectly printed check

The Print Checks window will reappear. From there, you can press Esc to cancel the check run. Checks numbered before the number you specify are recorded; checks numbered after the canceled run remain as written, but still pending printing.

Complete the fields in the Print Checks window again. In the Set Check Number window, for the next check number, enter the number of the first check in the series you have placed in the printer for the second printing.

WORKING IN THE CHECK REGISTER

Money you receive from your customers and deposit in your bank account also appears in the Check register. These transactions are covered in Chapter 10.

The Check register lists all the activity in your checking account. To display the register for our sample checking account, select Check Register from the Checkbook submenu. Your register should look like the one shown in Figure 8.6. The number assigned to the checks we have written appears in the Num column. Pending checks appear with asterisks in place of a number.

To edit a transaction in the Check register, highlight it, type over the existing data, and then record your changes. To edit the account distribution, highlight the transaction and press Ctrl-S. When the account distribution window appears, make your changes and record them. To delete a line, highlight it and press Ctrl-D. Always use discretion when you are editing or deleting recorded transactions. Usually, it is best to create a reversing entry to keep your audit trail intact.

You can also add a check for QuickBooks to print, as long as it is not a check to pay one of your vendors (use the Pay Bills option on the Accounts Payable menu to add a vendor check). Record the check and account distribution

FIGURE 8.6:

The Check register

DATE	NUM	◆PAYEE · MEMO · ◆ACCOUNT	PAYMENT	C	DEPOSIT	BALANCE
9/01 1993	Memo:	Opening Balance ◆Acct [Open Bal Equity]		X	25,382 90	25,382 90
9/15 1993	1001 SPLIT	CASH Set up Petty Ca◆[1210]	200 00			25,182 90
9/15 1993	1002 SPLIT	Kenneth M. Wade 9/14 Expense Re◆5110	152 90			25,030 00
9/20 1993	1003 SPLIT	Four Paws Pet Center DS3629 [2000]	1,180 00			23,850 00
9/20 1993	1004 SPLIT	Kat Kastle TTC4069 [2000]	1,000 00			22,850 00
9/22 1993	***** SPLIT	Loans-R-Us 31-7921 [2200]	886 50			21,963 50

1000

in the register, and leave the Num field filled with asterisks. QuickBooks will recognize it as an unprinted check and print it with your next check run.

If you want to return a printed check to checks-to-be-printed status, type an * (asterisk) over the existing check number (QuickBooks will fill the field with asterisks). You can then reprint that check along with your other pending payments.

VOIDING A PRINTED CHECK

Use caution when selecting to void a check. You are not given a chance to confirm your intention or change your mind.

After QuickBooks records correctly printed checks, you may need to void a check. Perhaps you put a stop payment on a lost or damaged check. When you void a check, your audit trail shows what happened to the check.

To void a check, highlight it in the Check register, press F3 (Find/Edit), and select Void Transaction. Then record the change. The check remains listed in the register, but the word VOID appears on the transaction.

RECORDING MANUAL CHECKS

Sometimes you need to pay for something at the time you buy it. You can handwrite a check, then record it later in the Check register.

We bought some office supplies from the local stationary store. This store requires everyone to pay cash for purchases, so we wrote a manual check.

Follow these steps to record the manual check in the Check register:

1. If the register is not already on your screen, select Checkbook from the Main menu, and then choose Check Register.

2. In the Check register, press Ctrl-End to display a blank entry line.

3. Enter **092393** as the Date we wrote the check.

4. In the Num field, enter **945**, the number of the check.

5. Enter **Office Mart** in the Payee field (the stationary store is not in our Payee List).

6. Enter **64.87**, the amount of the check, in the Payment field.

7. In the Memo field, enter **M487**, the number on the receipt from the stationary store.

8. In the Account field, press Ctrl-L and select 5160 (Office Supplies) to indicate what type of expense this check paid.

9. At the prompt, press ↵ to record the manual check.

To enter the date, you may need to press the spacebar through both lines in the Date field, then press Back Tab to go to the first line. Enter 09/23, press ←twice on the second line, and enter 1993.

HANDLING MANUAL CHECKS TO ACCOUNTS PAYABLE VENDORS

Although you can record a manual check written to an Accounts Payable vendor in the Checkbook, the transaction will not affect the vendor history (it won't appear with the vendor transaction history when you print the Vendor List), nor the vendor balance.

If you do write a manual check for an invoice you already entered in the Accounts Payable register, the only way to reduce the balance in the vendor record is to delete the transaction from the register. When you enter the manual check, be sure to charge the appropriate Expense account for the payment.

MAKING ADVANCE PAYMENTS TO VENDORS

An advance payment is not included in the records for our sample company.

You may need to write a check in advance of receiving an invoice from one of your established vendors. For example, suppose that the transmission failed in your old delivery truck, and you had it towed to your regular repair shop. The manager says you must pay in advance for special-order parts. You gave him a down payment of $400 for a rebuilt transmission. You will get an invoice including the parts and labor when the repair is complete.

When you record the manual check, charge it to a prepaid expense account for advance payments to vendors. Figure 8.7 shows the original deposit made by writing a manual check and charging it to Advance Payments, an asset account in the general ledger.

When you receive the invoice for the repairs, enter the invoice in the Accounts Payable register. In the Owed field, enter just the balance (275.80), the amount left after you subtract the deposit from the total cost (675.80).

Select to split the invoice, and enter the Advance Payments account number with a minus amount to reverse the original entry. Then enter the Auto Expense account number, and charge the entire cost of the repairs to this account. Figure 8.8 shows the invoice entry for the balance due on the invoice, with the account distribution reversing the amount in the Advance Payments account and charging the entire expense (deposit and remaining balance) to the Auto Expense account.

FIGURE 8.7:

Recording an advance payment in the asset account

DATE	NUM	◆PAYEE · MEMO · ◆ACCOUNT	PAYMENT	C	DEPOSIT	BALANCE
9/22 1993	***** SPLIT	Loans-R-Us 31-7921 [2200]	886 50			21,963 50
9/23 1993	945	Office Mart M487 5160	64 87			21,898 63
9/25 1993	SPLIT	Petty Cash Replenish Fund 5110	51 75			21,846 88
9/25 1993		Phyllis Rocklin Sept Draw [3015]	1,500 00			20,346 88
9/30 1993	946 Memo: ◆Acct	Jin's Auto Repair Deposit on Transmission Work [1240]	400 00			19,946 88
9/30 1993						
		END				

MEMORIZING AUTOMATIC DEDUCTIONS IN THE CHECK REGISTER

Some withdrawals from your checking account aren't made by check. For example, the bank takes service charges and some obligations are satisfied by automatic deductions.

FIGURE 8.8:

Reversing the advance payment and charging the expense account

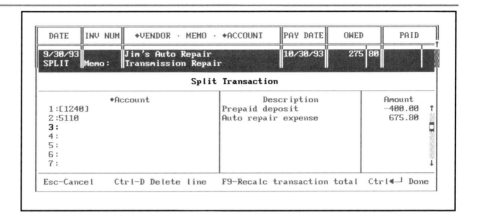

The loan payment for our delivery truck is deducted automatically each month from our checking account. Follow these steps to memorize that transaction:

1. If the Check register is not already on your screen, select Check Register from the Checkbook submenu.

2. Enter **092593** in the Date field. The bank deducts our loan payment on the twenty-fifth of each month.

3. Skip the Num field (check numbers are not used in automatic deductions), and enter **Countrywide Loans** as the Payee.

4. In the Payment field, enter **260,** the amount of our monthly payment.

5. In the Memo field, enter **28032-4,** the number of our loan.

6. Enter **2310** (Truck Loan) as the account in which we record payments on this long-term liability.

7. When you are prompted to confirm recording the transaction, press ↵.

8. Highlight the recorded transaction, and then press Ctrl-M to memorize it.

9. At the prompt, press ↵ to confirm that you want QuickBooks to memorize the highlighted fields.

10. Press Esc to return to the Checkbook submenu.

To enter the payment next month, we can recall the memorized transaction instead of keying it into the register as we just did. Chapter 13 describes how to recall memorized transactions.

WRITING CHECKS FOR SPECIAL PURPOSES

Two types of checks you will write are for special business purposes. When you need to put more money into your petty cash fund, you should record the amounts spent at the same time as you write a check to replenish the fund. This way, you can account for the expenditures and end up with the same amount of cash on hand.

Another check you may write regularly is to the owner or owners of the business. Most owners take an amount of cash out of the business on a monthly basis.

REPLENISHING THE PETTY CASH FUND

Our company used petty cash to buy a birthday cake for an employee, to get gasoline, and to pay the paper boy. The account distribution is shown in Figure 8.9.

Follow these steps to record the expenditures and replenish the fund:

1. From the Checkbook submenu, choose Write/Print Checks.

FIGURE 8.9:

Replenishing the petty cash fund

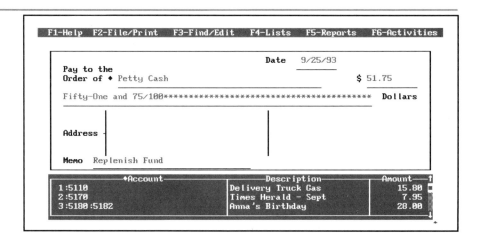

2. Press Back Tab to move to the Date field and enter **092593**. When you are writing checks for your own company, you usually can accept the system date as the date of the transaction.

3. In the Pay to the Order Of field, enter **Petty Cash**.

4. In the $ field, enter **51.75**, the total of the receipts in the cash box. The receipts and the cash left in the box should equal the original $200 fund.

5. Enter **Replenish Fund** in the Memo field.

6. In the Account field, press Ctrl-L and select 5110 (Auto/Truck Expense) as the account in which to record the gasoline purchase.

7. Enter **Delivery Truck Gas** in the Description field.

8. In the Amount field, press Ctrl-Backspace to erase the amount and enter **15.80**, which is the amount we spent on gas.

9. On the next line in the Account field, press Ctrl-L and then press 5 to move the cursor to the first account that starts with that number.

10. Move the cursor to account number 5170 (Subscriptions) and select it. This account is the one in which we record what we pay for the newspaper.

11. Enter **Times Herald - Sept** in the Description field.

12. Enter **7.95** as the amount we paid the paper boy.

13. On the third line in the Account field, press Ctrl-L, and then press Ctrl-End to move the cursor to the last account.

14. Select 5182 (Meals Expense) for the birthday cake.

15. For the Description, enter **Anna's Birthday**. The remainder of the check, 28.00, appears in the Amount field.

16. To accept the amount (the cake cost $28) and record the check, press Ctrl-↵.

TAKING OWNER DRAWS

In a single proprietorship or a partnership, each principal has a drawing account to record how much he or she takes out of the business. As profits are distributed to the principals, their capital accounts increase. This transaction is recorded in a drawing account, which acts as a contra account (an offset) to the principal's capital account.

Follow these steps to record a capital withdrawal by the owner of our company:

1. Leave the 9/25/93 entry in the Date field and enter **Phyllis Rocklin** in the Pay to the Order Of field.

2. In the $ field, enter **1500**, the amount of cash she is withdrawing.

3. Enter **Sept Draw** in the Memo field.

4. In the Account field, press Ctrl-L and select 3015 (Owner's Draw) as the account where we record money received by Phyllis.

5. Press F10 to record your entries.

In this chapter, you learned how to use the QuickBooks Checkbook to write and print checks. Remember, to maintain your vendor accounts properly, you should make your payments to Accounts Payable vendors through the Pay Bills option on the Accounts Payable submenu. Then you can print the checks to your vendors at the same time as your print the checks you wrote directly in the Checkbook.

The next chapter deals with a subject that is important to any business: sales. You will learn how to create and print invoices.

CHAPTER

9

Recording Sales

Sales are the lifeblood of your company. Whenever you sell a product or a service, you need to record the transaction. You will want to keep track of what is sold, the income generated from those sales, and if any items are returned for a refund or credit. You will also want to print invoices and statements. QuickBooks handles sales through its Invoicing/Receivables option.

CREATING INVOICES

To select an invoice type, from the Main menu, choose Set Up/Customize, then Customize Current Company, then Options.

To record a sale in QuickBooks, you enter an invoice. All invoices have two formats: the one you see on the screen and the one that prints. The screen format includes fields for information you use internally; the printed format is used for the customer's invoice.

You specify the type of invoice that QuickBooks should use for your business through the company options, as explained in Chapter 2. The three available invoice types are Service, Professional, and Product.

Product invoices contain the following fields, both in the screen and printed formats:

Invoice Number	Description
Invoice Date	Rate
Bill To	Amount
PO Number	Ship To
Terms	Sales Rep
Project	Ship Date
Quantity	Ship Via
Item Code	FOB

From an invoice-entry screen, press F8 to display the more detailed screen format.

Service invoices do not include the Ship To, Sales Rep, Ship Date, Ship Via, or FOB fields. The Item Code field can appear on the screen, but it does not appear on the printed invoice.

Professional invoices exclude the same fields as Service invoices, as well as the PO Number field. The printed format does not contain the Terms, Project, Quantity, Item Code, and Rate fields. These invoices have more space for a detailed description.

For our sample company, we chose the Service invoice. The invoice-entry screen that we will see when we record sales will contain all the fields listed above, except for those that relate to shipping products.

RECORDING A PAYMENT WITH THE INVOICE

When a customer pays for a product or service in cash or by a credit card, you record the payment along with the sale. If an established customer (one for whom you have set up a customer record in QuickBooks) pays in cash occasionally, you should enter the transaction on the customer's account rather than as a one-time cash sale. Then you will have an accurate figure for total sales to this customer. The purchase and payment will appear on the customer's statement.

The first sale we will record is for a dog-grooming service. Sales tax usually doesn't apply to services. One of our cash customers brought in a dog for grooming. The completed invoice is shown in Figure 9.1.

FIGURE 9.1:

Entering a cash sale

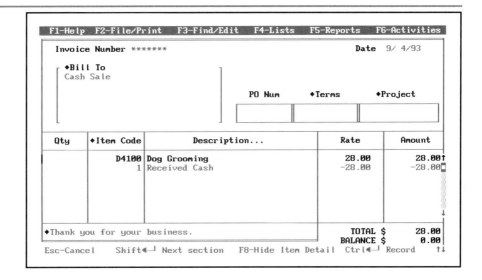

Follow these steps to record the sale and payment:

1. Select the Invoicing/Receivables option from the Main menu, and then choose Write/Print Invoices from the submenu.

The invoice-entry screen that appears does not contain the Item Code field. This is how the Service invoice format will look when it is printed. Let's change to the on-screen, more detailed format.

2. Press F8 to view the detailed input screen.

Now the invoice includes the Item Code field. QuickBooks doesn't assign numbers to invoices until you print them, so the Invoice Number field contains asterisks. The system date appears in the Date field.

3. Press BackTab to move to the Date field and enter **090493**, the date we issued the invoice.

4. In the Bill To field, enter **Cash Sale.** The Customer Not Found window appears.

5. Select One-Time Customer. This sale is to a customer who is not set up in our Accounts Receivable records.

6. Press Shift-⏎ twice to skip down to the Qty field.

7. Press ↵ in the Qty field. Unless you make an entry in this field, QuickBooks assumes that the quantity is one.

8. In the Item Code field, press Ctrl-L. The Item List appears.

9. Type **D** three times to move the cursor to each of the item codes starting with D. Press ↵ when D4100 (Dog Grooming) is highlighted, as shown in Figure 9.2.

When you select an item code from the Item List, QuickBooks fills in the Description, Rate, and Amount fields. The description and price are from the item record, and the Amount field is based on the figure in the Qty field and the amount in the Rate field. You can override the program-supplied entries. Your overrides do not affect the record from which the entry came; they change only the current invoice.

10. Press ↵ five times to accept the entries in both the Rate and Amount fields and move to the Item Code field on the next line.

11. Press Ctrl-L and type **1** to move the cursor to the code for the item defined as Received Cash, and then press ↵ to select it.

12. On the invoice-entry screen, move the cursor to the Rate field and enter **28**. QuickBooks precedes the number with a minus sign to indicate that it is a subtraction from the invoice (a payment).

FIGURE 9.2:

Selecting an item code from the Item List

```
╔═══════════════════════════════════════════════════════════════════╗
║ ▄▄▄▄▄▄▄▄▄▄▄▄▄▄▄▄▄▄▄▄▄▄▄▄▄▄▄▄▄▄▄▄▄▄▄▄▄▄▄▄▄▄▄▄▄▄▄▄▄▄▄▄▄▄▄▄▄▄▄         ║
║                           Item List                               ║
║                                                                   ║
║   Item Code    Type         Description          Price Each       ║
║  ───────────────────────────────────────────────────────────     ║
║   SubTot      Subt    Taxable Item Subtotal                 ↑     ║
║   B2159       Part    Sunflower Seed Mix            4.000         ║
║   C7341       Part    Diet Specific Cat Food        8.400         ║
║   D4112       Part    Dog Leash                     5.200         ║
║   D4165       Part    Flea Shampoo                  6.550         ║
║   H1000       Part    Alfalfa Hay                 165.000   ▓     ║
║ ▶ D4100       Service Dog Grooming                 28.000         ║
║   H1002       Service Pasture Rental              150.000         ║
║   Deliver     Charge  Delivery Charge               0.000         ║
║   Price Disc  Disc    20% Discount for Quantity   -20.000%  ▒     ║
║   1           Paymt   Received Cash                              ║
║   2           Paymt   Paid by Check                        ↓     ║
║  ───────────────────────────────────────────────────────────     ║
║   Esc-Cancel            F7-Actions            Ctrl◀┘ Done        ║
╚═══════════════════════════════════════════════════════════════════╝
```

13. Press ↵ to accept the entry in the Amount field. The balance, at the bottom of the screen, is now zero.

14. Press Shift-↵ to move the cursor to the memo line at the bottom of the invoice.

15. Press Ctrl-L to display the Invoice Memo List.

16. When the list appears, press End, then ↑ to move to the *Thank you for your business* memo.

17. Press ↵ to place the memo in the field.

18. Press F10 to record the invoice. QuickBooks displays a blank invoice-entry screen so that you can continue recording your sales.

When you create an invoice for a cash sale, QuickBooks records it in two places:

◆ It enters the quantity sold in the item record. You can see this information in the Sales report. (Chapter 15 describes how to print a Sales report.)

◆ It records the income in the general ledger account designated in the item record (Pet Services in our example).

Your checking account balance will not be increased by the amount of the payment until you deposit it, as explained later in this chapter. Although QuickBooks lists the undeposited amount as an asset on your Balance Sheet report, it does not add an account with this designation to your chart of accounts.

When a customer pays by check or credit card, follow the same steps outlined above, but select the item code for paid by check or paid by credit card.

> **TIP** *You may want to print a cash-sale invoice immediately and give it to the customer as a receipt. Printing invoices is covered later in this chapter.*

RECORDING A TAXABLE SALE TO BE BILLED

When you sell a product, you usually must charge state sales tax. With QuickBooks, you can create subtotals on your invoice and record the required sales tax.

Our customer is buying several cases of cat food, some pet shampoo, and two leashes, which are all taxable items. We have set up a customer record for this customer, and she doesn't pay at the time of purchase. The completed invoice is shown in Figure 9.3.

Entering an invoice for taxable items

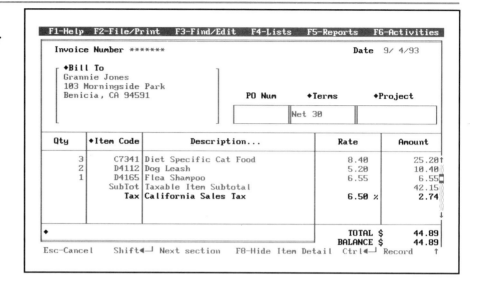

```
 F1-Help  F2-File/Print   F3-Find/Edit   F4-Lists   F5-Reports   F6-Activities

  Invoice Number ******                          Date  9/ 4/93

   ◆Bill To
   Grannie Jones
   103 Morningside Park
   Benicia, CA 94591              PO Num     ◆Terms       ◆Project

                                            Net 30


  Qty   ◆Item Code        Description...        Rate        Amount

     3       C7341 Diet Specific Cat Food       8.40         25.20↑
     2       D4112 Dog Leash                    5.20         10.40
     1       D4165 Flea Shampoo                 6.55          6.55
        SubTot Taxable Item Subtotal                         42.15
           Tax California Sales Tax             6.50 %        2.74

  ◆                                         TOTAL $         44.89
                                            BALANCE $       44.89
  Esc-Cancel     Shift◀┘ Next section    F8-Hide Item Detail  Ctrl◀┘ Record   ↑
```

Follow these steps to record a taxable sale:

The invoice-entry screen retains the last date keyed into the Date field.

1. In the Bill To field of the invoice-entry screen, press Ctrl-L to select from the Customer List.

2. Select Grannie Jones as the person to whom we made the sale.

If the customer provides you with a purchase order, you could enter the number in the PO Num field. In the Terms field, the program supplies the terms code from the customer record. You can override the terms code if you are using different terms for a particular invoice. If you chose to use projects, in the Project field, you could enter the predefined project that is responsible for this sale.

3. Press Shift-↵ to skip down to the Qty field.

You can delete an entire invoice line if you make an error. Place the cursor on the line you want to remove and press Ctrl-D.

4. In the Qty field, enter **3**, for three cases purchased.

5. In the Item Code field, press Ctrl-L and select C7341 (Diet Specific Cat Food) from the Item List. QuickBooks fills in the Description, Rate, and Amount fields for this item.

6. Press Tab four times to move to the next line and enter **2** in the Qty field.

7. Enter **D4112** in the Item Code field, the stockkeeping number of our dog leashes. QuickBooks enters the description and rate defined in the product record and calculates the amount.

8. Press ↵ in both the Rate and Amount fields to accept the entries and move to the next line.

9. Enter **1** in the Qty field. Although QuickBooks will assume this quantity if you leave the field blank, you must enter it if you want it to print on the invoice.

10. In the Item Code field, enter **D4165**, the number we assigned to flea shampoo.

11. Accept the information from the product record and move the cursor to the next line.

Next we will subtotal the taxable items and record the tax amount. You can view the Item List while the cursor is in the Qty field.

12. Press Ctrl-L and select SubTot from the Item List. The program totals all the preceding lines.

13. Move the cursor to the next line and press Ctrl-L in the Qty field.

14. When the Item List appears, press End and select Tax from the bottom of the list. QuickBooks multiplies the tax rate in the item record by the subtotal and enters the amount of the tax on the invoice.

15. Press F10 to record the completed invoice.

When you create an invoice for the sale of taxable items to an established customer, QuickBooks records it as follows:

◆ Records the customer invoice amount in the Accounts Receivable account.

◆ Increases the balance in the customer record.

◆ Notes the item quantities sold; you can see these quantities in your Sales report.

◆ Records the sale of these products in the general ledger income account specified in each item record (Pet Products in our example).

◆ Records the tax in your sales tax liability account in the general ledger (with a notation of the customer name) to indicate how much you owe the government taxing agency.

ADDING OTHER CHARGES TO INVOICES

You may need to add extra charges that are not for products or services, such as fees for delivery or shipping insurance, to a customer invoice. The next sale we will enter includes a delivery charge. The completed invoice is shown in Figure 9.4.

Follow these steps to create an invoice for the sale and delivery of hay:

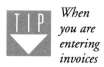

When you are entering invoices or working in the Accounts Receivable register, you can view the customer's record by pressing Ctrl-V.

1. In the Bill To field of the invoice-entry screen, press Ctrl-L and select Pony Pen, the customer making this purchase.

2. Enter **PO# 694** in the PO Num field.

3. Press ↵ to accept the terms code the program supplies from the customer record. It calculates the amount of discount the customer is allowed to take when paying within the discount days and how many days from the invoice date the invoice is due in full, based on the terms code.

4. Press Shift-↵ to skip to the Qty field and enter **3**, the number of hay bales the customer ordered.

5. In the Item Code field, press Ctrl-L, and then type **H** to move the cursor to item code H1000 (Alfalfa Hay). Press ↵ to select that item.

FIGURE 9.4:

Entering other charges on an invoice

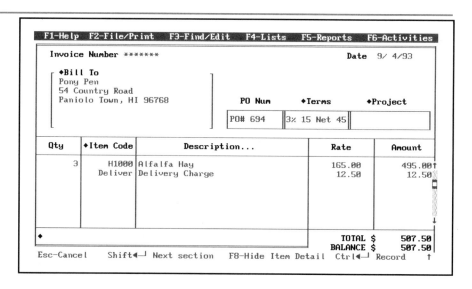

6. Move to the next line on the invoice, press Ctrl-L in the Qty field and select Delivery Charge from the Item List. Since we did not set up an amount in the item record, QuickBooks leaves the Rate field blank.

7. Press Tab to reach the Rate field and enter **12.50**, the amount we will charge for this trip to deliver the hay.

8. Press F10 to record the invoice.

SELLING SPECIAL-ORDER ITEMS

Now and then, you may place a special order for a customer and sell an item you do not intend to stock. In QuickBooks, you can handle this in one of two ways:

◆ You can set up an item record for special orders, as recommended in Chapter 6. If you want to record sales of different items in different Income accounts, you will need to define an item code related to each account, because you can assign only one Income account to each item code.

◆ Through the company options, you can choose not to require an item code for every line item on an invoice, as explained in Chapter 2.

If you do not create an item record that designates a specific income account to credit for sales of nonstock items, QuickBooks will create an account called Income, Other and record undefined items in it. This account designation will appear on your Profit and Loss Statement and on other reports, but QuickBooks will not add the Income account to your chart of accounts.

Our company does not intend to stock ponies, but one of our customers requested a pony from the sale of wild ponies at Chincoteague Island. We require an item code on all lines, but have not yet set up an item record for special orders. We will add a special item code for this sale. The completed invoice for this special order is shown in Figure 9.5.

Follow these steps to record the invoice for the pony:

1. On the invoice-entry screen, press Back Tab to reach the Date field and enter **090893**, the day we are creating this invoice.

2. In the Bill To field, press Ctrl-L and select Pony Pen.

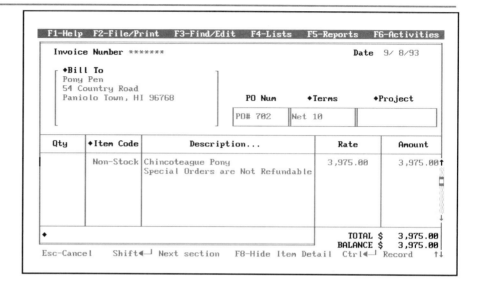

3. In the PO Num field, enter **PO# 702**.

4. Press Ctrl-Backspace to erase the entry in the Terms field.

5. Press Ctrl-L and select Net 10 from the Terms List. We don't allow discounts on special orders, and we require that the invoice be paid within 10 days of the invoice date.

6. Skip the Qty field (we sold one item) and move the cursor to the Item Code field.

7. Enter **Non-Stock** in the Item Code field. QuickBooks displays the Item Not Found window.

8. Select Add to Item List.

9. For Item Type, select Part.

10. In the Add New Part Item window, enter **4020** (Equine Products) as the account in which we want to record this income.

11. Leave the Price Each field blank, and enter **Chincoteague Pony** in the Description field.

12. Press F10 to record the new item. You return to the invoice-entry screen.

13. In the Rate field, enter **3975** as the price for the pony.

14. Press ↵ to accept the entry in the Amount field.

15. In the Description field, enter **Special Orders Are Not Refundable.** This message will print on the invoice. If we intended to use the message frequently, we would add it to the Invoice Memo List.

16. Press F10 to record the invoice.

PROCESSING SALES RETURNS

It's a fact of life: customers return purchased items for one reason or another. When you enter a sales return, QuickBooks does four things for you:

◆ Subtracts the amount from your general leger sales account.

◆ Subtracts the quantity from the total items sold.

◆ Subtracts the sales tax (if any) from your sales tax liability.

◆ Credits the customer's account or writes a refund check.

One of our customers purchased bulk bird seed. When the shipment arrived (after the invoice was paid), one sack contained weevils. The customer is requesting a refund. The completed sales return information is shown in Figure 9.6.

FIGURE 9.6:

Recording a customer return and refund

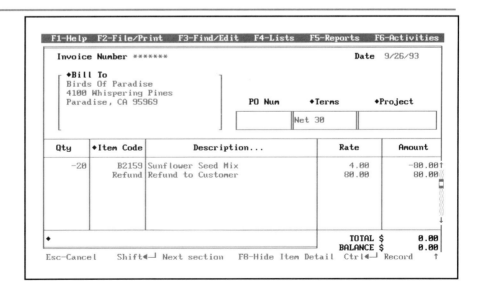

Follow these steps to record the return and refund:

1. In the Date field on the invoice-entry screen, enter **092693**, the date of the return.

2. In the Bill To field, press Ctrl-L and select Birds of Paradise.

3. Enter **−20** in the Qty field. This represents the 20 pounds of seed that were infested. You must precede the quantity with a minus sign to credit the customer for the return.

4. Enter **B2159**, the code for sunflower seed mix, in the Item Code field.

QuickBooks will subtract the quantity from the number sold and update the product record. The negative quantity shown in the Amount field will be subtracted from the Income account for bird seed sales (Pet Products), as well as from the customer's balance. In this case, it leaves a credit balance because nothing else is owed. The credit could be applied against future purchases, but our customer wants a cash refund. Sales returns that are not taken as a refund appear as an open credit memo on the customer record, reducing what the customer owes.

5. Press ↵ to reach the Item Code field of the second line, press Ctrl-L, and type **R** to move the cursor down the Item List. Then select Refund.

6. In the Rate field, enter **80**, to have QuickBooks write an $80 check to the customer.

7. Press ↵ in the Amount field. The program updates the Balance field at the bottom of the screen.

8. Press F10 to record the refund.

If you charged sales tax on an item that was returned, you would also enter a sales tax item with a minus amount. The sales tax percentage would be computed against the negative amount to obtain a reversing entry for tax. The negative tax amount would be deducted from your sales tax liability account, reducing what you owe the government taxing agency. Be sure that you return the same amount of tax you originally collected on the item.

VIEWING TRANSACTION INFORMATION

All invoices—printed and unprinted—can be viewed on the invoice-entry screen and in the Accounts Receivable register. Let's take a look at our sales-return transaction (a "reverse" invoice) in the Accounts Receivable register. Follow these steps:

> **TIP**
> *You can access the register quickly by pressing Ctrl-R. From the register, you can press Ctrl-H to display transaction history for the current transaction.*

1. From the invoice-entry screen, press F6 (Activities). The options on this menu provide quick access to other functions.

2. Select Register from the pull-down menu.

3. In the Accounts Receivable register, highlight the last transaction for Birds of Paradise and press F3 (Find/Edit). The options on this menu allow you to locate a transaction, alter the current transaction, use the Notepad, or exit to the customer record for the current transaction.

4. Select Transaction History from the menu. QuickBooks displays the information, as shown in Figure 9.7.

In the Type field, the credit shows as an INV (invoice), followed by XFER, which is the refund. The XFER represents a transfer to another balance sheet account. In this case, the credit was transferred to the Checkbook; Quick-Books created a check when we used the Refund item type. At this point, you could press Esc to return to the Accounts Receivable register. However, we will use the Goto option, noted at the bottom of the Transaction History window, to review the transfer that took place.

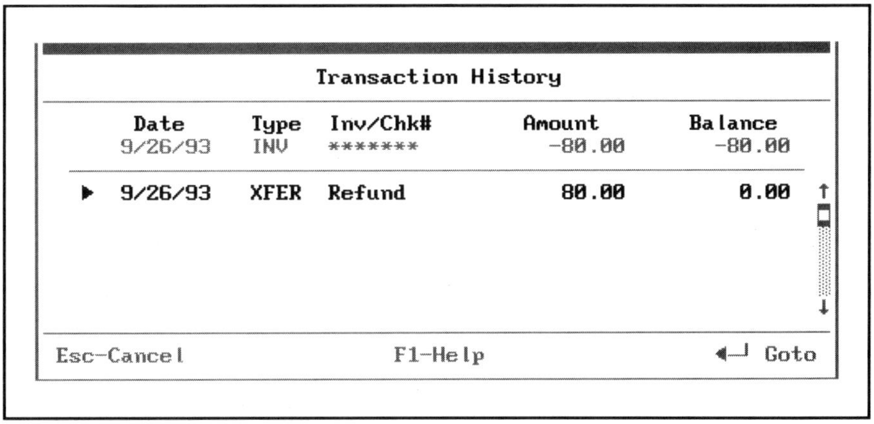

FIGURE 9.7:

Viewing transaction history

```
                        Transaction History

          Date      Type   Inv/Chk#       Amount      Balance
          9/26/93   INV    *******        -80.00       -80.00

     ►    9/26/93   XFER   Refund          80.00         0.00      ↑
                                                                   ▯
                                                                   ↓

     Esc-Cancel              F1-Help                   ◄─┘ Goto
```

5. Press ↵ to see the Check register with the check created from the refund entry, as shown in Figure 9.8.

FIGURE 9.8:

Viewing the refund check in the Checkbook

The asterisks indicate the check is waiting to be printed. The account number in brackets, [1100], indicates that the transaction is a transfer from the Accounts Receivable account.

6. Press Esc to exit the register and return to the Main menu.

The check could be printed now, but we'll include it in our next group check run.

CORRECTING SALES ENTRIES

When you change or delete a recorded sales entry, no record of how the entry once was remains.

You can correct or delete an invoice after you have processed it, and even after you have printed it, and QuickBooks will adjust the customer's balance and general ledger accounts accordingly. However, if a customer made a payment on an invoice and you deposited that payment, you cannot delete that invoice.

Note that when you print an invoice, the invoice number is used by the program. If you later delete the invoice, QuickBooks does not automatically reuse the number, and it will not show that the invoice number once existed in your transactions.

PRINTING INVOICES

After you enter your invoices, you can print them individually to hand to the customer, or in a group for mailing. QuickBooks allows you to select from the following paper types for your invoices:

To order supplies from Intuit, press F2 and select Print Supplies Order Form.

◆ **11-Inch Form:** Prints information on an invoice form preprinted with your company name and column headings. You can order these forms from Intuit.

◆ **Blank Paper with Lines:** Prints boxes around column headings and your company name and address in the heading.

◆ **Blank Paper without Lines:** Prints column headings and the invoice body without boxes, and your company information in the heading.

◆ **Letterhead with Lines:** Prints boxed column headings, but no company heading.

◆ **Letterhead without Lines:** Prints freestanding column headings, without a company heading.

For our example, we will print on blank paper so you don't waste your real forms. Place blank paper in your printer and follow these steps to print the invoices we have created:

You can press Ctrl-P to print invoices from the invoice-entry screen.

1. From the Main menu, select Invoicing/Receivables, and then choose Write/Print Invoices.

2. From the invoice-entry screen, press F2 (File/Print). This menu also contains options for printing statements and labels.

3. Select Print Invoices. QuickBooks notes how many invoices are waiting to be printed.

4. Override the system date in the Print Invoices Dated Through field by entering **092693**.

5. Override the A in the Print All/Selected Invoices field by entering S. Although we will print all the invoices, we want to view the list of invoices that are ready.

6. In the Paper Type field, press Ctrl-L and select Blank Paper w/o Lines.

7. In the Print To field, choose from your list of printers. You can also send the invoice information to a .TXT file (ASCII) for transfer to a word processor.

When you are printing invoices for your own company, after completing the Print To field, you can press F9 to print a form-alignment test to make sure that the invoices are properly placed in the printer. The procedure is similar to the procedure for printing a sample check (see Chapter 8), but varies depending on the type of paper you chose and the printer you are using. QuickBooks prints a sample, unnumbered invoice and marks it as void.

Print extra invoice copies to serve as "packing slips" for shipped merchandise.

8. Press ↵ in the Additional Copies field. If you want to print more than one copy of the invoices, for example to have an extra copy to enclose with the order, enter the number of extra copies you want.

In the Select Invoices to Print window, all invoices through the date we selected are marked to print. The invoice to Birds of Paradise has a zero balance, because of our refund entry. You can move the cursor to any invoice and press the spacebar to toggle between print and don't print. However, we will print all our invoices.

9. Press Ctrl-↵ to exit the window. The Set Invoice Number window appears, with the next invoice number already supplied.

10. If the invoice number is not 1001, enter **1001**. QuickBooks assigns the numbers as it prints the invoices.

11. Press ↵ to begin printing. QuickBooks prints the invoices, notes the numbers used, and asks if the invoices printed correctly.

12. If the invoices did *not* print correctly, follow the instructions in the next section. If the forms printed correctly, at the prompt

First incorrectly printed invoice:

press ↵ to exit the invoice-printing function.

REPRINTING INCORRECTLY PRINTED INVOICES

If any invoice did not print correctly (perhaps you ran out of paper), you can take one of two actions depending on how many invoices you were printing. If you printed more than one invoice, you must respond to the prompt

First incorrectly printed invoice

Enter the number of the first invoice in the series you want to cancel. You will be returned to the Print Invoices window. Invoices printed before the number you entered will be assigned numbers in the Accounts Receivable register; invoices printed with or after that number will remain unnumbered and waiting to be printed.

If you printed only *one* invoice, select No at the prompt

Did Invoices Print OK?

After responding to the appropriate prompt, complete the fields in the Print Invoices window again. In the Set Invoice Number window, enter the number of the first invoice to be reprinted in the Next Invoice Number field.

REPRINTING CORRECTLY PRINTED INVOICES

After verifying the correct printing of your invoices, you can still reprint one, with or without its original number. To reprint an invoice, select Write/Print Invoices from the Invoicing/Receivables submenu and press PgUp to move to that invoice.

If you want to reprint the invoice with its original number, enter **R** in the Invoice Number field. You will see (Reprint) below the number. The same notation will appear in the register and the customer history.

To print the invoice with a new number, type an asterisk (*) in the Invoice Number field. The original number will be replaced by asterisks, and a new invoice number will be assigned to the invoice when it is printed again.

After changing the entry in the Invoice Number field, record the invoice. When you choose to print invoices again, the invoices will be included in the list of those that are ready to print.

MEMORIZING INVOICES

Any invoice you send to a customer on a regular basis can be set up as a *recurring invoice.* Just as you can use the QuickBooks memorize function for checks that you write, you can have the program memorize invoices you need to produce repeatedly.

Our company bills one customer monthly for pasture rental. Figure 9.9 shows the completed invoice being memorized.

Follow these steps to create and memorize the invoice:

1. In the Date field on the invoice-entry screen, enter **092593**.

2. In the Bill To field, press Ctrl-L and select Carol Hendrickson. QuickBooks displays the warning message

   This customer has outstanding past due invoice(s) totaling $150.00. Cancel this invoice (Y/N)?

 *Depending on your system date, you may not see this warning.*

If you were entering this invoice at the point of the sale, you could refuse to complete the sale and demand payment of the overdue balance. However, we are billing the customer in advance for next month's rent, and her check for her previous bill is in today's mail, so we will continue.

3. Enter **N** at the prompt to indicate that we don't want to cancel the invoice.

4. Press Shift-↵ to reach the Qty field and enter **1.5**, for one and one-half acre. The customer is renting slightly more space from us beginning this month.

5. In the Item Code field, enter **H1002**, the code for Pasture Rental. QuickBooks fills in the Description, Rate, and Amount fields.

Memorizing an invoice

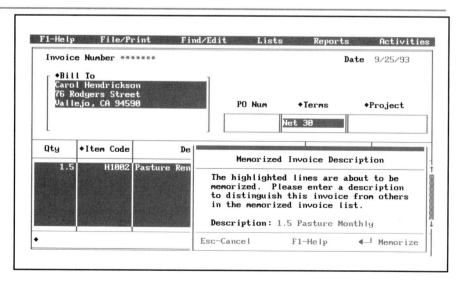

The program multiplies the rate of $150 per acre times 1.5 to arrive at the price for one and one-half acres.

6. Press ↵ through the fields to accept the program-supplied information.

7. Press Ctrl-M to memorize the invoice so we can use it again next month. QuickBooks displays the Memorized Invoice Description window.

8. In the Description field of the window, enter **1.5 Pasture Monthly**. The description will appear in the Memorized Invoice List.

9. Press ↵ to memorize the invoice.

10. Press Ctrl-↵ to record the invoice for this month's billing.

In Chapter 13, we will recall and use the invoice for next month's billing.

GIVING PRICE DISCOUNTS

If the customer's payment terms allow an early payment discount, that discount is in addition to the discount you give on the price.

In Chapter 6, we set up a price discount to be applied to large quantity purchases. One of our customers purchased 60 pounds of bird seed. Figure 9.10 shows the completed invoice, which includes the 20 percent discount.

Follow these steps to enter the invoice and discount:

1. In the Date field on the invoice-entry screen, enter **092793**.

2. In the Bill To field, press Ctrl-L and select Birds of Paradise.

3. Press Shift-↵ to reach the Qty field and enter **60**, for 60 pounds of bird seed.

4. In the Item Code field, enter **B2159**, the code for Sunflower Seed Mix.

QuickBooks enters the sales price from the product record in the Rate field. Even when you want to charge the customer a reduced price, it is good accounting practice to charge full price for the item, then give the customer a discount (on the next line) to reduce the actual cost.

5. Press ↵ through the fields to accept the program-supplied information.

FIGURE 9.10:

Entering a price discount

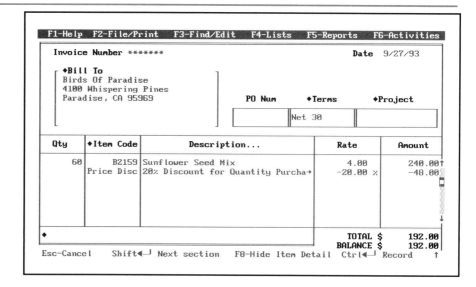

6. In the Qty field of the next line, press Ctrl-L, type **P** to move the cursor to the Price Discount item on the Item List, and press ↵ to select it.

QuickBooks supplies the description, discount percentage, and discount amount (preceded by a minus sign to indicate a subtraction from the invoice total). If you had several items you wanted to discount at the same rate, you would need to create a subtotal before entering the line for the price discount. Subtotaling discounted items is similar to calculating the sales tax on several items, as we did in an earlier example.

7. Press ↵ through the remaining fields to accept the program's calculations.

8. Press F10 to record the invoice.

9. Press Esc until you return to the Main menu.

CREATING CREDIT MEMOS

Occasionally, you may want to create credit memos for your customers to apply against their accounts. You might issue a credit memo for damaged merchandise, promotions, or to appease a dissatisfied customer.

Under some circum-stances, QuickBooks will automatically create an open credit in the customer account, as explained in Chapter 10.

A credit memo is like an invoice, but with a negative amount. Credit memos reduce the balance in both the customer's record and the Accounts Receivable account in the general ledger (which is an accumulation of all the customers' balances).

Our company offers our existing customers a $15 credit for referring a new customer to us. First, we need to create a discount item to use on the invoice. Then we can issue a credit memo to any customer who brings us new business.

CREATING AN ITEM CODE FOR CREDIT MEMO ENTRIES

Follow these steps to set up an invoice item that allows credit entries on our customers' accounts:

Promo-tional activities are actually an expense related to advertising.

1. Select Company Lists from the Main menu, and then choose Items/Parts/Services from the submenu.

2. From the Item List, press Ctrl-Ins to add a new item.

3. For Item Type, select Discount.

4. In the Code field, enter **Promo**.

5. In the Account field, press Ctrl-L and select Miscellaneous Expense (5150).

6. In the Price Each field, enter **15**.

You can change the amount on the invoice if the specific promotion is worth more or less. Notice this differs from our price discount, which calculates a percentage of the preceding invoice line item to determine the amount by which the invoice is reduced.

7. In the Description field, enter **Promotional Credit**.

8. Press F10 to record the new code.

9. Press Esc until you return to the Main menu.

PLACING A CREDIT MEMO ON A CUSTOMER'S ACCOUNT

You can press Ctrl-PgDn to display a blank invoice-entry screen.

The credit we established does not apply to a specific invoice. The customer can use it at any time. It will appear on the customer's statement and account as a stand-alone open item.

One of our customers referred a new dog-grooming customer to us. The completed credit memo is shown in Figure 9.11.

Follow these steps to issue a credit memo to her for the referral:

Although the program supplies terms, which may indicate a discount, they are irrelevant because it does not calculate a discount on credit memos nor are they "due" in any number of days. Credit memos are always available until used.

1. Select Invoicing/Receivables from the Main menu, and then choose Write/Print Invoices.

2. In the Date field, enter **092893**, the date we are issuing the credit memo.

3. In the Bill To field, press Ctrl-L and select Carol Hendrickson.

4. Respond **N** if QuickBooks asks if you want to cancel the invoice due to other past-due charges.

5. Press ↵ to move through the PO Num, Terms, and Project fields.

6. In the Qty field, enter **1**, for one credit memo.

7. In the Item Code field, enter **Promo**, the code we just created.

FIGURE 9.11:

Entering a credit memo

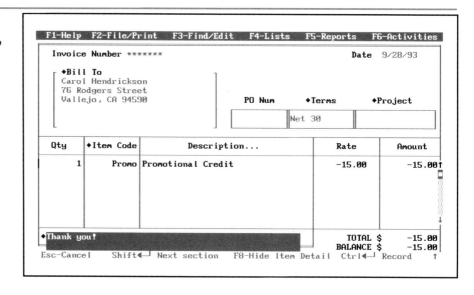

The Rate and Amount fields show −15. A credit memo amount must be preceded by a minus sign.

8. Press Shift-⏎ to reach the memo line, press Ctrl-L, and select *Thank you!* from the Invoice Memo List.

9. Press F10 to record the credit memo.

10. Press Esc to return to the Invoicing/Receivables submenu.

The credit memo will appear as an open item in the customer record.

KEEPING TRACK OF BACK ORDERS

QuickBooks does not provide a back-orders function, but you can still use it to keep track of your back-ordered items. To record a back order, create an invoice and complete the heading (Bill To, PO Num, Terms, and Project fields) as usual. Then skip to the Description field and type an explanation, such as *Backorder 3 Cat Condos @ $29.95*. Do not make any entries in the Item, Rate, and Amount fields. This is simply a notational document. Record the invoice.

Next, print two copies of the invoice, one for the customer, the other for your manually maintained back-order file. Regularly check that file against the merchandise you receive. When the stock arrives, create an invoice to charge the customer for the item you can now deliver.

REVIEWING THE ACCOUNTS RECEIVABLE REGISTER

Now that we have entered Accounts Receivable transactions, let's see how the transactions appear in the register. We also will print the remaining invoices. Follow these steps:

1. Select View A/R Register from the Invoicing/Receivables submenu. Your register should look like the one shown in Figure 9.12.

FIGURE 9.12:

The Accounts Receivable register

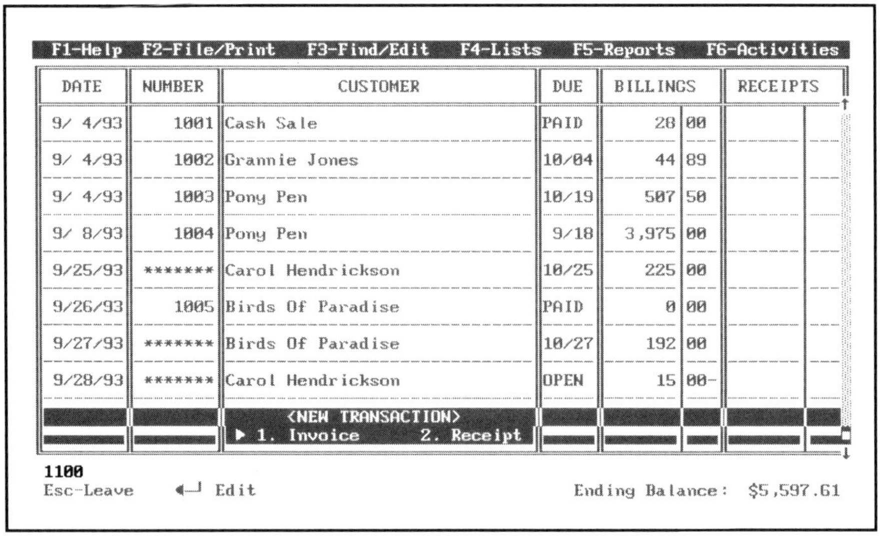

```
 F1-Help  F2-File/Print   F3-Find/Edit   F4-Lists    F5-Reports    F6-Activities

   DATE      NUMBER            CUSTOMER        DUE    BILLINGS      RECEIPTS

  9/ 4/93      1001  Cash Sale              PAID       28 00
  9/ 4/93      1002  Grannie Jones          10/04      44 89
  9/ 4/93      1003  Pony Pen               10/19     507 50
  9/ 8/93      1004  Pony Pen                9/18    3,975 00
  9/25/93    *******  Carol Hendrickson      10/25     225 00
  9/26/93      1005  Birds Of Paradise      PAID        0 00
  9/27/93    *******  Birds Of Paradise      10/27     192 00
  9/28/93    *******  Carol Hendrickson      OPEN       15 00-
                         <NEW TRANSACTION>
                       ▶ 1.  Invoice      2.  Receipt

 1100
 Esc-Leave      ◀┘  Edit                          Ending Balance:  $5,597.61
```

The unprinted invoices and credit memos appear with asterisks in the Number field. Invoices without any balance due, because they were paid (number 1001) or because a refund was issued on the same invoice as a sales return (number 1005), are marked PAID in the Due field. The credit memo appears as OPEN, with a negative amount in the Billings field.

If your system date is earlier than the transaction dates we are using, you will see a double line after the date nearest your system date. Also, a Current Balance field will appear in addition to the Ending Balance field. The current balance refers to the balance as of your system date, as opposed to the ending balance in the Accounts Receivable account after all transactions are considered. Don't be concerned about the difference.

You can go directly from the register to the invoice-entry (Invoice) or Receive Payments (Receipt) screen, as noted at the bottom of the screen.

2. Type **1** to switch to the invoice-entry screen.

3. Press Ctrl-P to print the remaining invoices.

4. In the Print Invoice window, enter **09/28/93** for the date.

5. Enter **A** to print all the remaining invoices.

6. In the Paper Type field, accept Blank Paper w/o Lines.

7. Select your printer and press Ctrl-↵.

8. Press ↵ to accept 1006 as the next invoice number and print the invoices.

9. Verify that the invoices printed correctly and press ↵.

10. Press Esc to return to the Accounts Receivable register, then again to return to the Main menu.

In this chapter, you learned how to record your sales by entering invoices. You can record cash and company credit sales, miscellaneous charges, special orders, and price discounts. Invoices can be printed separately or in batches. You also can keep track of returns and credits through the invoicing function.

In the next chapter, you will learn how to record payments from your customers and deposits to your bank accounts.

10

Recording Payments and Deposits

any businesses do not extend credit to their customers. They require payment either in cash or by credit card whenever a purchase is made. If your company works this way, you will record the payment when you create the invoice, and then record the deposit of the payments.

However, when you let customers charge their sales, a few more steps are necessary. Purchases sit unpaid on customers' accounts until the customers tender payment. Then you must apply their payments to their accounts.

RECORDING CUSTOMER PAYMENTS

When a customer pays at the time of the sale, you can record the payment on the invoice-entry screen when you create the invoice, as explained in Chapter 9. However, when a customer pays after the invoice is recorded, you enter the payment through the Receive Payments option on the Invoicing/Receivables submenu.

RECORDING PAYMENT FOR THE FULL INVOICE AMOUNT

The way that QuickBooks handles payment entries depends on which method you are using to apply payments. Through the company options, you can choose the Balance Forward method of applying payments, as we did for our sample company, or the Open Item method. With the Balance Forward method, you enter the payment and QuickBooks calculates the amount to be applied to each outstanding invoice, beginning with the oldest unpaid invoice. If you chose the Open Item method, the program does not supply payment amounts when you enter a receipt; you must manually enter the amount you want to apply to each invoice.

The first payment we will enter is for the full amount of the customer's invoice. Figure 10.1 shows the completed information on the Receive Payments screen.

Follow these steps to record the payment:

1. From the Main menu, select Invoicing/Receivables, and then choose Receive Payments from the submenu.

2. In the Customer field, press Ctrl-L and select Birds of Paradise from the Customer List.

FIGURE 10.1:

Recording a customer payment

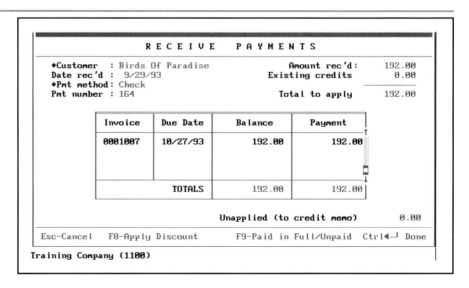

```
                    R E C E I V E    P A Y M E N T S

  ♦Customer   : Birds Of Paradise        Amount rec'd :     192.00
  Date rec'd  :  9/29/93                  Existing credits     0.00
  ♦Pmt method : Check                                     ──────────
  Pmt number  : 164                       Total to apply     192.00


            ┌──────────┬──────────┬──────────┬──────────┐
            │ Invoice  │ Due Date │ Balance  │ Payment  │
            ├──────────┼──────────┼──────────┼──────────┤
            │ 0001007  │ 10/27/93 │  192.00  │  192.00  │
            │          │          │          │          │
            │          │          │          │          │
            ├──────────┴──────────┼──────────┼──────────┤
            │              TOTALS │  192.00  │  192.00  │
            └─────────────────────┴──────────┴──────────┘

                            Unapplied (to credit memo)      0.00

  Esc-Cancel    F8-Apply Discount       F9-Paid in Full/Unpaid  Ctrl⏎ Done

  Training Company (1100)
```

3. In the Amount Rec'd field, enter **192**, the full balance of the invoice.

4. Override the system date in the Date Rec'd field by entering **092993**, the actual date of the payment. This date will appear in the Accounts Receivable register and on the customer statement.

5. In the Pmt Method field, press Ctrl-L and select Check from the Payment Method List.

6. Enter **164**, the number on the check received from the customer, in the Pmt Number field. This reference will appear on reports to help identify the transaction.

The detail window shows information about the customer's open invoices. The Invoice field contains the invoice numbers, the Due Date field shows when the net invoice should be paid (according to the terms on the original transaction), and the Balance field shows the amount still unpaid on each invoice.

What you see in the Payment field depends on whether you are using the Balance Forward or Open Item method of applying payments, as explained at the beginning of this section. Because we chose the Balance Forward method, QuickBooks supplied the payment for invoice 1007, $192.00.

7. Press F10 to process the payment. The payment will reduce the balance in the customer record and will appear on the customer statement.

SELECTING THE INVOICE TO PAY

If you are using the Balance Forward method of applying payments, and the customer is not paying the invoice in full or not paying the oldest invoice, you must override the payments supplied by QuickBooks.

QuickBooks uses the invoice date, not the invoice payment due date, to age invoices. Therefore, when QuickBooks pays the "oldest" invoice, it may apply the payment to an invoice that is not yet due, leaving one that *is* due unpaid.

One of our customers made a payment to be applied to an invoice for a special order (the pony we recorded as a nonstock sale, in Chapter 9).

Instead of using the due date to determine the oldest invoice, QuickBooks uses the invoice date.

Follow these steps to record the payment as the customer intended it to be applied:

1. In the Customer field of the Receive Payments screen, press Ctrl-L and select Pony Pen.

2. In the Amount Rec'd field, enter **3975**. The customer is not paying the total account balance.

3. Override the system date in the Date Rec'd field by entering **092993**.

4. In the Pmt Method field, enter **Ch**. QuickBooks will complete the field with the closest match, Check, in the Payment Method List. Press ↵.

5. Enter the customer's check number, **5589**, in the Pmt Number field.

> ***NOTE*** *The program does not retain the last payment date entry, as it does when you are writing checks.*

QuickBooks applies the payment to the oldest invoice and places the remainder on the special-order invoice. We must override those entries to apply the payment as the customer intended.

Notice that QuickBooks considers invoice 1003 as the oldest invoice. This is because is has an invoice date of 9/4/93. However, its terms are 3% 15 Net 45, which means that it is not due until 10/19/93. Invoice 1004 has an invoice date of 9/8/93, with terms of Net 10. It is due 9/18/93, so it should be paid first.

6. To erase the payment supplied on the line for invoice 1003, press F9. The F9 key is a toggle, which switches between payment in full and no payment on an invoice.

7. On the line for invoice 1004, press F9 to clear the original payment amount supplied by QuickBooks.

8. Press F9 again beside invoice 1004 to pay it in full, using the entire amount shown in the Total to Apply field. Figure 10.2 shows the screen at this point.

9. Press F10 to process the payment.

FIGURE 10.2:

Selecting an invoice to pay

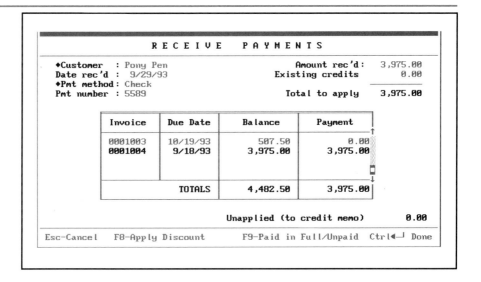

```
                    R E C E I V E     P A Y M E N T S

    ◆Customer   : Pony Pen              Amount rec'd :   3,975.00
    Date rec'd  :  9/29/93             Existing credits     0.00
    ◆Pmt method : Check                                _____
    Pmt number  : 5589                  Total to apply    3,975.00


        ┌───────────┬───────────┬────────────┬────────────┐
        │ Invoice   │ Due Date  │ Balance    │ Payment    │
        ├───────────┼───────────┼────────────┼────────────┤
        │ 0001003   │ 10/19/93  │    507.50  │      0.00  │
        │ 0001004   │  9/18/93  │  3,975.00  │  3,975.00  │
        │           │           │            │            │
        │           │           │            │            │
        │           │  TOTALS   │  4,482.50  │  3,975.00  │
        └───────────┴───────────┴────────────┴────────────┘

                            Unapplied (to credit memo)      0.00

    Esc-Cancel    F8-Apply Discount      F9-Paid in Full/Unpaid  Ctrl◄─┘ Done
```

USING AN OPEN CREDIT

QuickBooks automatically creates an open credit, which reduces the amount the customer owes you, in two cases:

◆ When you enter a sales return for which no refund is issued

◆ In the unlikely event that a customer pays more than he or she owes

The credit memos you create through the invoice-entry screen, as explained in Chapter 9, also appear as open credits.

An open credit on the customer's account must be applied to an unpaid invoice at some point. When you apply an open credit to an invoice, the cash account is not affected by this entry. You are merely transferring a previously received payment or a credit memo to an invoice; no money is coming in or going out.

The customer who received a $15 credit for referring a new customer has made a payment on an invoice. We can apply the open credit while recording the payment, as shown in Figure 10.3.

Follow these steps to record the payment and apply the credit:

1. In the Customer field of the Receive Payments screen, press Ctrl-L and select Carol Hendrickson.

2. Enter **150** in the Amount Rec'd field.

NOTE NOTE
Although we are entering a payment at the same time we are using an open credit, you do not have to enter a new payment to use existing credits.

*Applying an open credit
to an unpaid invoice*

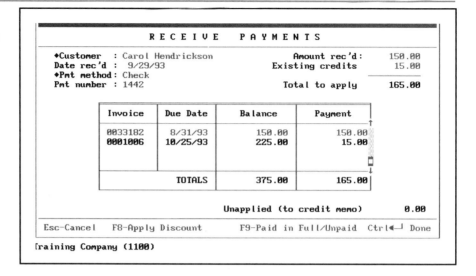

```
                R E C E I V E    P A Y M E N T S

 ◆Customer   : Carol Hendrickson       Amount rec'd:     150.00
  Date rec'd :  9/29/93             Existing credits      15.00
 ◆Pmt method: Check                                    ──────────
  Pmt number : 1442                    Total to apply    165.00


        ┌──────────┬──────────┬──────────┬──────────┐
        │ Invoice  │ Due Date │ Balance  │ Payment  │
        ├──────────┼──────────┼──────────┼──────────┤
        │ 0033182  │ 8/31/93  │  150.00  │  150.00  │
        │ 0001006  │ 10/25/93 │  225.00  │   15.00  │
        │          │          │          │          │
        │          │          │          │          │
        ├──────────┼──────────┼──────────┼──────────┤
        │          │ TOTALS   │  375.00  │  165.00  │
        └──────────┴──────────┴──────────┴──────────┘

                          Unapplied (to credit memo)      0.00

 Esc-Cancel   F8-Apply Discount      F9-Paid in Full/Unpaid  Ctrl◄┘ Done

 Training Company (1100)
```

The amount of all open credits on a customer's account appears in the Existing Credits field. You do not see individual credits listed separately.

3. Enter **092993** in the Date Rec'd field.

4. In the Pmt Method field, press Ctrl-L and choose Check.

5. Enter **1442** in the Pmt Number field.

QuickBooks distributes the payment and the credits among the existing invoices. If you wanted to use less than the full amount of the credit, you would enter that amount in the Payment field for invoice 1006. To leave the credit unapplied, you would remove the amount from the Payment field. You cannot match credit memos to specific invoices automatically. You must specify how much of the amount in the Existing Credits field to use on which invoice.

6. Press Ctrl-↵ to accept and record the payments supplied by QuickBooks.

RECORDING A DOWN PAYMENT

If a customer places a special order and makes a down payment on that order, you must record that you received the money. If you know how much the charges are going to be, you can create an invoice (on the invoice-entry screen) and enter the down payment along with the invoice. But if you do not know the exact amount, you enter the down payment through the Receive Payments option.

Even if you don't intend to allow the customer to make payments on invoices, you must set up a customer account for the advance payment transaction. The deposit will leave a credit balance on the account.

A Training Company customer is placing a $100 deposit (charged to his credit card account) on a special order. The completed entries for the down payment are shown in Figure 10.4.

Follow these steps to record the advance payment:

1. Select Receive Payments from the Invoicing/Receivables submenu.

2. In the Customer field, enter the customer's name, **John Eugene**. QuickBooks displays the Customer Not Found prompt.

3. In the Customer Not Found window, select One-Time Customer.

4. Enter the down payment, **100**, in the Amount Rec'd field.

5. Enter **092993** in the Date Rec'd field.

FIGURE 10.4:

Entering an advance payment

```
                    R E C E I V E    P A Y M E N T S

  ◆Customer  : John Eugene              Amount rec'd :    100.00
  Date rec'd :   9/29/93                Existing credits    0.00
  ◆Pmt method: VISA
  Pmt number : 49 3216                  Total to apply    100.00

       ┌───────────┬───────────┬───────────┬───────────┐
       │ Invoice   │ Due Date  │ Balance   │ Payment   │↑
       │           │           │           │           │
       │           │           │           │           │
       │           │           │           │           │
       │           │           │           │           │▯
       │           │  TOTALS   │    0.00   │    0.00   │↓
       └───────────┴───────────┴───────────┴───────────┘

                            Unapplied (to credit memo)   100.00

  Esc-Cancel   F8-Apply Discount      F9-Paid in Full/Unpaid  Ctrl◀─┘ Done

  Training Company (1100)
```

6. In the Pmt Method field, press Ctrl-L and select **VISA**.

7. In the Pmt Number field, enter **49 3216**, the last six digits on the credit card slip.

Because the account does not have any open invoices, the $100 payment does not appear in the Payment field. However, the amount is shown in the Unapplied (to Credit Memo) field in the bottom-right corner of the screen.

The customer's copy of the credit card slip is his receipt. For a customer who pays cash, you must prepare a handwritten receipt. QuickBooks does not allow you to print a cash-receipt slip as proof of a payment entered though the Receive Payments screen.

8. Press Ctrl-⏎ to indicate you are finished with your entries. Again, QuickBooks tries to find the customer and displays the Customer Not Found window.

9. Once again, select One-Time Customer. QuickBooks displays a message to inform you that the amount has not been applied to any invoice, and that it will create a credit memo for this amount, as shown in Figure 10.5.

10. Press ⏎ to create the credit on the customer's account.

If this customer had any other open credits, the advance payment amount would be added to the account's existing credit amount.

FIGURE 10.5:

Creating a credit memo for an unapplied receipt

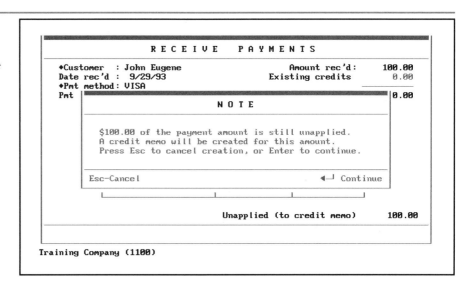

```
               R E C E I V E    P A Y M E N T S
 ◆Customer   : John Eugene          Amount rec'd:    100.00
 Date rec'd  :  9/29/93             Existing credits    0.00
 ◆Pmt method : VISA
 Pmt ┌────────────────────────────────────────────────┐ 0.00
     │                  N O T E                         │
     │                                                  │
     │   $100.00 of the payment amount is still unapplied. │
     │   A credit memo will be created for this amount.    │
     │   Press Esc to cancel creation, or Enter to continue. │
     │                                                  │
     │  Esc-Cancel                       ◀─┘ Continue   │
     └────────────────────────────────────────────────┘

                           Unapplied (to credit memo)   100.00


 Training Company (1100)
```

If the customer had any open invoices, and you are using the Balance Forward method of applying payments, QuickBooks would apply the advance payment amount to those invoices. You would need to override the payment entries (by moving the cursor to the Payment field of each invoice and pressing F9 to remove the payment), and then record the advance payment without applying any of it to existing invoices.

ALLOWING AN EARLY PAYMENT DISCOUNT

> N O T E
> N O T E *The invoice your customer receives notes the discount percent allowed, but it does not print the discount amount to be taken for early payment.*

When a customer pays an invoice in time to get an early payment discount (according to the terms you established), you apply the discount when you record the payment. One of QuickBooks quirks is to calculate the early payment discount on the *total* invoice. This means the discount has been applied not only to the items you sold, but to the sales tax as well. Most companies do not discount sales tax, so you may need to override the discount amount calculated by the program.

The folks from Pony Pen gave a check for a previous invoice to one of our stable hands when they picked up the special-order pony. It was an early payment, but the employee forgot to turn it in to our office. In order to ensure that the customer receives the early payment discount, we must adjust the date. The entries for applying a discount are shown in Figure 10.6.

FIGURE 10.6:

Allowing an early payment discount

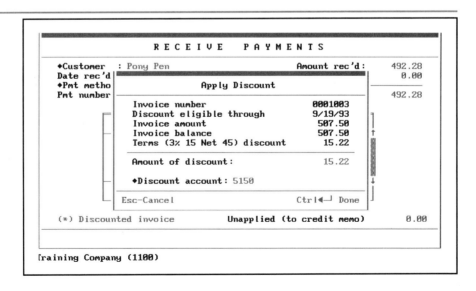

Follow these steps to allow an early payment discount with a customer payment:

1. In the Customer field of the Receive Payments screen, press Ctrl-L and select Pony Pen.

2. In the Amount Rec'd field, enter **492.28**, the net amount due after a 3 percent discount of 15.22 is subtracted from the $507.50 invoice.

3. Enter **091093** in the Date field. The payment was made within the 15-day limit.

4. In the Pmt Method field, enter **Check**.

5. Enter 5574 in the Pmt Number field.

6. Press F8 to apply a discount to the payment. The Apply Discount window appears.

The Discount Eligible Through field contains the date the discount expires according to the terms on the invoice. QuickBooks leaves the discount available beyond the allowable time, so you have the option of giving the discount after the eligible time period. If, on the invoice, you entered terms that allow an early payment discount, the Terms and Amount of Discount fields show the discount for the *total* invoice, as explained at the beginning of the section.

You can enter the discount you actually want to give the customer (excluding the sales tax from the calculations) in the Amount of Discount field. If the customer takes more than the allowed discount, you can enter the actual amount in the Amount of Discount field. If you don't want to give the extra discount, enter only what you allow, leaving a balance due on the invoice.

7. In the Amount of Discount field, press ↵ to accept 15.22, the amount of the discount taken by the customer on the second invoice.

8. In the Discount Account field, enter **5150** (Miscellaneous Expense). An early payment discount is an expense because it costs revenue to accept less than what was billed on the invoice. QuickBooks records the discount and indicates that a discount was taken by placing an asterisk beside the amount in the Balance column on the Receive Payments screen.

9. Press Ctrl-↵ to record the payment.

10. Press Esc to return to the Invoicing/Receivables submenu. Quick-Books displays a prompt asking if you want to make a deposit now.

11. Press ↵ to accept the N for No.

MAKING DEPOSITS

After you enter payments on customers' accounts, you record deposits so that your checking account will reflect the amounts you received. You usually deposit cash and checks on one deposit slip and payments made by credit card on a separate slip, because you are usually charged a fee for credit card deposits. You record deposits through the Make Deposits option on the Invoicing/Receivables submenu.

DEPOSITING CHECKS AND CASH

Follow these steps to make a deposit of the checks and cash we have received from our customers:

1. Choose Make Deposits from the Invoicing/Receivables submenu. The Deposit Summary screen appears. It lists the payments we entered through the Receive Payments screen.

2. Override the system date in the Deposit Date field by entering **092993**, the date the deposit will reach the bank.

3. In the Account for Deposit field, press Ctrl-L to select from the valid accounts.

Your only choices for the Account to Deposit field are a Checking, Current Asset, or Fixed Asset account. Typically, you would not use a Current Asset or Fixed Asset account as a repository of money deposited in a bank account.

4. Select 1000, our Countrywide Bank checking account. This is the account in which we wish to deposit the money. The cursor moves to Dep field.

The type, date, customer, and amount for each payment you recorded appears. The Type field indicates the payment method. The one-time customer entries do not include the customer name, but the name will appear with the transaction in your Accounts Receivable register.

As on other selection screens, the spacebar acts as a toggle key. Press it to include and exclude payments in the deposit. You can also use the Ctrl-spacebar combination to include or exclude all payments of the type highlighted.

5. Press the spacebar to include the Cash entry.

6. Beside the first Check entry, press Ctrl-spacebar to include all the payments of this type in the deposit.

7. Leave the VISA entry blank. We will not include it with this deposit.

8. To print the Deposit Summary information before recording the items selected for deposit, press Ctrl-P and select your printer.

9. Compare the Deposit Summary information with the documents being deposited. We are depositing five items.

A good accounting control is to balance the amount you deposit into your bank account each day with the amount of cash and credit card payments posted to your customer accounts.

Use the printed information to verify that every item on the deposit slip you make up for the bank is entered in your QuickBooks records. If there is a difference between the deposit slip and the Deposit Summary information, you can make corrections, as explained later in the chapter.

10. When you have determined that the Deposit Summary information and the documents to deposit agree, press F10 to record the deposit.

QuickBooks records the deposit in the Check register. It is identified in the Payee field as Deposit from A/R. The account balance is updated to include the deposit. The deposit is also noted in the Accounts Receivable register.

DEPOSITING CREDIT CARD SLIPS

We deposit credit cards separately because we must compute the fee that the bank assesses for accepting the cards. Follow these steps to record the deposit amount:

1. Choose Make Deposits from the Invoicing/Receivables submenu. The payments you already chose to deposit no longer appear on the Deposit Summary screen.

2. Enter **092993** in the Deposit Date field. We will deposit the cash, check, and credit card payments on the same day.

3. In the Account for Deposit field, enter **1000**. We deposit our credit cards into the same account as we deposit cash, although the deposit slips must be made up separately for our records.

4. In the Dep column, press the spacebar to select the credit card payment for deposit.

5. Press Ctrl-P and select the printer to print the Deposit Summary information.

6. Press F10 to record the deposit.

VIEWING DEPOSITS IN THE ACCOUNTS RECEIVABLE REGISTER

QuickBooks includes a record of your deposits in the Accounts Receivable register. To view the entries for our deposits in that register, select View A/R Register from the Invoicing/Receivables submenu. Press PgDn to reach the end of the register.

The register now includes the two deposits. The Number field contains the notation DEPOSIT, along with the number of the general ledger account that received the deposit and the amount.

Highlight the $4837.28 deposit and press ↵. The deposit detail appears, as shown in Figure 10.7. When you are finished reviewing the deposit information, press Esc until you return to the Main menu.

CORRECTING DEPOSIT ENTRIES

You can correct deposit entries before or after they are recorded. If the Deposit Summary information does not match your deposit slip and you have not recorded the deposit yet, you can take one of the following actions:

◆ If you forgot to include a deposit amount or marked an amount that isn't being deposited, make changes on the Deposit Summary screen. Highlight the item you want to include or exclude and press the spacebar.

◆ If the amount on the deposit slip is wrong, simply rewrite the deposit slip.

FIGURE 10.7:

Viewing detail on a recorded deposit

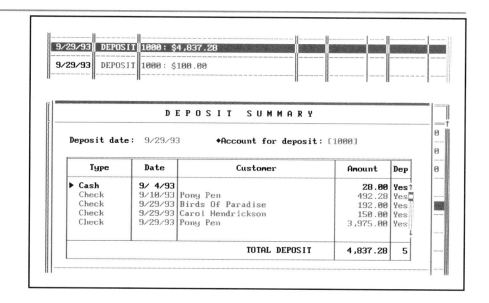

- ◆ If the deposit slip is right and you entered a payment in the customer's account incorrectly, you must change the payment in QuickBooks.

To correct a recorded customer payment, press Esc to cancel the deposit procedure, and then display the Accounts Receivable register. Highlight the payment with the error and press ↵ to display the Receive Payments screen. In the Amount Rec'd field, press Ctrl-Backspace to erase the entry, and then enter the correct amount. Review how the payment is applied to the invoices and make any necessary changes.

After you have edited the payment entry, press F10 to save your changes. QuickBooks will update the customer and Accounts Receivable account balances. Finally, repeat the steps for making deposits. The corrected payment will appear on the list of items ready to be deposited.

You can change a recorded deposit by adding or removing items. After you have recorded a deposit, the Deposit Summary screen will reappear with all items that comprised that deposit marked YES in the Dep field. Any undeposited items will also be listed. To include or exclude an item, highlight it and press the spacebar. The deposit total will change, and QuickBooks will update the Accounts Receivable register notation, as well as the deposit amount and balance in the Check register.

ADJUSTING FOR A CREDIT CARD FEE

The bank automatically deducts the credit card company fee from your account on a monthly basis. You can record the fee individually with each deposit, or you can wait until you get your bank statement and enter it as a monthly total. To subtract the credit card fee, you enter it directly in your Check register.

You must indicate the number of the general ledger account you use to record credit card company expenses. For our sample company, we enter this expense in the Miscellaneous Expense account. In your actual company, you might want to maintain a separate Expense account for each credit card to determine how much it costs you to accept a specific card.

To record the fee, follow these steps:

1. From the Main menu, select Checkbook, and then choose Check Register. Notice that the two deposits we just completed are also recorded here.

2. Enter **092993** in the Date field.

3. In the Payee field, enter **VISA**, the name of the credit card company that extracts the discount.

4. In the Payment field, enter **4.50**, the discount fee for the $100 credit card slip we deposited.

5. Enter **Visa Fee** in the Memo field.

6. In the Account field, enter **5150**, the Expense account in which we record the amount the credit card company charges us for accepting its card.

7. Press ↵ to record the transaction, and then press Esc to return to the Main menu.

RECORDING MISCELLANEOUS RECEIPTS

You record money from a source other than a customer directly in the Deposit field of the Check register. Amounts you receive that are not generated by a sale, such as the return of a security deposit, a refund for overpayment of payroll taxes, or a commission check for a vendor's promotion, are referred to as *miscellaneous receipts*.

The entry in the Check register increases your cash balance. The other general ledger account affected by the transaction could be an Income account, such as Commissions Received. If someone returned a deposit, you could be reducing another asset account, such as Prepaid Deposits.

Money you record directly in the Check register does not appear on the Deposit Summary screen. That screen lists only payments received from customers.

In this chapter, you learned how to record customer payments, apply credits, and handle down payments. After entering payments, you record your deposits to your bank accounts.

The next chapter will help you understand how to manage your Accounts Receivable customers. You will learn how to assess finance charges, print customer statements, and generate aging reports.

CHAPTER

11

Managing Accounts Receivable

anaging your accounts receivable requires more than entering invoices and recording payments. You will want to know how much is owed to you and who isn't paying. You will need to assess finance charges, collect delinquent accounts, and deal with uncollectible accounts and bad checks.

QuickBooks can help you manage your accounts receivable. You can print reports on the status of your customers' accounts and produce customer statements and address labels.

AGING YOUR CUSTOMER BALANCES

Aging a customer's account means separating invoice amounts by due date into time periods that reflect how current or past due each invoice is. You should review the customer aging regularly. In QuickBooks, you can view an individual customer's aging on the screen, or generate a report showing the aging of all your customers.

VIEWING CUSTOMER AGING ON THE SCREEN

The QuickBooks Customer Aging Status window shows your customer's balance separated into 30-day time periods. Follow these steps to see the aging information about one of our customers:

1. Select Company Lists from the Main menu, and then choose Customers from the submenu.

2. Highlight Grannie Jones on the Customer List and press Ctrl-E to edit the record.

3. When the record appears, press F8 to review the aging. Your screen should look similar to the one shown in Figure 11.1.

The window displays the five aging periods, from current to over 90 days, and the total balance due. The last field keeps a running tally of how much the customer purchased in the last 12 months (counting backward from today).

4. Press Esc to return to the Main menu.

FIGURE 11.1:

Viewing the aging in the customer record

```
                    Customer Aging Status


        Current            44.89
        1-30 Days          62.10
        31-60 Days          0.00
        61-90 Days          0.00
        Over 90 Days        0.00
                         ─────────
        Balance Due       106.99

        Sales in last 12 months:    106.99


     Esc-Cancel          F1-Help         ◄┘ Continue
```

PRINTING AN ACCOUNTS RECEIVABLE AGING REPORT

The Accounts Receivable Aging report separates your customer balances into the time periods you designate. It also shows a grand total for each period and for all outstanding bills.

The report can help you determine which accounts are past due and the number of days they are delinquent. You can use the information to assess finance charges, which are meant to discourage late payments and repay you for the extra cost of collections.

Follow these steps to print an Accounts Receivable Aging report that reflects the data we have recorded for our sample company:

1. From the Main menu, select Reports, then A/R Reports, then Aging Report.

2. In the Report Title field, press ↵ to accept the QuickBooks report name as the heading of the report.

3. In the Create Report As Of field, enter **100193**, the day we send statements. QuickBooks uses this date to calculate whether an item is past due.

4. Press ↵ in the Show Aging at Intervals Of field to accept 30, for 30-day periods. If you wanted to see the amounts separated into semimonthly periods, you would enter 15.

5. In the Through field, press ↵ to accept 90. The report will have columns representing 30 days each up to 90 days, and amounts over 90 days past 10/01/93 will be grouped into one column titled >90. Current invoices are in their own column.

6. Press ↵ to accept No in the Select Customers to Include field. We want to include all the customers who meet the criteria.

7. Press ↵ to accept A (for All) in the Use All/Selected A/R Accounts field. In our company, we have only one Accounts Receivable account. QuickBooks generates the report and displays it on the screen, as shown in Figure 11.2.

Quick-Books should automatically wrap the report onto a second page if your printer or printer settings won't accommodate wide reports.

On the report, advance payments and unapplied credits appear according to the date of the transaction, and they reduce the amount due in that time period. Invoice due dates are compared with the as of date, 10/01/93. Invoices that are

FIGURE 11.2:
Viewing the Accounts Receivable Aging report

```
                        A/R AGING REPORT

                         As of 10/ 1/93
Training Company-1100
10/ 1/93

   Customer        Current   1 - 30   31 - 60   61 - 90    > 90

Carol Hendrickson    210.00     0.00     0.00     0.00      0.00
Grannie Jones         44.89    62.10     0.00     0.00      0.00
Pony Pen               0.01     0.00     0.00     0.00      0.00
Ted Costa              0.00     0.00     0.00     0.00    456.12
One-Time Customers     0.00  -100.00     0.00     0.00      0.00

OVERALL TOTAL        254.90   -37.90     0.00     0.00    456.12
```

due *after* 10/01/93 are listed as current. Invoices due *before* 10/01/93 are past due and listed according to how late they are.

8. To view the rest of the wide report, off the right side of the screen, press →.

9. To print the report, press Ctrl-P. The Print Report window appears.

10. In the Print To field, press Ctrl-L and select the printer and orientation combination that uses compressed print or landscape orientation to accommodate the wide report.

NOTE *See Chapter 2 for more information about printer settings.*

If you did not set up a format for wide reports, press F9 from the list of available printers to change the printer setup. Highlight the printer you want to define as the printer for wide reports and press ↵. In the Set Up Printer window, move the cursor to Report Styles and press Ctrl-L to see a list of the styles your printer supports. Select a landscape style if possible. Otherwise, choose a style with compressed print (15 or more cpi).

11. After the report prints, press Esc until you return to the Main menu.

GENERATING FINANCE CHARGES

Finance charges are amounts added to past-due customer accounts. Quick-Books does not automatically calculate or enter these charges. You must

Federal guidelines establish the maximum percentage you can assess for finance charges annually.

determine which invoices are past due and how much you want to charge.

You might want to assess a finance charge for each past-due amount listed on the Accounts Receivable Aging report. To calculate finance charges, subtract the Current column amount from the Overall Total amount. Multiply the result times the percentage you charge for past-due accounts.

After determining the amount you want to charge, create a debit memo (through the invoice-entry screen) to bill the customer for the late fees. Use the Other Charges item that you set up specifically for finance charges.

PRINTING CUSTOMER STATEMENTS

Some customers will make payments when they receive an invoice; others will wait until you send a statement of all their activity for the month. After the close of business on the last day of the month, the Training Company prints an Accounts Receivable Aging report, enters late charges, and then prints statements.

Invoices that have not been printed will not appear on the statement.

On the statement, invoices and open credit memo amounts are listed by date. Any payments or credits applied to an invoice are noted. The total due appears with a notation in separate columns of amounts delinquent 30, 60, or 90 or more days.

You can print statements on letterhead, preprinted forms, or plain computer paper. For this example, use blank computer paper.

Follow these steps to print statements for our company's customers:

1. From the Main menu, select Invoicing/Receivables, and then choose View A/R Register.

2. From the Accounts Receivable register, press F2 (File/Print) and select Print Statements. You can also choose to print statements from the invoice-entry screen. The Print Statements window appears.

3. Enter **090193** and **093093** in the Statement Period From and Through fields. Transactions dated between and including the two dates will be printed on the statement and included in the balance.

4. Press ↵ in the Select Specific Customers to Include field to accept N. We will print statements for all our customers.

If you separate your Customer List into four sections, you can print statements for one section each week. Mailing statements every week to one-fourth of your customers generates a steady cash flow.

To print statements for only certain customers, you would enter Y to select specific customers. Then use the spacebar to mark or unmark one customer at a time, or Ctrl-spacebar to toggle between marking all the customers to print or not to print.

5. Press ↵ in the next two fields to print all statements, without past-due balance or balance amount restrictions.

To save time, forms, envelopes, and postage costs, you might want to send statements to only the customers who owe you enough to make statement production worthwhile. You can enter Y to print statements for just past-due accounts, and send them as a reminder to customers who have not paid on time. Sending a statement to someone who owes less than a dollar is actually costing you more money than you will gain. You can enter a minimum balance amount and print statements for only the accounts that match that criterion.

6. In the Print To field, press Ctrl-L and select the printer to use for statements.

7. In the Paper Type field, press Ctrl-L and select Blank Paper w/o Lines. When you use letterhead or preprinted forms, you can press F9 to test the alignment before completing the fields in the Print Statements window.

8. Press ↵ to accept 0 (zero) in the Additional Copies field. For your own work, you may want to print an extra copy of the statement for your files, in case you need to refer to it later.

9. Press Esc to return to the Main menu. The statements will print immediately.

If necessary, you can reprint statements by repeating the steps above. You might want to print only those customer statements that did not print correctly the first time.

MANAGING COLLECTIONS

If your business allows customers to charge their purchases, you may need to remind them to pay their bills. You can print the Collections report to see which customers have past-due balances. If you have talked to the customer about the problem, you may want to make a note of your conversation. You can use the Notebook to enter the notes to go with the customer's account.

PRINTING THE COLLECTIONS REPORT

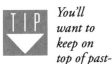

You'll want to keep on top of past-due accounts. Studies and experience prove that the longer an account sits on your books, the less chance you have of ever getting your money.

The Collections report includes the name and phone number of the contact in the customer record. It also lists each past-due invoice, with its number, date of issue, due date, and amount unpaid. This report gives you the information you need to personally contact customers with delinquent accounts. Print it regularly for your collection department to use as a worksheet.

To print the Collections report, select Reports from the Main menu, then choose A/R Reports, then Collections Report. You can accept the QuickBooks report title or enter your own. At the prompt

Show customers who are   or more days past due as of

Enter a number of days and a past-due date that allow the customers a reasonable amount of time to have received and responded to their statements. For example, to see which customers ignored your October 1 statement, enter 8 days as of **10/08/93.**

Then choose whether to include all the customers who meet your criteria and which Accounts Receivable accounts to use. When the report appears on the screen, press Ctrl-P to print it.

MAKING NOTES IN A CUSTOMER'S ACCOUNT

When you want to jot down some information about a customer, you can add a note to that customer's record. One of our customers responded by phone to our billing. Follow these steps to make a note of the conversation:

1. Select Company Lists from the Main menu, and then choose Customers from the submenu.

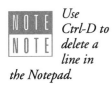

Use Ctrl-D to delete a line in the Notepad.

2. Highlight Grannie Jones and press Ctrl-E.

3. When the record appears, press Ctrl-N to display the Notepad.

4. Press F9 to paste the system date into the note.

5. Type **Social security check late. Will pay ASAP.**

6. Press Ctrl-↵ after entering the note.

7. From the View/Edit Customer window, press F10 to record the Notepad entries in the record.

8. Press Esc to return to the Main menu.

When you want to see the note you recorded in the Notepad, display the customer record and press Ctrl-N.

WRITING OFF A BAD DEBT

Like it or not, some accounts are uncollectable. When you finally give up and decide it is costing you more to try to collect than the account is worth, it's time to remove the balance from Accounts Receivable.

Our collections report shows Ted Costa's account has been past due since 12/30/92. We must set up a bad-debt item, create a credit to write off the debt, and close the customer's account.

SETTING UP A BAD DEBT INVOICE ITEM

Follow these steps to create an invoice item to handle bad-debt write offs.

1. Select Company Lists from the Main menu, and then choose Items/Parts/Services from the submenu.

2. From the Item List, press Ctrl-Ins and select to add a new Other Charges item.

3. In the Code field of the Add New Other Charge Item window, enter **Bad Debt**.

You should consult your accountant about the best way to handle bad-debt write offs.

4. In the Account field, press Ctrl-L and choose account 5150 (Miscellaneous Expense). For your actual company, you should add a Bad Debts Expense account to your chart of accounts and charge the item to that account.

5. Press ↵ to leave the Price Each field blank.

6. Enter **Bad Debt Write Off** in the Description field.

7. Press F10 to record the new item.

GENERATING A CREDIT TO WRITE OFF THE DEBT

To reduce the customer's balance and the Accounts Receivable account, you must create a credit to the customer's account, and then apply that credit to the old invoice. Figure 11.3 shows the completed credit memo for the bad debt.

Follow these steps to enter the bad-debt credit:

1. Select Invoicing/Receivables from the Main menu, and then choose Write/Print Invoices from the submenu.

2. In the Date field, enter **100193**, the date we are closing the customer's account.

3. In the Bill To field, press Ctrl-L and select Ted Costa. Terms don't apply to credits, so ignore the Terms field.

4. When the warning about the customer being over his credit limit appears, enter **N** to continue recording the invoice.

5. In the Item Code field, press Ctrl-L and select Bad Debt.

6. Enter − (minus) **456.12** in the Rate field. We are creating a credit memo, so the amount must be negative.

7. Press F10 to record the credit memo.

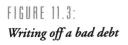

FIGURE 11.3:

Writing off a bad debt

```
 F1-Help  F2-File/Print   F3-Find/Edit    F4-Lists   F5-Reports   F6-Activities

 Invoice Number *******                                 Date 10/ 1/93

  ◆Bill To
  Ted Costa
  #1 Flakey Jake Road
  Sacramento, CA 95814          PO Num     ◆Terms        ◆Project

                                          Net 30

  Qty    ◆Item Code       Description...        Rate        Amount

          Bad Debt  Bad Debt Write Off         -456.12      -456.12↑
                                                               ▯
                                                               ↓
  ◆                                              TOTAL $    -456.12
                                               BALANCE $    -456.12
 Esc-Cancel    Shift◀⏎ Next section   F8-Hide Item Detail  Ctrl◀⏎ Record   ↑↓
```

You can print recorded invoices whenever the invoice-entry screen is displayed.

8. Press Ctrl-P to print the credit memo. We want to keep a paper copy of the transaction in the customer's file for future reference.

9. When the Print Invoices window appears, replace the system date with **100193**. Then press Ctrl-↵ to accept the other QuickBooks entries.

10. If the Next Invoice Number field does not contain 1009, enter that number.

11. Press ↵ to print the memo, and then verify that the form printed correctly.

12. Press Esc to return to the Invoicing/Receivables submenu.

CLOSING THE CUSTOMER'S ACCOUNT

Now that we have created the bad-debt credit memo, we can apply it to the unpaid items in the customer's account to bring the amount due to zero. Figure 11.4 shows the completed entries on the Receive Payments screen.

Follow these steps to apply the credit and close the customer's account:

1. Select Receive Payments from the Invoicing/Receivables submenu.

2. In the Customer field, press Ctrl-L and select Ted Costa.

FIGURE 11.4:

Clearing the customer's account

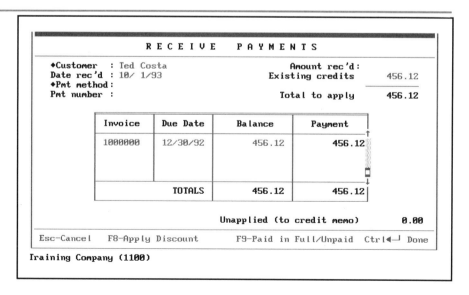

Although the Customer List shows this customer's balance as zero, the Receive Payments screen displays two open items: the past-due invoice and the recent credit memo. Our credit memo to write off the bad debt appears as the amount in the Existing Credits field.

3. In the Date Rec'd field, enter **100193**.

4. Move to the Payment field and press F9 to apply the credit to the unpaid invoice.

5. Press F10 to record the transaction.

6. Press Esc to return to the Invoicing/Receivables submenu.

These two transactions will close the customer's account and transfer the amount from the Accounts Receivable account to a Bad Debt Expense account. Your accounts receivable asset is reduced (because you will probably never receive the money), and you have recorded an expense that reduces the profit you once recorded when the sale was first made.

ADJUSTING FOR A RETURNED CHECK

When a customer's check is returned to you by a bank, you must adjust your records by entering a *debit memo* on the customer's account. A debit increases the customer's balance to show what is still owed and decreases your checking account balance. A debit memo is like an invoice, but for miscellaneous charges instead of product or service sales.

One of our customers gave us a check that bounced. Now we must set up an invoice item for other charges and create a debit memo to adjust our records. Figure 11.5 shows the completed entries.

Follow these steps to record the returned check:

1. From the Invoicing/Receivables submenu, choose Write/Print Invoices.

2. In the Bill To field of the invoice-entry screen, press Ctrl-L and select Carol Hendrickson, the customer whose check was returned.

*Adjusting your records
for a returned check*

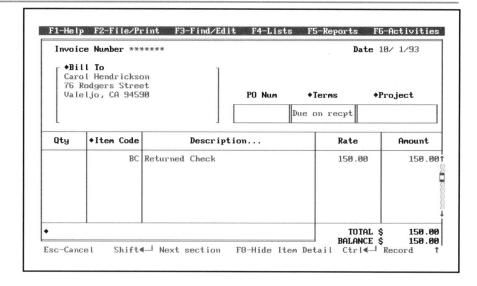

```
  F1-Help  F2-File/Print   F3-Find/Edit   F4-Lists   F5-Reports   F6-Activities

  Invoice Number *******                              Date 10/ 1/93

     ◆Bill To
      Carol Hendrickson
      76 Rodgers Street
      Valejo, CA 94590               PO Num    ◆Terms      ◆Project

                                             ║Due on recpt║

   Qty    ◆Item Code        Description...              Rate        Amount

              BC  Returned Check                       150.00      150.00↑

                                                                         ▓

   ◆                                            TOTAL $   150.00
                                                BALANCE $  150.00
   Esc-Cancel   Shift◀─┘ Next section   F8-Hide Item Detail  Ctrl◀─┘ Record   ↑
```

3. Override the entry in the Terms field by pressing Ctrl-L and selecting
   Due on Recpt from the Terms List. Debit memos are not usually discounted, and returned check charges are due immediately.

4. In the Item Code field, enter **BC**, a new code for Bounced Check.
   When prompted, select to add the new item and assign it the
   Other Charges type.

5. In the Account field, enter the general ledger account number representing the bank account that was charged for the check, **1000**.

When you are recording a returned check, you want to reduce the account
for the bank account to which it was originally deposited. If you do not, your
general ledger balance and your bank account balance will not reconcile.

6. Enter **Returned Check** in the Description field and record the
   new item.

7. In the Rate field of the invoice-entry screen, enter **150**, the amount
   of the check.

8. Press F10 to record the debit memo.

9. Press Esc until you return to the Main menu.

*You may
want to set
up an in-
voice item
for charging cus-
tomers a fee for
returned checks.
Record the amount
in a general ledger In-
come account. You
could record the fee
on the same debit
memo you enter for
the returned check.*

This debit memo will increase the customer's balance and decrease the balance in the checking account indicated in the Other Charges record. The debit will appear as an unpaid item on the customer statement.

PRINTING CUSTOMER LABELS

You may want to print customer labels for mailings or reference. For example, you can use them when you notify customers of a big sale, or put them on index cards for your salesperson's tickler file.

The labels QuickBooks prints include the information in the five lines in the Bill To field of the customer record, which are usually the customer name and address. The program prints two labels across, which are 4 inches wide and 1 inch deep.

If your printer won't accept labels, print on blank paper and copy the output onto label forms.

To print labels, from either the invoice-entry screen or the Accounts Receivable register, press F2 (File/Print) and select Print Mailing Labels. Then choose whether you want to sort the labels by zip code (enter Z) or by name (enter N). If you are printing labels for a mailing, you will probably want to sort them by zip code.

Next, choose whether to print labels for all or specific customers. If you enter Y to print all the customers, QuickBooks ignores any criteria you enter in the following fields.

Press Ctrl-L in the Customer Type Matches field to display the Customer Type List and select the type of customer. For example, you could select Individual from our company's list to print labels for only the customers whose records are defined with this type.

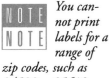

You cannot print labels for a range of zip codes, such as 94590 to 95610. You can match only one zip code.

In the last two fields, you can limit the selections to a specific zip code and to a minimum purchase amount. For example, you might want to mail sale notices to only local customers who made significant purchases.

Finally, select the printer that has the label forms loaded. Then you can print the labels.

This chapter reviewed common accounts receivable maintainenance tasks. You learned how to display and print the Accounts Receivable Aging report, which groups the amounts due to you by time periods, and the Collection report, which lists customers with delinquent accounts. The chapter described how to print customer account statements and labels. You also learned how to write off bad debts and record returned checks.

In the next chapter, you will learn how to keep your bank and credit card accounts current. It covers checking account and credit card statement reconciliation.

12

Reconciling Bank and Credit Card Statements

ou can use QuickBooks to reconcile your checking and credit card accounts. The reconciliation procedure involves marking items as cleared by your bank or credit card institution.

The success of your reconciliation depends on how carefully you have recorded transactions in your registers. If you have kept accurate, up-to-date information, your records should agree with your statements.

RECONCILING YOUR BANK STATEMENT

Balancing a checkbook seems to be the last thing anyone wants to do. Quick-Books has made this chore a simple task. Now you can be sure of your bank balance and avoid bouncing checks.

PRINTING THE CHECK REGISTER

Before we begin the reconciliation, we will print the Check register to review

Quick-Books provides Help text for each screen. For more information about the fields on the Print Register window, press F1.

the transactions we have recorded. Follow these steps to print the register:

1. Select Checkbook from the Main menu, and then choose Check Register from the submenu.

2. Press Ctrl-P to print the register. The Print Register window appears.

3. In the Print Transactions From and To fields, enter **080193** and **093093**.

4. In the Print To field, press Ctrl-L and select a printer with a landscape format, if possible. Otherwise, choose a compressed print format.

5. Enter **Y** in the Print One Transaction per Line field.

6. Enter **N** in the next two fields. The report prints immediately. Your printout should look similar to the one shown in Figure 12.1.

The report shows that checks 1001 through 1004 were written and printed. Check 945 is the manual check we entered directly in the register. The Num field is blank for deposits and withdrawals that did not involve a check, and it has asterisks for checks that have been written but not printed. Obviously, the checks that have not been distributed yet have not been cashed.

We will be comparing the entries in the Check register with the entries on the checking account statement from the bank.

FIGURE 12.1:

The Check register printout

```
                                    1000 - Register
1000                                                                       Page 1
10/ 1/93

     Date    Num       Payee          Memo       Account    Amount   C  Balance
   -------- -----  --------------  ----------  ----------  ---------- - ----------
    9/ 1/93         Opening Balance             [Open Bal   25,382.90 X  25,382.90
    9/15/93 1001    CASH            Set Up Pet  [1210]        -200.00    25,182.90
    9/15/93 1002 S  Kenneth M. Wade 9/14 Expen  5110         -152.90    25,030.00
    9/20/93 1003 S  Four Paws Pet Cen DS3629    [2000]      -1,180.00    23,850.00
    9/20/93 1004 S  Kat Kastle      TTC4069     [2000]      -1,000.00    22,850.00
    9/22/93 *****S  Loans-R-Us      31-7921     [2200]        -886.50    21,963.50
    9/23/93 945     Office Mart     M487        5160          -64.87    21,898.63
    9/25/93         Countrywide Loans 28032-4   [2310]        -248.33    21,650.30
    9/25/93 *****S  Petty Cash      Replenish   5110          -51.75    21,598.55
    9/25/93 *****   Phyllis Rocklin Sept Draw   [3015]      -1,500.00    20,098.55
    9/26/93 *****   Birds Of Paradise Refund to [1100]         -80.00    20,018.55
    9/29/93         Deposit from A/R            [1100]       4,837.28    24,855.83
    9/29/93         Deposit from A/R            [1100]         100.00    24,955.83
    9/29/93         VISA            Visa Fee    5150           -4.50    24,951.33
```

RECONCILING YOUR RECORDS WITH THE BANK STATEMENT

You cannot cancel the reconciliation process once you begin it, but you can exit and leave the reconciliation incomplete.

You begin the reconciliation process from the register of the bank account you want to reconcile. You enter bank account statement information, and then mark entries as cleared by the bank.

Follow these steps to compare our records with the bank statement:

1. Select Chart of Accounts from the Main menu.
2. Highlight the bank account you want to reconcile, Countrywide Bank (1000), and press ↵.
3. Press F6 (Activities) and select the Reconcile option.

The Reconcile Register with Bank Statement window appears. The Bank Statement Opening Balance field contains the amount we recorded when we set up QuickBooks. After you complete your first bank account reconciliation, the opening balance will be calculated from your previous reconciliation.

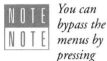

You can bypass the menus by pressing Ctrl-Y to begin reconciliation.

4. Enter **28304.48** in the Bank Statement Ending Balance field.
5. In the Service Charge field, enter **9.40**, the service charge the bank assessed for handling our account.

QuickBooks will record the service charge amount in the Check register. If you want to keep service charges separate from check-printing charges, record the first charge in the Service Charge field now, and record the other charges in the register later.

6. In the Account field, enter **5150** (Miscellaneous Expense), which is the general ledger Expense account in which we record bank charges.
7. Enter **093093** as the date the bank charged our account. Your bank account information should match the entries in the window shown in Figure 12.2.

If this were a savings account or an interest-earning checking account, you would enter the amount of the interest in the Interest Earned field, the account in which you record interest income in the Account field, and the date

Entering
bank statement
information

```
╔════════════════════════════════════════════════╗
║                                                  ║
║        Reconcile Register with Bank Statement    ║
║                                                  ║
║                                                  ║
║      Bank statement opening balance: 25,382.90   ║
║      Bank statement ending balance : 28,304.48   ║
║                                                  ║
║      ────────Transaction to Be Added (Optional)──────── ║
║        Service Charge : 9.40                     ║
║        ◆Account : 5150                           ║
║        Date :  9/30/93                           ║
║                                                  ║
║        Interest Earned :                         ║
║        ◆Account :                                ║
║        Date : 10/ 2/93                           ║
║                                                  ║
║            F9-Print Last Reconciliation Report   ║
║      Esc-Cancel          F1-Help          Ctrl◄┘ Done ║
╚════════════════════════════════════════════════╝
```

the bank posted the increase to your bank account in the Date field (over-riding the system date in that field). QuickBooks would record the interest amount in the Income account you specified.

8. Press Ctrl-↵ to skip the remaining fields and record your entries.
The reconciliation screen appears, as shown in Figure 12.3.

This screen lists the open transactions in your Check register. The asterisk (*) in the C field of the service charge line indicates that this amount has been cleared. The ↑ and ↓ along the right side of the screen mean that there are more transactions, which you can see by moving the cursor down past the last transaction that appears.

To reconcile your account, you mark each check and deposit listed in your bank statement as cleared. You can press ↵ to mark individual items, or use F8 to mark a range of checks. The spacebar toggles between marking items as cleared and unmarking items.

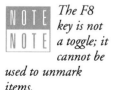 *The F8 key is not a toggle; it cannot be used to unmark items.*

9. Press F8 to display the Mark Range of Check Numbers as Cleared window. It contains the prompt

Mark items numbered   to   with an *.

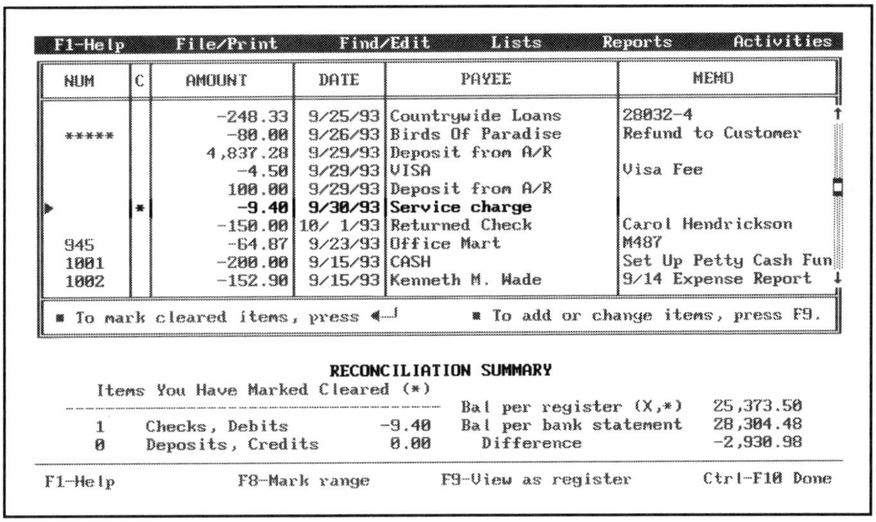

FIGURE 12.3:

Beginning the reconciliation

```
 F1-Help      File/Print      Find/Edit      Lists      Reports      Activities

 ┌─────┬──┬──────────┬─────────┬────────────────────┬──────────────────────────┐
 │ NUM │C │  AMOUNT  │  DATE   │       PAYEE        │           MEMO           │
 ├─────┼──┼──────────┼─────────┼────────────────────┼──────────────────────────┤
 │     │  │  -248.33 │ 9/25/93 │Countrywide Loans   │28032-4                  ↑│
 │*****│  │   -80.00 │ 9/26/93 │Birds Of Paradise   │Refund to Customer        │
 │     │  │ 4,837.28 │ 9/29/93 │Deposit from A/R    │                          │
 │     │  │    -4.50 │ 9/29/93 │VISA                │Visa Fee                  │
 │     │  │   100.00 │ 9/29/93 │Deposit from A/R    │                          │
 │►    │ *│    -9.40 │ 9/30/93 │Service charge      │                          │
 │     │  │  -150.00 │10/ 1/93 │Returned Check      │Carol Hendrickson        ║│
 │ 945 │  │   -64.87 │ 9/23/93 │Office Mart         │M487                      │
 │1001 │  │  -200.00 │ 9/15/93 │CASH                │Set Up Petty Cash Fun     │
 │1002 │  │  -152.90 │ 9/15/93 │Kenneth M. Wade     │9/14 Expense Report      ↓│
 └─────┴──┴──────────┴─────────┴────────────────────┴──────────────────────────┘
  ■ To mark cleared items, press ◄─┘      ■ To add or change items, press F9.

                            RECONCILIATION SUMMARY
      Items You Have Marked Cleared (*)
 ───────────────────────────────────────── Bal per register (X,*)    25,373.50
      1    Checks, Debits          -9.40   Bal per bank statement     28,304.48
      0    Deposits, Credits        0.00   Difference                 -2,930.98

  F1-Help          F8-Mark range       F9-View as register       Ctrl-F10 Done
```

10. Enter **1001**, then **1003**. An asterisk will appear in the C column beside 1001, 1002, and 1003.

11. Highlight the withdrawal for Countrywide Loans and press ↵ to mark it as having been deducted by the bank.

12. Highlight the first deposit on 9/29 and press ↵ to mark it as showing on the bank statement.

13. Skip the VISA entry (the bank has not yet deducted this fee), move the cursor to the $100 deposit, and press ↵ to mark it.

14. Move the cursor to mark the returned check and press ↵ to mark it.

15. Press ↵ to mark check 945. This is the last item we will mark.

16. Press PgDn to view the remaining entries. Check 1004 has not been cashed yet. Several unprinted checks are at the bottom of the list. They do not, of course, appear on the bank statement.

As you mark the items, QuickBooks totals the checks or debits and deposits or credits that have been posted by your bank and shows the result in the Reconciliation window beneath the list of transactions. These items are used to adjust the ending balance in your register to reconcile it with the new balance on your statement. The difference should be zero when you have completed the reconciliation.

However, the Reconciliation window indicates that our difference is 10.20, as shown in Figure 12.4. We did not mark check 1004 as cleared, and looking again at the bank statement, we verify that the VISA discount has not yet been subtracted from our account by the bank. But now we see the check-printing charge of $10.20, which we didn't enter in the Check register. Fortunately, you can make entries in the register during the reconciliation process, as we will do next.

FIGURE 12.4:

Reconciling a bank account

```
                          RECONCILIATION SUMMARY
        Items You Have Marked Cleared (*)
        ----------------------------------   Bal per register (X,*)   28,314.68
            7    Checks, Debits    -2,005.50  Bal per bank statement   28,304.48
            2    Deposits, Credits  4,937.28  Difference                  10.20

        F1-Help           F8-Mark range      F9-View as register     Ctrl-F10 Done
```

CORRECTING ERRORS IN THE CHECK REGISTER

As you review your statement during the bank account reconciliation procedure, you may discover errors in your register. For example, you may have written a manual check and forgotten to enter it in the register, or you could have recorded an amount that differs from the amount actually on the check. You might also need to record an automatic charge that doesn't qualify as a service charge.

From the reconciliation screen, you can display the Check register and add, edit, or delete transactions. We need to record the bank charge for printing checks. Follow these steps to enter that transaction:

1. From the reconciliation screen, press F9 to view the Check register.

2. Press Ctrl-End to move past the last transaction. You will see that the service charge we entered during reconciliation already appears in the register.

3. Press Back Tab to reach the Date field for the new entry and enter **092793**, the date the bank posted the check-printing charge.

4. In the Payee field, enter **Countrywide Bank**, the institution we are paying for the printed checks.

5. Enter **10.20**, the amount we were charged, in the Payment field.

6. In the C field, enter * (an asterisk) to indicate this charge has cleared the bank.

7. In the Memo field, enter **Check printing charge**.

8. In the Account field, enter **5150**, which is the number of the account (Miscellaneous Expense) in which we record the expense.

9. When QuickBooks asks if it should record the transaction, press ↵. The transaction appears in the register according to its date.

10. To return to the reconciliation screen, press F9. Now the check-printing charge is included in the list.

CORRECTING BANK STATEMENT INFORMATION ERRORS

During the reconciliation process, you may discover that the bank statement ending balance you entered in the Reconcile Register with Bank Statement window (Figure 12.2) is incorrect. To change the ending balance amount, from the reconciliation screen, press F9 to display the register. Then press F6 (Activities) and select the Reconcile option again. The Reconcile Register with Bank Statement window will reappear. You can correct the ending balance amount (but not the service charge or interest-earned amount) and record your change to return to the reconciliation screen.

If you entered the bank service charge or interest-earned amount incorrectly, edit those transactions in the Check register, not in the Reconcile Register with Bank Statement window or on the reconciliation screen. Press F9 from the reconciliation screen and make the necessary changes. Then press F9 to return to the reconciliation process.

COMPLETING THE RECONCILIATION AND PRINTING A REPORT

When your bank statement and Check register are balanced, the Difference field in the Reconciliation Summary window will show a difference of zero. You can exit the reconciliation process and print a Reconciliation report.

Now that we have adjusted our Check register, our bank statement and register are balanced. Follow these steps to complete the reconciliation and print a report:

The next time you reconcile your checking account, press F9 from the Reconcile Register with Bank Statement window to print a report showing the transactions that were outstanding after your previous reconciliation.

1. Press Ctrl-F10 to exit the reconciliation process. QuickBooks changes the asterisks in the C field to X's and asks if you want to print a reconciliation report.

2. Enter **Y** to print the report. The Print Reconciliation Report window appears.

3. Select which printer to use.

4. In the Reconcile Date field, enter **093093**, the ending date on our bank statement. This date prints on the report.

5. In the Report Title field, enter **September Statement**. This report heading explains the range of activities included in the reconciliation.

6. Press ↵ to accept S (for Summary). We want to print a summary report, which includes totals for all transactions and detail for the uncleared transactions.

If you wanted to see totals and detail for both cleared and uncleared transactions, you would enter F to print a full report.

The report prints immediately, but the Print Reconciliation Report window remains. You could now choose to print a full report (if you selected a full report the first time, you could print a summary report after that report printed).

7. Press Esc until you return to the Main menu.

HANDLING A CHECKING ACCOUNT THAT WON'T BALANCE

If you want to exit the reconciliation process without balancing, press Esc. QuickBooks displays the Reconciliation is Not Complete window, as shown in Figure 12.5. Choose to leave the reconciliation, and QuickBooks will save the work you have done. Your entries remain intact, the asterisks stay in the C field (indicating the reconciliation process is incomplete), and the reconciliation attempt remains unbalanced.

*Selecting to exit before
an account balances*

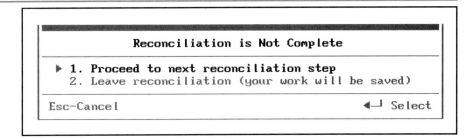

After you research the difference, begin the reconciliation again and complete the process. Note that you should not enter the service charge again when you are continuing a previously attempted reconciliation.

If you press Esc from the reconciliation screen and then choose to proceed rather than leave, QuickBooks will notify you that the register and statement do not agree. Selecting to proceed when the account doesn't balance is the same as pressing Ctrl-F10 when the Difference field shows an amount other than zero.

*You
should not
arbitrarily
make an
adjustment to force
your records to
balance with your
bank statement. You
should make every
effort to locate the
error and make the
appropriate
corrections.*

In both cases, QuickBooks displays a window warning you that a problem exists. This window lists possible reasons for the difference, as shown in the example in Figure 12.6. Check your statement against the information you have entered, and correct your Check register or bank statement information, as described earlier in the chapter.

You can also force the account to balance by pressing ↵ from the warning window and allowing QuickBooks to enter an adjustment in the register. You will see the Adding Balance Adjustment Entry window, as shown in Figure 12.7. You can verify that you want to make the adjustment and enter an

------

FIGURE 12.6:

*Completing
reconciliation before
an account balances*

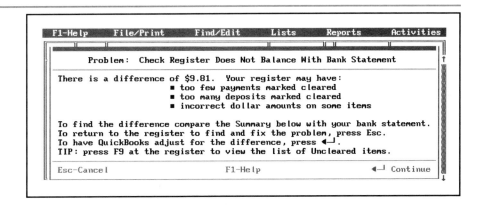

FIGURE 12.7:

Making an adjustment to force a bank account to balance

```
                  Adding Balance Adjustment Entry

                       Difference: $9.81

    QuickBooks is about to add an entry to your register to make
    it agree with the statement.  The entry will appear as a
    "Balance Adjustment" payment for $9.81.

    Note: The only reason you should take this step is if you are
          unable to resolve the difference with your bank.
          To avoid all chance for error, cancel this operation
          by pressing Esc, and fix the difference yourself.
          This may require reconciling previous months'statements
          if you have skipped any.

    Add Balance Adjustment to register (Y/N):

    ◆Account:

  Esc-Cancel                    F1-Help              Ctrl◀┘ Done
```

account to charge the adjustment against. Alternatively, you can press Esc to cancel the adjustment, as QuickBooks suggests. Adjustments and transactions appear differently on reports.

RECONCILING YOUR CREDIT CARD ACCOUNT

To reconcile your credit card account, you compare your credit card statement with your entries in the Credit Card register. At the end of the reconciliation process, you can choose to pay your credit card bill.

RECONCILING YOUR RECORDS WITH THE CREDIT CARD STATEMENT

You begin the reconciliation process from the register of the Credit Card account you want to reconcile. You enter credit card statement information, and then mark the entries that appear on the statement.

We will reconcile the transactions in our sample company's Credit Card register. The completed credit card statement information entries are shown in Figure 12.8.

FIGURE 12.8:

Entering credit card statement information

F1-Help	F2-File/Print	F3-Find/Edit	F4-Lists	F5-Reports	F6-Activities

DATE	REF	◆PAYEE · MEMO · ◆ACCOUNT	CHARGE	C	PAYMENT	BALANCE
		▅▅▅▅ BEGINNING ▅▅▅▅				
9/01 1993		Opening Balance [Open Bal Equi→	15 80	X		15 80
9/12 1993		Hans' Auto Service 1DWE846 5110	19 95			35 75

Follow these steps to begin the reconciliation process:

1. Choose the Chart of Accounts option from the Main menu. On the Chart of Accounts screen, select Dutch Oil. The Credit Card register appears, as shown in Figure 12.9.

2. Press F6 (Activities) and select the Reconcile/Pay Bill option. The Credit Card Statement Information window appears.

3. In the Charges, Cash Advance field, enter **19.95**, the total of all our charges and cash advances.

The charges and cash advances amount does not include the opening balance nor any finance charges. As noted in the window, finance charges are handled separately.

NOTE
NOTE

You must make an entry in the Payments, Credits field, even if you have not made any payments on your account and the company has not posted any credits.

4. In the Payments, Credits field, enter **0**.

5. Enter **35.99** in the New Balance field. You must enter the new or *ending* balance from the statement, not the beginning balance.

6. In the Finance Charges field, enter **.24**, the amount we were charged this month.

7. In the Account field, press Ctrl-L and select 5150 (Miscellaneous Expense), which is the account we use to keep track of interest paid. For your own company, you might want to set up an individual Expense account for interest and finance charges (for tax reporting purchases).

8. In the Date field, enter **100393**, the date we want the finance charge to appear in our Credit Card register.

The Credit Card register

```
┌────────────────────────────────────────────────────────┐
│ ▄▄▄▄▄▄▄▄▄▄▄▄▄▄▄▄▄▄▄▄▄▄▄▄▄▄▄▄▄▄▄▄▄▄▄▄▄▄▄▄▄▄▄▄▄▄▄▄▄▄▄▄▄▄▄  │
│              Credit Card Statement Information           │
│  ──────────────────────────────────────────────────     │
│                                                          │
│     Charges, Cash Advances: 19.95                        │
│       (other than finance charges)                       │
│     Payments, Credits    : 0.00                          │
│     New balance          : 35.99                         │
│                                                          │
│     ──────Transaction to Be Added (Optional)──────       │
│       Finance Charges: 0.24                              │
│       ◆Account: 5150                                     │
│       Date: 10/03/93                                     │
│  ──────────────────────────────────────────────────     │
│            Enter statement information.                  │
│   Esc-Cancel             F1-Help         Ctrl◄─┘ Done    │
└────────────────────────────────────────────────────────┘
```

After you complete the last field in the Credit Card Statement Information window, the reconciliation screen appears. It shows the open transactions in your Credit Card register. The asterisk (*) in the C field of the finance charge line indicates that this amount has been cleared. The Reconciliation Summary window below the transactions shows the totals of the charges and payments that have cleared. These items are used to adjust the ending balance in your register to reconcile it with the new balance on your statement. The difference should be zero when you have completed the reconciliation.

You mark cleared items on this screen in the same way that you mark items on the screen for reconciling a checking account. Press ↵ to mark individual items, or use F8 to mark a range of items (based on their beginning and ending dates). The spacebar toggles between marking and unmarking items.

9. Highlight the charge from Hans' Auto Service and press ↵ to mark it as appearing on your statement.

Our records and statement balance, as shown by the zero in the Difference field in the Reconciliation Summary window.

CORRECTING ERRORS IN THE CREDIT CARD REGISTER

As you review your credit card statement, you may find that there are errors in your Credit Card register. For example, you may have forgotten to enter a charge in the register, or you entered the wrong amount because the carbon copy was difficult to read.

From the reconciliation screen, you can switch to the Credit Card register and make changes. Press F9 to display the register, and then add, edit, or delete transactions as necessary. To return to the reconciliation screen, press F9 again.

CORRECTING CREDIT CARD STATEMENT INFORMATION ERRORS

If you discover that you entered the credit card statement information incorrectly, you can change that information. From the reconciliation screen, press F9 to display the register. Then press F6 (Activities) and select the Reconcile/Pay Bill option again. The Credit Card Statement Information window (Figure 12.6) will reappear.

You can change the entries in the Charges, Cash Advances field and the Payments, Credits field. However, if you entered the wrong amount in the Finance Charges field, you must edit that transaction line in the register.

COMPLETING RECONCILIATION AND MAKING A PAYMENT

NOTE
NOTE

You can originate a payment from your bank account to your credit card at any time. This transaction (a transfer) will appear in your Credit Card register automatically.

When your credit card statement and register agree (the Difference field shows zero), you can complete the reconciliation process. Optionally, you can make a payment at the same time. The payment can be a manual check or a check generated by QuickBooks. If you don't want to make a payment after reconciling your actual credit card account, just press Esc from the Make Credit Card Payment window.

Our statement and register balance, and we want to pay our credit card bill now. Follow these steps to finish reconciling and make a payment:

1. From the reconciliation screen, press Ctrl-F10. The Make Credit Card Payment window appears.

2. Press Ctrl-L to select the bank account from which to make the payment.

3. Select our only checking account, 1000.

4. In the Hand-Written Check field, press ↵ to indicate that this payment is *not* to be made with a manual check. QuickBooks writes and displays the payment check, as shown in Figure 12.10.

QuickBooks has filled in the amount as the balance due on the credit card statement and charged the payment to the Credit Card account. You can override the amount if you do not want to pay the full balance.

5. Override the system date in the Date field by entering **100593**, the date we want the check processed.

6. Press F10 to record the check.

If you choose to write the payment check by hand (by entering Y in the Handwritten Check field), QuickBooks will display the Check register with the transaction for the credit card payment already entered for payment in full. You can complete the transaction with a check number, description, and

FIGURE 12.10:

*The program-generated
credit card payment*

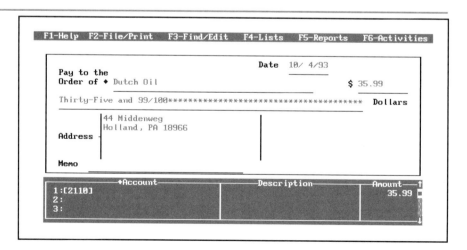

memo. If you are making a partial payment, override the Payment field entry by entering the actual amount of the check.

If you press Ctrl-F10 from the reconciliation screen before your credit card statement and Credit Card register balance (while an amount remains in the Difference field), QuickBooks will display the Adjust Register to Agree with Statement window, as shown in Figure 12.11.

Instead of making the adjustments, you should try to locate the difference and record the missing transactions in the register. Press Esc to exit the reconciliation process without balancing the account. Check your statement against the information you have entered, and correct your Credit Card register or credit card statement information as described earlier in the chapter. After correcting your errors, begin the reconciliation process again.

Alternatively, you can press ↵ and allow QuickBooks to create an adjusting entry to force the balance in your register to agree with the credit card statement. You can enter an account to charge the adjustment against.

In this chapter, you learned how to reconcile your checking account by comparing the statement from your bank with the entries in your Check register. You reconcile a credit card account by comparing your credit card statement with the transactions in your Credit Card register.

The next chapter describes how memorized transactions can make your work more efficient. You will learn how to recall and group the checks, payments, and other transactions memorized by QuickBooks.

FIGURE 12.11:

*Making an adjustment
to force a credit card
account to balance*

```
                 Adjust Register to Agree with Statement.

    QuickBooks is about to make the following entries in your register,
    So that your records will balance with the statement.

      ── Description ──        ── Amount ──              ◆Account ──
    ■ Adjust for opening           137.00
      balance difference
    ■ Register was missing         -56.00
      one or more payments
    ■ Register was missing         -45.00
      one or more charges

        Press ◄─┘ to make the adjustments, or Escape to cancel.

    Esc-Cancel                     F1-Help                  Ctrl◄─┘ Done
```

13

Recalling and Grouping
Memorized Transactions

emorized transactions can make your work more efficient and accurate. After you create a memorized transaction, you don't have to reenter the information when you want to record another occurrence of that transaction. When you recall a memorized transaction, QuickBooks fills in the fields for you.

If you regularly process several similar transactions at once, you can save time by memorizing those transactions and then grouping them. Then you will be able to record those transactions by selecting the group that contains them from the list of transaction groups.

WORKING WITH MEMORIZED TRANSACTIONS

QuickBooks can memorize three types of transactions:

◆ Checks you write regularly, such as a monthly check to your landlord for building rent

◆ Recurring entries in a register, such as an automatic deduction from your checking account for your monthly insurance premium

◆ Customer invoices you issue repeatedly, such as an invoice for a weekly gardening service

To have QuickBooks memorize a transaction, after you enter it but before you record it, press F4 and select the Memorize Transaction option, or use the Ctrl-M shortcut to bypass the menu. You can also memorize a transaction you already recorded by highlighting it and then choosing to memorize it.

The definition of the recurring transaction remains in a memorized transaction file. When you are ready to use one of your recurring register entries or invoices, you select it from a list of memorized transactions.

RECALLING MEMORIZED TRANSACTIONS

If you change the amount of a transaction that has been split, the amount of the change will be included in the split as an uncategorized entry. Press Ctrl-S to view the account distribution and change it as necessary for the new transaction amount.

You can recall a memorized transaction whenever you need it by selecting Recall Transaction from the F4 menu (or by pressing Ctrl-T) and choosing the transaction from the list. You can access your memorized Checkbook transactions from the check-writing screen or the Check register. The list of memorized invoices, which is separate from memorized Checkbook transactions, is available through the invoice-entry screen or the Accounts Receivable register.

A transaction is not specific to one account. In other words, you can define a check for one bank account and recall it to use in another bank account. Logically, however, memorized transactions should affect the same account every time.

When you recall a memorized transaction, you can record it without changes or edit it for the current entry. For example, you can change the amount of the transaction for the current entry or enter a different memo.

Any changes you make to the current transaction will not affect the stored definition for the memorized transaction.

RECALLING A MEMORIZED CHECK

In Chapter 8, we had QuickBooks memorize a check for a monthly loan payment. Now we will recall that check, make some changes, and record it for this month's payment. The completed check is shown in Figure 13.1.

Follow these steps to recall the memorized transaction:

1. Select Checkbook from the Main menu, and then choose Write/Print Checks from the submenu.

2. From the check-writing screen, press F4 (Lists) and select Recall Transaction from the menu. The Standard Memorized Transaction List appears, as shown in Figure 13.2.

3. Highlight the check to Loans-R-Us and press ↵. QuickBooks fills in the check with the memorized information.

The cursor waits in the Amount field, in case you want to change it. However, our payments are the same each month.

4. Press Back Tab to reach the Date field and override the system date by entering **102293**, the date our payment is due.

5. Press Shift-↵ to move the cursor to the Memo field.

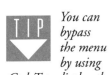 *You can bypass the menu by using Ctrl-T to display the list of memorized transactions.*

 FIGURE 13.1:

Editing a recalled check

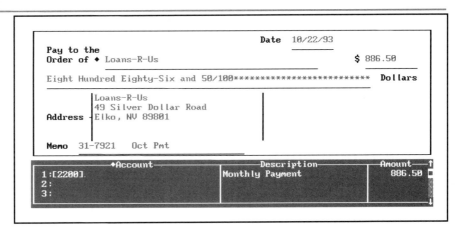

```
┌─────────────────────────────────────────────────────────────────┐
│                Standard Memorized Transaction List                │
│   ........................................................        │
│        Name             Memo          Account      Type :Amt      │
│  ▶ Countrywide Loans   28032-4       [2310]       Pmt:    248 ↑   │
│    Loans-R-Us          31-7921       [2200]       Chk:    886 ▯   │
│                                                                   │
│                                                                   │
│                                                                   │
│                                                                   │
│                                                                   │
│                                                                   │
│                                                                   │
│                                                                 ↓ │
│   Esc-Cancel               F7-Actions            Ctrl◀┘ Done      │
└─────────────────────────────────────────────────────────────────┘
```

6. Use the → key to move past the loan number in the Memo field, and then enter **Oct Pmt** to indicate which month's payment we are making.

The payment is still recorded in our Current Liability account (2200), so we do not need to change the information in the account-distribution window.

7. Press F10 to record the check.

The check is now ready to print, along with any other checks you are writing.

RECALLING TRANSACTIONS IN A REGISTER

Another memorized transaction we created in Chapter 8 is for the monthly deduction the bank takes from our checking account for our delivery truck loan. We will recall that transaction to record the entry for this month in the Check register. The completed entry is shown in Figure 13.3, which also shows the memorized check we recalled in the previous section.

Follow these steps to recall the memorized register entry:

1. From the Checkbook submenu, choose Check Register.

FIGURE 13.3:

Recalling a memorized transaction in the Check register

F1-Help F2-File/Print F3-Find/Edit F4-Lists F5-Reports F6-Activities

DATE	NUM	◆PAYEE · MEMO · ◆ACCOUNT	PAYMENT	C	DEPOSIT	BALANCE
9/29 1993		VISA Visa Fee 5150	4 50			24,941 13
9/30 1993		Service charge 5150	9 40	X		24,931 73
10/01 1993		Returned Check Carol Hendricks→[1100]	150 00	X		24,781 73
10/05 1993	*****	Dutch Oil [2110]	35 99			24,745 74
10/22 1993	***** SPLIT	Loans-R-Us 31-7921 Oct Pmt [2200]	886 50			23,859 24
10/25 1993	Memo: ◆Acct	Countrywide Loans 28032-4 [2310]	248 33			

TIP *If you memorized a Check register entry for an automatic deduction but now have to write checks for your payments, you can recall that memorized transaction from the check-writing screen instead of from the Check register.*

2. Press Ctrl-End to move the cursor to a blank transaction line in the register. If you recall a memorized transaction while the cursor is on a register entry, the recalled transaction will overwrite the existing transaction.

3. Press Ctrl-T to display the Standard Memorized Transaction List.

4. Highlight the Countrywide Loans transaction and press ↵.

QuickBooks fills in the fields in the register with the stored definition. The only change we need to make is to the date. The account in which we record the payment for the truck loan, 2310 (our Long-Term Liability account) remains the same.

5. Press Back Tab to reach the Date field and enter **102593**, the date the bank deducts the payment from our checking account.

6. Press F10 to record the entry.

7. Press Esc until you return to the Main menu.

QuickBooks will update your checking account balance to reflect the amount of the transaction.

RECALLING RECURRING INVOICES

In Chapter 9, we had QuickBooks memorize a customer invoice for pastureland rental. We bill in advance for the rent, and now it's time to send the invoice for November. The customer also ordered some hay, and we will add this charge to the invoice. The completed invoice is shown in Figure 13.4.

Follow these steps to recall and edit the memorized invoice:

1. From the Main menu, select Invoicing/Receivables, and then choose Write/Print Invoices from the submenu.

2. From the invoice-entry screen, press Ctrl-T to display the Memorized Invoice Transaction List.

3. Highlight the invoice to Carol Hendrickson and press ↵. QuickBooks fills in the fields in the invoice.

4. Press Back Tab to move the cursor to the Date field and enter **102593**.

5. Press Shift-↵, and then press Tab until the cursor reaches the Item Code field below the line for pasture rental.

6. In the Item Code field on the second line, enter **H1000**, the code for hay. QuickBooks fills in the Description, Rate, and Amount fields. This addition appears on the new invoice, but it is not added to the memorized copy.

FIGURE 13.4:

Editing a recalled invoice

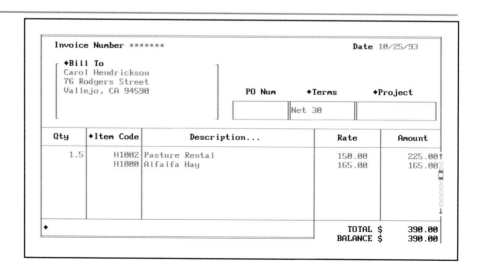

7. Press F10 to record this invoice.

8. Press Esc until you return to the Main menu.

The invoice is now ready to print, along with any other invoices you have entered but not printed yet.

GROUPING MEMORIZED TRANSACTIONS

Before you can create a transaction group, you must first create and memorize the transactions.

A *transaction group* is made up of several memorized transactions that you place in a group and recall for processing at the same time. You use the Transaction Group option on the F4 menu to access your transaction groups. All the transactions in a group must originate in the same general ledger account.

CREATING A TRANSACTION GROUP

We will group our two loan payments—the one for the delivery truck and the one for the printer—so that we can process them at the same time. Follow these steps:

1. From the Main menu, select Checkbook, and then choose Check register from the submenu.

2. From the Check register, press F4 and select Transaction Group from the menu.

3. From the Standard Transaction Group List, press Ctrl-Ins to add a new group. The Add New Standard Transaction Group window appears.

4. In the Group Name field, enter **Loan Payments** to describe this set of transactions.

You can bypass the menu by pressing Ctrl-J to display the list of transaction groups.

The group's name will appear on the list of transaction groups. You should make this name as descriptive as possible. For example, you might name one group Utility Bills and another Employee Checks.

5. Accept 1000 (our checking account number) as the account to load before executing.

QuickBooks supplies the number of the account whose register you were in when you chose the Transaction Group option. Since we were in our Check register, 1000 appears here. When we process this group, the check will be written and ready to print, and the automatic deduction will be added to the register.

If the transactions you are grouping are generic enough to be applicable to more than one account, leave this field blank. Then, before you choose to process the group, be sure that you are in the account that you want to affect.

6. In the Frequency field, select Monthly as how often we want to process these transactions.

If you specify a frequency and scheduled date for the group, QuickBooks will display a reminder when you start the program. If you do not want to be reminded about transaction groups processing, select None in the Frequency field.

The groups do not execute automatically on the scheduled date. You must select to process them, as explained in the next section.

7. In the Next Scheduled Date field, override the system date by entering **112593**. QuickBooks will calculate future scheduled dates according to the frequency you entered.

When you complete the fields in the window, the list of your memorized transactions appears so that you can select which ones you want to include in this group. The spacebar toggles between including or removing a transaction from the group. Remember to include only transactions that occur in the same account.

8. Highlight Countrywide Loans and press the spacebar to include it in the group.

If you press ↵ or Ctrl-↵ while a transaction group is highlighted on the list, QuickBooks will record the individual transactions in the group.

9. Highlight the next transaction, Loans-R-Us, and press the spacebar to mark it.

10. Press Ctrl-↵ to record the transactions in the group. The Standard Transaction Group List appears, as shown in Figure 13.5. It now contains the group name, number of transactions, frequency, and next scheduled date of our transaction group.

11. Press Esc to exit the Standard Transaction Group List without processing the new group.

*A transaction group
listing*

```
┌─────────────────────────────────────────────────────────────┐
│            Standard Transaction Group List                    │
│                                                               │
│     Group Name      Size   Frequency       Next Scheduled     │
│                                                               │
│ ▶ Loan Payments       2 │Monthly        │11/25/93 (Thursday) ↑│
│                                                               │
│                                                               │
│                                                               │
│                                                               │
│                                                               │
│                                                               │
│                                                               │
│                                                             ↓ │
│  Esc-Cancel              F7-Actions            Ctrl◀┘ Done    │
└─────────────────────────────────────────────────────────────┘
```

MAINTAINING A TRANSACTION GROUP

To edit a transaction group, press Ctrl-J from the check-writing screen; the invoice-entry screen; or the Accounts Receivable, Accounts Payable, or Check register. When the list of transaction groups appears, move the cursor to the group you want to edit and press Ctrl-E.

You can change the name of the group, as well as the account to use, frequency, and scheduled date. If you want to remove or add memorized transactions to the group, press Ctrl-┘ to display the list of memorized transactions. Then use the spacebar to add or delete transactions. Press Ctrl-┘ when you are finished editing the transaction group. Press Esc to leave the list without processing the transactions.

To delete a transaction group, press Ctrl-J to display the Standard Transaction Group List. Highlight the group you want to remove, press Ctrl-Del, and then confirm the deletion. QuickBooks deletes the group definition, but retains the individual memorized transactions (they will still appear on the Standard Memorized Transaction List).

PROCESSING TRANSACTION GROUPS

After you have defined a transaction group, you can process it at any time, regardless of the scheduled date. Where you begin processing a transaction group depends on the memorized transactions it contains:

◆ If the transactions are a group of billings, begin from the invoice-entry screen.

◆ If the transactions are checks, begin from the check-writing screen.

◆ If the transactions are a mixture of checks and routine checking account entries, begin from the Check register.

After you process a transaction group, you can edit the individual transactions that were recorded.

RECALLING A TRANSACTION GROUP

Follow these steps to process the group of loan payments we just created:

1. In the Check register, press Ctrl-End to move to move to a blank transaction line.

2. Press Ctrl-J to display the Standard Transaction Group List.

3. Highlight the Loan Payment group and press ↵ to select it.

4. Press ↵ to accept 11/25/93 as the date of the group. This date will appear on the transactions in the register. You can edit the date for individual transactions after they are recorded.

QuickBooks flashes a message letting you know that the transactions are being processed. When the process is complete, it notifies you that the first transaction from the group is highlighted, so you can quickly locate and edit it if necessary.

5. Press ↵ to return to the register.

The check that is included in the group is entered with asterisks, ready to print, and the automatic deduction is also recorded. Because we recorded the transactions with a future date, they appear beneath a double line, which denotes the last transaction on or before the current date.

6. Press Esc until you return to the Main menu.

After you process a transaction group, QuickBooks sets the next scheduled date according to the frequency you established.

EDITING PROCESSED TRANSACTIONS

You can change the individual transactions resulting from processing a group. Your modifications to these transactions do not affect the memorized transaction definition, nor the transaction group.

For example, you might have a group of checks set up for your water, garbage, electricity, gas, and telephone bills. Each month the amounts differ, but the payee, address, and general ledger account remain constant. You can record the checks through a transaction group, and then change the amounts to match this month's statements before you print them. You might also want to change the amount or other information on a processed invoice or register entry.

This chapter described how to use memorized transactions. You learned how to recall memorized transactions individually and create transaction groups to recall several transactions simultaneously. The next chapter explains how to make entries to general ledger accounts.

CHAPTER

14

Working with Your General Ledger

uickBooks enters all the activity resulting from your Check-book, Accounts Payable, and Accounts Receivable transactions into the appropriate accounts in your general ledger. The few transactions that you must enter directly in the general ledger accounts are usually adjustments that take place at the end of a period. Your accountant can advise you as to the need for monthly or yearly entries.

Entries you make directly to a general ledger account are those that are unrelated to sales, purchases, or cash transactions. These entries do not affect a specific vendor or customer. For example, you may enter capital investments by the principals, depreciation, reduction of prepaid expenses, or distribution of profits among the owners.

MAKING PERIODIC ADJUSTMENTS

An *adjusting entry* is a transaction to record certain changes in your financial status. For example, an adjusting entry to record depreciation notes the wear and tear on a fixed asset and reduces its book value. If you have paid for an asset in advance, such as prepayment for an insurance policy, you make periodic adjustments to devalue it.

Adjusting entries often involve accruals. An *accrual* is an amount that accumulates over time, such as the liability for wages owed to your employees for the current, incomplete pay period. Other accruals pertain to expenses and assets.

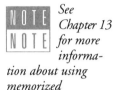 *See Chapter 13 for more information about using memorized transactions.*

Recurring general ledger transactions are those that repeat entries to the same accounts for the same amounts over a period of time. Prepaid expenses, accrued revenue, and depreciation (if you use the straight-line method) are typical examples of recurring transactions.

After you enter an adjustment, you can have QuickBooks memorize it before you record it. Then you will be able to generate it at any time. If the amounts do not remain constant, you can edit the memorized transaction after you have recalled it.

ENTERING DEPRECIATION

When you purchase an asset, you record it in a Fixed Asset account. Assets such as equipment deteriorate with use and must be replaced eventually. This deterioration is recorded as an expense called *depreciation*.

Rather than reducing the original value of the asset, the depreciation is captured in a contra account called Accumulated Depreciation. When you print your balance sheet, the accumulated depreciation is subtracted from the original value to give a book value. Depreciation should be recorded regularly to give a true picture of the value of your assets.

 *Consult your accountant regarding various depreciation methods and regulations.*

The Training Company makes adjusting entries quarterly. Our fixed assets are our delivery truck and our laser printer. Because we use a declining-balance formula for calculating the depreciation, the amount differs each period. We will enter the combined depreciation in the Accumulated Depreciation account register. The completed entries are shown in Figure 14.1.

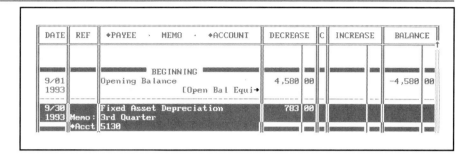

Follow these steps to record the fixed-asset depreciation:

1. Select Chart of Accounts from the Main menu.
2. Highlight account 1315 (Accumulated Depreciation) and press ↵ to display the register.
3. Enter **093093**, the date we want the depreciation to show in the account.
4. Enter **Fixed Asset Depreciation** in the Payee field. Since we aren't paying anyone, we can use this field for a notation.
5. In the Decrease field, enter **783**, the amount by which we need to reduce our fixed-asset value this quarter.
6. Enter **3rd Quarter** in the Memo field to identify the period for which the depreciation is being recorded.
7. In the Account field, press Ctrl-L and select 5130 (Depreciation Expense). Depreciation is a *paper expense* that is never paid out in cash, but nonetheless reduces our profit.
8. At the prompt, press ↵ to record the transaction.

We could have QuickBooks memorize this transaction and then recall it for next quarter's depreciation entry. However, because our depreciation isn't the same for each period, we would need to remember to change the amount.

ENTERING PREPAID EXPENSES

Prepaid expenses are also recorded as adjustments. Our company paid a year's insurance premium in advance. This is a prepaid expense whose devaluation is a recurring transaction.

When we originally paid the insurance, we decreased one asset account, Cash, and increased another asset account, Prepaid Insurance. As each month goes by, we record one-twelfth the amount as an increase to the Insurance Expense account and a reduction of the deposit. The balance of the prepayment remains refundable if we cancel the coverage before the year is up, thus prepaid insurance is defined as an asset (something that can be turned into cash). Figure 14.2 shows the entries to adjust the prepaid expense.

Follow these steps to reduce the amount paid in advance for a year's worth of insurance coverage:

1. On the Chart of Accounts screen, highlight account 1220 (Prepaid Insurance) and press ↵ to display the register.

2. Enter **093093**, the date we want to record the expense.

3. In the Payee field, enter **Triple A Insurance**, the company to whom the premium was originally paid. Again, because we are not writing a check, we can use this field for reference information.

4. In the Decrease field, enter **289.95**, the amount of premium we use each quarter.

5. Enter **3rd Qtr Premium Expended** in the Memo field to explain the transaction.

6. In the Account field, press Ctrl-L and select 5140 (Insurance Expense). This is the offsetting account for the transaction. It "cost" us $289.95 for insurance coverage this quarter.

7. At the prompt, ↵ press to record the transaction.

This adjustment is a good candidate for a memorized transaction. We could have chosen to memorize it before recording it, so that we could recall it at the end of each quarter.

FIGURE 14.2:

Reducing the amount prepaid for insurance

DATE	REF	◆PAYEE · MEMO · ◆ACCOUNT	DECREASE	C	INCREASE	BALANCE
		BEGINNING				
9/01 1993		Opening Balance [Open Bal Equi→			544 00	544 00
9/30 1993		Triple A Insurance Memo: 3rd Qtr Premium Expended ◆Acct 5140	289 95			

HANDLING ACCRUALS

An *accrual* records an event before money changes hands. You should record some forms of income, even though you have not received the cash. For example, you make an adjustment for accrued revenue, which is money you have earned but not yet received. In the same way, some expenses should be recorded when you have not paid the obligation. For example, you should enter any wages your employees have earned but not been paid.

Recording Accrued Revenues

Accrued revenue could be interest on an investment that accumulates over time but is not received until the investment matures, or the value of work you perform under a long-term contract that you do not receive payment for until the job is complete. The entries to record accrued revenue are similar to those for selling merchandise on credit.

You record accrued revenue as a receivable until you actually have the money in hand. You enter the transaction in an asset account, Accrued Interest Receivable, as an increase, and select Interest Revenue, an income account, as the offsetting account. When you actually receive the money, you reduce the Accrued Interest Receivable account, leaving a zero balance, and increase the Cash account to record the money you received.

Entering Accrued Salary Expense

At the end of a period, you should enter wages your employees have earned but not been paid as a liability to reflect your true financial situation. You also include the wages as an expense when calculating your profit and loss for the period. To record these wages, enter a transaction in a liability account, Accrued Salaries, and select Payroll Expense as the offsetting account. When you enter the transaction, have QuickBooks memorize it, because you will need to reverse the accrual.

NOTE
NOTE

See Appendix C for more information about using QuickBooks for payroll.

When the new month begins, reverse the entries of the original transaction. This reversal prevents you from duplicating amounts as you record the specific expenses and liabilities incurred when the payroll checks are written.

WORKING WITH EQUITY ACCOUNTS

Equity accounts record transactions involved in the ownership of a business. When you invest in your business you enter the transaction in your capital account. When you withdraw funds from the business for your personal use, you record the transaction in your drawing account. Periodically, you record profit or loss in a retained earnings account.

ADDING A PARTNER TO THE BUSINESS

When a new partner invests in your business, you need to add a capital account to record the investment. As explained in Chapter 3, a capital account is an Equity account.

The Training Company is taking a partner into the business. The new partner is retiring from his own saddle and bridle shop, and is investing in our company by contributing his remaining merchandise. Additionally, he will work a few hours a week in the store. For his time and investment, we have agreed he is entitled to 15 percent of our company's profits. The entries to set up the new account are shown in Figure 14.3.

Follow these steps to record our new partner's investment in the business:

1. From the Chart of Accounts screen, press Ctrl-Ins and choose to add a new Equity account.

2. Enter **3020** as the name for this account.

3. Skip to the Description field and enter **Owner's Capital** (**FL**) to identify the account and the owner, Frank Loomis. Remember, we have another Owner's Capital account for Phyllis Rocklin, the original sole proprietor.

FIGURE 14.3:

Recording a partner's investment

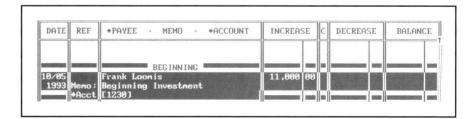

4. In the Notes/Account Number field, enter **Frank**. QuickBooks adds the new account to the Chart of Accounts screen.

5. With the new account highlighted, press ↵ to display the register.

6. In the Date field, enter **100593**, the date Frank joined our business.

7. In the Payee field, enter **Frank Loomis**. This is for our reference, since we are not actually paying him.

8. Enter **11000** in the Increase field. This is the value of the merchandise he is adding to our inventory.

9. In the Memo field, enter **Beginning Investment**.

10. In the Account field, press Ctrl-L and select 1230 (Inventory) as the offsetting account. Frank's investment has increased the value of our inventory by $11,000.

11. At the prompt, press ↵ to record the transaction.

When you add a new partner for your own business, you should also establish a drawing account to record that owner's cash withdrawals, as explained in Chapter 3.

CLOSING THE DRAWING ACCOUNT

NOTE
NOTE

Although the following examples typically occur at year-end, we are ending our activity in the Training Company on October 31, 1993, as if it were the end of our fiscal year.

Before assigning the earnings in a sole proprietorship or a partnership, you should transfer the balance from the drawing account into the capital account. Throughout the year, the drawing account acts as a contra account, which offsets the amount in the capital account to arrive at net equity. Closing this account and transferring the balance into the capital account actually reduces the balance in the capital account.

By starting the new year with a zero balance in the drawing account, you can check how much each partner has received during the year. Good management practices dictate that no one withdraw more than the expected profit he will be assigned at year-end.

Now we will close the drawing account of the Training Company's original partner. Figure 14.4 shows the entries to close this account.

Follow these steps to close the Owner's Draw account:

1. From the Chart of Accounts screen, highlight account 3015 (Owner's Draw) and press ↵ to display the register.

FIGURE 14.4:

Closing a drawing account

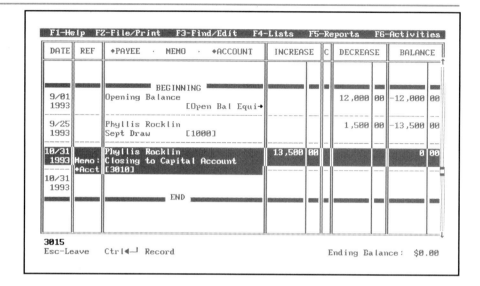

2. In the Date field, enter **103193**, the date we are closing the account.

3. In the Payee field, enter **Phyllis Rocklin**.

4. In the Increase field, enter **13500**, the amount showing as the balance in the account. We want to bring the balance to zero.

5. Enter **Closing to Capital Account** in the Memo field.

6. In the Account field, press Ctrl-L and select 3010 (Owner's Capital), as the account to which we are transferring this amount. In other words, we are recording the withdrawals directly in the capital account now that the accounting period is complete.

7. At the prompt, press ↵ to record the transaction.

8. Press Esc to return to the Main menu.

9. Select Chart of Accounts, highlight account 3010 and press ↵ to see the register. Verify that the drawing amount has been deducted from the owner's capital account.

TRANSFERRING PROFITS TO A RETAINED EARNINGS ACCOUNT

The purpose of being in business is to produce a profit for the owners. Periodically, you must assess if your company has done so. The results of your operation are recorded in an Equity account, either Current Earnings or Retained Earnings. A *Current Earnings* account records the profit or loss from current operations. The amount from current earnings is usually transferred to the *Retained Earnings* account at year-end.

Preparing for Year-End

Year-end transactions wrap up the activity for either the fiscal or calendar year, whichever you use in your business. Basically, closing the year means updating your Equity account with the resulting profit or loss for that year's operations. It is an essential part of the standard bookkeeping cycle.

Here are some of the year-end tasks you should perform:

Year-end reports might be the most important documents you produce in your business; investors, your board of directors, the bank, and the Internal Revenue Service will want to examine them.

◆ Enter all outstanding vendor invoices.

◆ Record all sales to your customers.

◆ Print all checks.

◆ Make all deposits.

◆ Reconcile all bank and credit card accounts.

◆ Make final adjusting entries (such as those discussed earlier in this chapter).

◆ Print final copies of your balance sheet and income (profit and loss) statement at the end of the year. QuickBooks can generate these reports for you.

Generating a Balance Sheet

The Balance Sheet report shows what your resources are, what your obligations are, and what your resulting ownership is. Follow these steps to print the Training Company's Balance Sheet report:

1. Select Reports from the Main menu, and then choose Balance Sheet from the submenu.

2. Leave the Report Title field blank to use the QuickBooks report name.

3. In the Show Balances As Of field, enter **103193**. All transactions dated through October 31 will be included in the balance (the total activity) of the balance sheet accounts.

4. When the report appears, press Ctrl-P to print it.

5. Select the printer you want to use.

6. After the report is printed, press Esc to return to the Main menu.

This report shows that the assets equal the combined liabilities and equity. Also, you can see the sales tax liability that was created when we charged tax on our sales. Figures preceded by a minus sign reduce the total amount of that category. The value of the fixed assets is reduced by the accumulated depreciation, and the original partner's ownership is reduced by her drawing account (the money she has already taken from the business).

The Current Earnings notation on the report is the amount of profit or loss as of the date shown. Although QuickBooks adds this notation, it does not record your profit or loss for you. The program does not create an account in your chart of accounts, nor is there a register in which you can view the transactions that make up the Current Earnings amount shown on the Balance Sheet report.

Producing a Profit and Loss Report

The Profit and Loss report (your income statement) shows how much you earned, how much you spent, and the profit (hopefully) resulting from those transactions. The amount at the bottom of the report is the profit you made after all income and expenses for the period were recorded. This is the same amount that shows on your Balance Sheet report as Current Earnings.

Follow these steps to print the Training Company's Profit and Loss report:

1. Select Profit & Loss from the Reports submenu.

2. In the Report on Months From and Through field, enter **0893** and **1093**, respectively. We want to include all the transactions occurring in August through October in the balance of the profit and loss accounts.

3. When the report appears, press Ctrl-P to print it.

4. Select the printer to which the report is to be sent.

5. After the report is printed, press Esc to return to the Main menu.

The amount at the bottom of the report, **$1,896.70,** is the profit we made after all income and expenses for the period were recorded. It is the same amount shown as Current Earnings on our Balance Sheet report. A loss would be preceded by a minus sign.

Closing Your Books

Closing your books in a conventional system means making an entry in each Income and Expense account to bring the account balance to zero. The difference, your gross profit, is posted to your Retained Earnings account as the offsetting entry to the ones that closed your Income and Expense accounts. This can be done on a monthly, quarterly, or yearly basis.

Unfortunately, QuickBooks does not provide a function that does this automatically. To record your profit for any period, you must make a manual entry after determining the amount by printing a Profit and Loss report for a date range that encompasses the entire period.

 Consult your accountant on how and when to record retained earnings.

First, however, you must set up an Expense account, which Quick-Books requires you to use to offset the profit. Follow these steps to set up the offsetting account:

1. From the Chart of Accounts screen, press Ctrl-Ins and choose to add an Expense account.

2. In the Name field, enter **9000**, a unique number that will always appear at the bottom of your account list.

3. In the Description field, enter **Offset to P&L.**

Through this utility account, you can keep a running balance in the Income and Expense accounts you have set up in QuickBooks. Use it to reduce the difference between the Income and Expense accounts to zero and record that difference in the Retained Earnings account.

Booking Retained Earnings

Your next year-end task is to transfer profits (or losses) into your Retained Earnings account. Figure 14.5 shows the completed entries for this account.

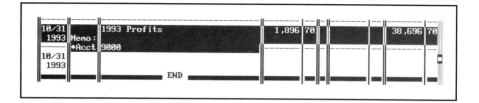

Follow these steps to transfer the Training Company's year-end profit amount:

1. On the Chart of Accounts screen, highlight 3500 (Retained Earnings) and press ↵ to view the register.

2. In the Date field, enter **103193**, the date we are recording the profit in our Equity account.

3. In the Payee field, as a notation, enter **1993 Profits**.

4. Enter **1896.70**, the amount of the current earnings, in the Increase field. If this were a loss, it would be recorded as a decrease to the account (in the Decrease field).

5. Skip to the Account field, and select our new offset account, 9000.

6. Record the entry. QuickBooks will update the balance of the Retained Earnings account.

If you printed a Profit and Loss report now, the total income and expense would be zero, as would the Current Earnings notation on the Balance Sheet report.

The Retained Earnings account balance will be increased. If the partners or shareholders are entitled to some of the profits, you must now distribute them, as explained in the next section.

DISTRIBUTING PROFITS

At the start of a new year, you should transfer the earnings from last year into the appropriate Equity accounts. Profit distribution should take place at the properly scheduled interval.

For our sample company, the Profit and Loss report as of 10/31/93 showed a profit of $1,896.70. We will distribute this profit according to the partnership agreement between Phyllis, the original proprietor, and Frank, the new partner. Phyllis keeps 65 percent; Frank gets 15 percent; and the company sets 20 percent aside for future growth. That $379.35 remains in the Retained Earnings account. Figure 14.6 shows the completed transactions.

Follow these steps to distribute the profits from the Retained Earnings account to the partners:

1. Display the register for account 3500 (Retained Earnings).
2. Change the date to **110193**, the date after the period in which we booked the retained earnings.
3. In the Payee field, enter **Phyllis Rocklin**, the partner to whom we are transferring earnings.
4. In the Decrease field, enter **1232.85**, the amount we are transferring to Phyllis.
5. In the Memo field, enter **65% of 1993 Profits**.
6. Enter **3010** in the Account field to transfer Phyllis' share of the profits to her capital account.

FIGURE 14.6:

Transferring profits to the business partners

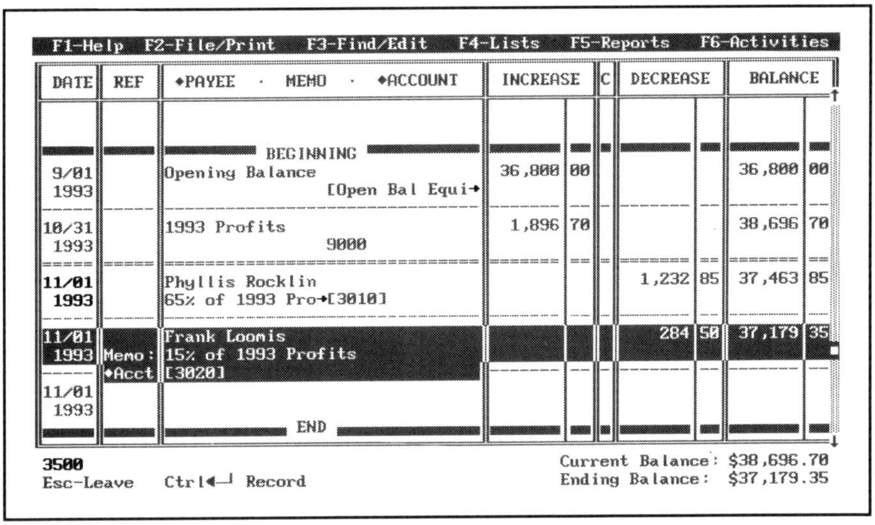

7. Record the transaction.

8. In the next transaction area of the same Retained Earnings account, verify that the date is 11/01/93.

9. In the Payee field, enter **Frank Loomis**, the other partner to receive a portion of the earnings.

10. In the Decrease field, enter **284.50**, the amount he receives out of the retained earnings.

11. In the Memo field, enter **15% of 1993 Profits**.

12. Enter **3020** in the Account field to transfer the profits to Frank's capital account.

13. Record the transaction.

The portion of the 1993 earnings that was not transferred to the partners remains in the Retained Earnings account with profits from prior periods.

In this chapter, you learned how to make entries that are necessary to maintain your general ledger. These entries include adjustments for depreciation, prepaid expenses, and accruals. You also learned how to handle Equity accounts, including those for owner investments and withdrawals and those to record profit or loss.

The next chapter explains how to generate the reports provided by QuickBooks. Some of these, such as the Accounts Receivable Aging and Collections reports, have been discussed in earlier chapters. Others, such as the Budget, Profit and Loss, and Balance Sheet reports, will be described in detail in the next chapter.

15

Producing Reports

**Q**uickBooks supplies many reports that provide information about your financial activities. You can use the standard reports to evaluate your business in a variety of ways.

Although you cannot actually design a report from scratch, you can control the format, subtotals, and data included in the report. QuickBooks provides options for customizing, filtering, and memorizing your report formats.

PROCESSING A STANDARD REPORT

Processing one of QuickBooks standard reports involves selecting the type of report you want and specifying its parameters. You can then view the report on the screen and choose to print it.

CHOOSING A REPORT

To choose a report to generate, select the Reports option on the Main menu. The Reports menu lists the following types of reports:

◆ **Profit & Loss:** Lists balances in Income and Expense accounts, subtotals by those account types, and notes the profit or loss for the period selected (see Chapter 14).

◆ **Balance Sheet:** Lists balances in Current Asset, Fixed Asset, Current Liability, Long-Term Liability, and Equity accounts, with subtotals by account type for the period selected (see Chapter 14).

◆ **A/R Reports:** Displays a submenu listing three reports.

    ◆ **Sales Report:** Lists the item code description, units sold, and the sales amount for each item, with a grand total of the sales for the period.

    ◆ **Aging Report:** Lists each customer's balance, with amounts divided by aging periods (see Chapter 11).

    ◆ **Collections Report:** Lists customers who are past due (see Chapter 11).

◆ **A/P Reports:** Displays a submenu listing three reports.

    ◆ **Aging Report:** Lists each vendor name and total due, with amounts divided by aging periods (see Chapter 7).

    ◆ **Sales Tax Report:** Shows sales tax districts, revenue in each district, and sales tax levied on that revenue.

    ◆ **1099 Report:** Lists vendor name, address, and taxpayer's identification, with the amount of payments made in the specified time frame.

The tax-payer ID number appears on the 1099 report only if you entered it into the Taxpayer ID Number field in the vendor record.

◆ **Cash Flow Forecast:** Lists projections of cash coming in and going out, based on data in your Accounts Receivable, Accounts Payable, and Checking accounts.

◆ **Payroll Report:** Totals income and expenses by payee, with subtotals by account, for all accounts identified as Payroll.

◆ **Budget Report:** Compares actual activity versus budgeted amounts in each Income and Expense account, with totals for each account type.

◆ **Other Reports:** Displays a submenu listing four reports.

    ◆ **Summary Report:** Prints subtotals and grand totals, but not the detail for transactions included in the report.

    ◆ **Transaction Report:** Shows detail for each transaction in the specified accounts, including date and number, the description, memo, and account affected, any notation in the Cleared (C) field of the register, and transaction amount.

In order to print a Project report, you must have chosen project tracking in the company options. See Chapter 2 for details.

◆ **Itemized Income/Expense Report:** Prints transaction detail, including Income and Expense accounts, and subtotals at the end of each account type (similar to the Transaction report).

◆ **Project Report:** Shows Income and Expense account activity by project, with totals for both account types.

◆ **Memorized Reports:** Displays a list of your memorized report formats.

After you choose a report and specify the parameters (a title and the periods or dates to include), QuickBooks displays the report on the screen. You can then store the report format, print the report, or press Esc to exit the report.

VIEWING A REPORT ON THE SCREEN

The report will print as it appears on the screen: truncated or in its entirety, depending on the column-width setting.

In some cases, QuickBooks displays a report in abbreviated form. For example, in the Transaction report shown in Figure 15.1, the information in some columns is truncated. To view the entire entries, press F9 to toggle between full and half column width.

When the report is either too wide or long to fit on the screen all at once, you can use the following keys to view it:

◆ PgUp or PgDn: Scrolls one page up or down

FIGURE 15.1:

The screen display of a truncated report

```
                        TRANSACTION REPORT

                     8/ 1/93 Through 9/30/93
Training Company-All Accounts
11/ 1/93

Date   Acct    Num    Description    Memo        Accts      Clr  Amount


              BALANCE  7/31/93                                    0.00

 9/ 1 1000-Co         Opening Balance            Open Bal Equit X  25,382.90
 9/15 1000-Co 1001 S  CASH             Set up Pet -SPLIT-       X    -200.00
 9/15 1000-Co 1002 S  Kenneth M. Wade  9/14 Expen -SPLIT-       X    -152.90
 9/20 1000-Co 1003 S  Four Paws Pet C  DS3629     -SPLIT-       X  -1,100.00
 9/20 1000-Co 1004 S  Kat Kastle       TTC4069    -SPLIT-          -1,000.00
 9/22 1000-Co *****S  Loans-R-Us       31-7921    -SPLIT-            -886.50
 9/23 1000-Co 945     Office Mart      M487       5160-Office Su X    -64.87
 9/25 1000-Co *****S  Petty Cash       Replenish  -SPLIT-             -51.75
 9/25 1000-Co *****   Phyllis Rocklin  Sept Draw  3015-Owner's D   -1,500.00
 9/25 1000-Co         Countrywide Loa  28032-4    2310-Truck Loa X   -260.00↓

Training Company-All Accounts
Esc-Create  Ctrl-M Memorize          F1-Help  Ctrl-P Print  F9-Full column width
```

◆ ↑ or ↓: Scrolls one row up or down

◆ → or ←: Shifts one column to the right or left

◆ Tab or Back Tab: Shifts one screen to the right or left

◆ Home or End: Moves to the upper-right or lower-left corner of the report.

SELECTING THE REPORT DESTINATION

When a report appears on the screen, you can print it by pressing Ctrl-P. To choose a destination for the report, move the cursor to the Print To field and press Ctrl-L to display the Available Printers List. The list contains the following destinations:

◆ **Default Printer:** Prints a hard copy.

◆ **Alternate Printer:** Prints a hard copy.

◆ **.TXT:** Prints to disk in ASCII format. You can import the file into a word processing application.

◆ **.WKS:** Prints to disk in Lotus 1-2-3 format. You can import the file into 1-2-3 or another spreadsheet application that accepts this format.

◆ **.PRN:** Prints to disk in a comma-delimited ASCII format. You can import the file into database, spreadsheet, and some word processing applications.

If you don't specify otherwise, QuickBooks will place a report that you print to disk in the directory in which your QuickBooks program is located. If you want to store the report in another directory, designate that location when you are prompted for the file name. You must specify a directory that already exists.

You define your printers by using the Set Up Printers option on the Set Up/Customize menu, as described in Chapter 1. If you are printing a hard copy, have your printer ready. The report prints as soon as you select a destination. If you need to reset the printer parameters before printing, move the cursor to the Print To field, press Ctrl-L, and then press F9. Select the printer from the list displayed. In the Set Up Printer window, choose the printer setting you want to alter.

After the report is sent to the print destination, it remains on your screen. You can press Ctrl-P again and send the report to a different destination. For example, you may want to save it on disk or print a second copy to hand out or file.

PROJECTING YOUR CASH FLOW

The Cash Flow Forecast report contains information from both your Accounts Payable and Accounts Receivable Aging reports. You can use this report to anticipate the cash you will have available over a period of time.

A Cash Flow Forecast report for our sample company is shown in Figure 15.2. It shows our projected balance for each week in September.

REVIEWING YOUR SALES FIGURES

You can use the Sales report to analyze which of your products and services are moving quickly and the amount of revenue each generates. You will want to note the quantity of items sold versus income. You can also see how much price discounts are costing overall.

FIGURE 15.2:

A Cash Flow Forecast report

```
              CASH FLOW FORECAST REPORT AT 7 DAY INTERVALS

                       9/ 1/93 Through 9/30/93
Training Company-All Checking/AR/AP Accounts
11/ 2/93
                      Accts      Accts     Checking     Net      Projected
     Date Range        Recv     Payable      Accts     Inflow     Balance

Checking balance                                0.00
Past due A/R & A/P     456.12      0.00

     As of  8/31/93    456.12      0.00         0.00                456.12

  9/ 1/93 -  9/ 7/93     0.00   -271.32    25,382.90  25,111.58   25,567.70
  9/ 8/93 -  9/14/93     0.00      0.00         0.00       0.00   25,567.70
  9/15/93 -  9/21/93     0.00      0.00    -2,532.90  -2,532.90   23,034.80
  9/22/93 -  9/28/93    62.10  -1,000.00   -2,853.32  -3,791.22   19,243.58
  9/29/93 -  9/30/93    50.00     -2.74     4,773.38   4,820.64   24,064.22

  9/ 1/93 -  9/30/93   112.10  -1,274.06   24,770.86  23,608.10

Training Company-All Checking/AR/AP Accounts
Esc-Create  Ctrl-M Memorize       F1-Help                    Ctrl-P Print
```

A Sales report for our sample company is shown in Figure 15.3. We sold 40 pounds of seed mix for less than $200, and one pony for almost $4,000. We wouldn't stop offering ponies because we sold only one this month, but we might consider our profit margin versus the amount of labor involved in producing and selling 40 pounds of seed.

FIGURE 15.3:

A Sales report

```
                              SALES REPORT
                         9/ 1/93 Through 9/30/93
              Training Company 3-1100
              11/ 2/93
                                         9/ 1/93-      9/30/93

                Item Code      Description        Units      Dollars

                B2159     Sunflower Seed Mix        40       160.00
                C7341     Diet Specific Cat Food     3        25.20
                D4100     Dog Grooming              1        28.00
                D4112     Dog Leash                 2        10.40
                D4165     Flea Shampoo              1         6.55
                Deliver   Delivery Charge           1        12.50
                H1000     Alfalfa Hay               3       495.00
                H1002     Pasture Rental            2       225.00
                Non-Stock Chincoteague Pony         1     3,975.00
                Price Disc 20% Discount for Quantity P  1   -48.00
                Promo     Promotional Credit        1       -15.00
                Other     Applied Discount          1       -15.22

              Training Company 3-1100
              Esc-Create  Ctrl-M Memorize      F1-Help           Ctrl-P Print
```

CREATING A BUDGET REPORT

NOTE NOTE *Budgets are not required; you can budget some accounts and not others.*

QuickBooks allows you to establish budgets for your accounts and generate a report that compares your budgeted amounts with your actual amounts. You can establish guidelines for each Income and Expense account in your chart of accounts. Your budget can project money that you expect to receive, as well as money you expect to spend.

A budget is specific to one account. Let's consider budgets for three of the Training Company's accounts. Suppose that $6000 is what we typically spend on office supplies in a year, and we want to restrict crop maintenance costs to $17,500 a year. We are also setting a goal for income from our new dog-grooming service.

SETTING ANNUAL BUDGETS

We want to spread our office-supply budget evenly across the entire year. Follow these steps to establish an annual budget for this account:

1. Select Budget Report from the Reports submenu. The Create Budget Report window appears.

2. Skip to the Set Budget Amounts field and enter **Y**.

3. Press Ctrl-⏎ to display the Specify Monthly Budget Amounts window. The list of our Income and Expense accounts appears.

4. Move the cursor to account 5160 (Office Supplies).

5. In the Budget Amount field, enter **500**, our monthly allowance. QuickBooks will duplicate this entry in each of the 12 calendar month fields.

You can view the budget detail by pressing Ctrl-E when the account is highlighted.

SETTING FLUCTUATING BUDGET AMOUNTS

We want to allot most of our crop-maintenance expenditures to the spring and fall planting and harvesting seasons. Follow these steps to enter a specific amount in each month for this account:

1. In the Specify Monthly Budget Amounts window, move the cursor to account 5120 (Crop Maintenance).

2. Press Ctrl-E to enter a budget amount.

3. When the list of months appears, move the cursor to April, the first month we want to budget. (No outside maintenance is necessary in the fields from November through March.)

4. Beside April, enter **3000**, the amount we expect to spend that month.

5. For May, enter **2000**.

6. Enter **1500** for June, and skip to August.

You can also use the F9 key to clear the months below the cursor if the cursor rests on a blank amount. Any month left blank in an account will show a zero budget on reports.

7. In the month of August, type **3000**, then press F9 (Fill w/Amt). QuickBooks fills the remaining months with the same amount that appears where the cursor resides.

8. For October, press Ctrl-Backspace to erase the entry and replace it with **4000**.

9. For November and December type **0** over the existing entry to reduce the budget to zero for those months. The result is shown in Figure 15.4.

10. Press ↵ to record your entries.

The Specify Monthly Budget Amounts window reappears. It shows the amount budgeted for the current month. When you enter varying amounts for other months, Yes appears in the Varies by Month field. You can press Ctrl-E to see the budget detail.

PROJECTING INCOME

Now we will enter our projections of the income from our new grooming service. Our goal is to do at least two groomings a day, Monday through

FIGURE 15.4:

Entering varying budget amounts

```
┌────────────────────────────────────────────────┐
│  ┌──────────────────────────────────────────┐  │
│  │                                          │  │
│  │   Monthly Budget For Account:    5120    │  │
│  │  ──────────────────────────────────────  │  │
│  │   Jan:                                    │  │
│  │   Feb:                                    │  │
│  │   Mar:                                    │  │
│  │   Apr: 3,000.00                           │  │
│  │   May: 2,000.00                           │  │
│  │   Jun: 1,500.00                           │  │
│  │   Jul:                                    │  │
│  │   Aug: 3,000.00                           │  │
│  │   Sep: 3,000.00                           │  │
│  │   Oct: 4,000.00                           │  │
│  │   Nov: 0.00                               │  │
│  │   Dec: 0                                  │  │
│  │  ──────────────────────────────────────  │  │
│  │  Esc-Cancel    F9-Fill w/Amt   ↵ Continue│  │
│  └──────────────────────────────────────────┘  │
└────────────────────────────────────────────────┘
```

Friday, at $28 each. Follow these steps to set up the budget:

1. Highlight 4030 (Pet Services) and press Ctrl-E.

2. Move the cursor to September, the month we first offered the service.

3. Type **1080** as our goal for September income.

4. Press F9 to fill the remaining months with the same amount.

5. Press Ctrl-↵ to record the four-month budget.

NOTE
NOTE

Quick-Books does not retain budget history for previous years.

If business increases dramatically, you can change the budget amounts for any month at any time. The new figure overrides the old and will be used in future reports. One set of monthly budget data must suffice for every year. If your budget for next year differs, print a Budget Report for the year-end, and then set up new amounts for next year's budget.

GENERATING A BUDGET REPORT

The Budget Report lists only the accounts in which transactions have been recorded. It includes the amount you actually spent or earned, the amount of your budget, and the difference. Income and Expense accounts are listed and totaled separately.

Follow these steps to print a Budget Report that includes our company's activity for September:

1. Select Budget Report from the Reports submenu.

2. Accept the QuickBooks title for the report.

3. Enter **090193** as the beginning of our date range and **093093** as the ending date.

4. In the Column Headings field, press Ctrl-L to view the subtotal options.

5. Accept None to total all transactions in the date range together.

If you select other subtotal options, QuickBooks accumulates or divides the monthly budget amounts according to the column headings you select. For example, if you request a quarterly report, QuickBooks adds January, February, and March together for the first budget-to-actual comparison. If you select a period of less than one month, QuickBooks performs some intricate calculations to arrive at a daily amount specific to that month. The results vary with the time period you request.

6. Enter **N** in the Set Budget Amounts field. We do not want to view or edit the budget amounts prior to printing the report.

7. Press ↵ to accept A to include activity from all of our general ledger accounts. The report appears on the screen, as shown in Figure 15.5.

The Diff column shows the difference between the actual activity in the account and the amount budgeted. A minus preceding an amount indicates you are under the amount of your budget. In the case of an Income account (Pet Services in our example), being under budget means you have not earned as much as you had hoped. When an Expense account has a minus in the Diff column, you have spent less than expected. If you incur expenses in a zero month, the report will indicate that you are over your budget for that month.

8. Press Esc to return to the Main menu.

Instead of including activity from all your accounts, you can compare the budget amount against one or several accounts. For example, perhaps you record office-supply purchases in your Checking, Petty Cash, and Credit Card

FIGURE 15.5:

Viewing the Budget report

```
                                    BUDGET REPORT
                              9/ 1/93 Through 9/30/93
              Training Company-All Accounts
              10/ 5/93
                                      9/ 1/93       -        9/30/93
                    Inc/Exp Description  Actual    Budget      Diff

              INCOME/EXPENSE
                INCOME
                  4010-Pet Products        202.15     0.00      202.15
                  4020-Equine Products   4,707.50     0.00    4,707.50
                  4030-Pet Services         28.00 1,080.00   -1,052.00

                TOTAL INCOME            4,937.65 1,080.00    3,857.65

                EXPENSES
                  5000-Merchandise Purchases  509.85    0.00    509.85
                  5110-Auto/Truck Expense      92.85    0.00     92.85
                  5120-Crop Maintenance     1,000.00 3,000.00 -2,000.00
                  5140-Insurance Expense        0.00    0.00      0.00

              Training Company-All Accounts
              Esc-Create  Ctrl-M Memorize        F1-Help              Ctrl-P Print
```

accounts. The Office Supply account amount will include amounts from all three accounts. The Office Supply budget remains constant, but you can compare the budgeted amount to the combined expenditures recorded in just the Checking and Credit Card accounts. Then any supplies bought with petty cash money will not be considered in the actual-to-budget comparison.

PREPARING 1099 FORMS

The 1099 information is only a report. You must prepare the actual forms to send to the vendor and the government yourself.

The Internal Revenue Service requires you to submit a 1099 form at the end of the calendar year for certain vendors you pay more than a given amount during the year. Recently, the amount has been $600, but it is subject to change. Check your IRS regulations.

QuickBooks does not print the forms, but it does provide a report containing the necessary information for you to fill in the forms manually. To print the 1099 report, select Reports from the Main menu, then A/P Reports, then 1099 Report. You can produce the report for all your vendors or for the specific vendors you select from the Vendor List. QuickBooks does not eliminate vendors who have received less than the current $600 limitation for reporting.

After you choose all or specific vendors, the report appears on your screen. Press Ctrl-P, load regular paper in the printer, select the printer to use, and then press ↵ to print the report.

CUSTOMIZING REPORTS

QuickBooks defines *customizing a report* as selecting records to appear on the report. The program will organize information on the report according to the criteria you designate. By alternating the column headings, you can obtain subtotals for time periods or for other criteria, such as customer, vendor type, or payee. After you set the parameters for a custom report, you can save the report format for future use.

Depending on the report you are customizing, you have several choices, including a date range, the fields you want included (row headings), how you want the report to subtotal (column headings), and which account or accounts you want included in the report (all, selected, or current).

The following reports can be customized:

- Profit and Loss
- Balance Sheet
- Payroll
- Summary
- Itemized Income/Expense
- Project
- Transaction

Figure 15.6 shows an example of the screen for customizing a report. That screen is for creating a Summary report, but your options are the same for all the reports listed above.

CHOOSING ROW AND COLUMN HEADINGS

Row headings print down the left side of the report. The row heading you choose determines how the report will be sorted. In reports that offer row

FIGURE 15.6:

Criteria for customizing a report

```
                        Create Summary Report

   Report title (optional):

   Restrict transactions from:  8/ 1/93 through: 10/31/93

   ◆Row headings (down the left side): Income/Expense Account

   ◆Column headings (across the top): Totals only

   Report on Cash (received) or Accrual (billed) basis (C/A): A

   Use Current/All/Selected balance sheet accounts...(C/A/S): A

   Esc-Cancel    Ctrl-M Memorize    F8-Options    F9-Filter   Ctrl◄┘ Done
```

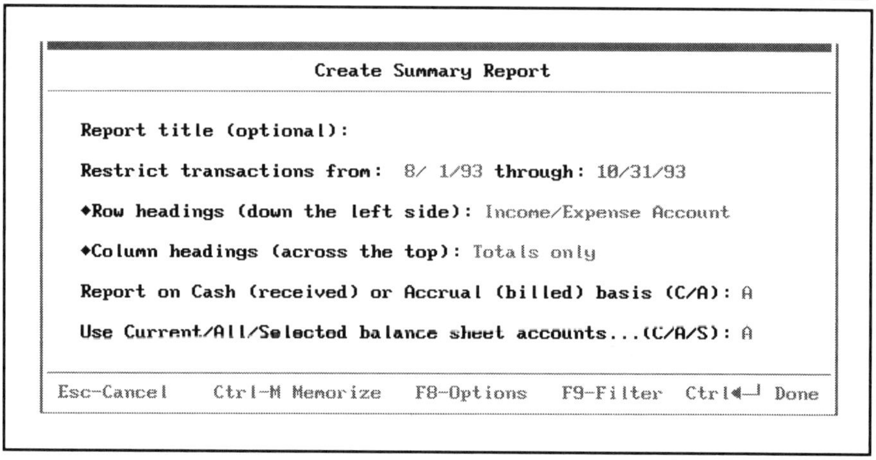

headings, you can select from the following:

Income/Expense account	Payee
Customer	Project
Customer type	Vendor
Item	Vendor type
Employee	

Column headings print across the top of the page. The column heading you choose controls when the report will subtotal. All reports allow you to select how you want to subtotal your data, but your choices depend on the type of report you are printing. Select one column heading from the following:

None	Account
Totals only	Income/Expense account
Day	Customer
Week	Customer type
Two weeks	Employee
Half month	Payee
Month	Project
Quarter	Vendor
Six months	Vendor type
Year	

CHOOSING CASH-BASIS OR ACCRUAL REPORTING

NOTE
NOTE

See Chapter 16 for descriptions of the cash-basis and accrual bookkeeping methods.

You choose to report on transactions using a cash-basis or accrual method of viewing the activity by your response to the prompt

Report on Cash (received) or Accrual (billed) basis

Enter C for cash-basis reporting, or A for accrual reporting.

Cash-basis reporting does not include a customer transaction until you receive the money, nor a vendor transaction until you pay the bill. Accrual reporting shows all recorded customer billings and all vendor invoices, regardless of when payment is received.

CHOOSING ACCOUNTS TO INCLUDE

You select which accounts you want included in the report by your response to the prompt:

Use Current/All/Selected balance sheet accounts

You can enter C for the current account only, A for all accounts in the current company, or S for selected accounts in the current company.

If you enter S for selected accounts, QuickBooks will display a list of your accounts. Press the spacebar to mark accounts to include or exclude.

USING REPORT FILTERS

A *filter* is a method of excluding the records that do not meet your selection criteria. The following reports can be filtered:

◆ Profit and Loss

◆ Payroll

◆ Budget

◆ Summary

◆ Transaction

◆ Itemized Income/Expense

◆ Project

To filter a Profit and Loss, Payroll, Itemized Income/Expense, or Project report, press F8 (Customize) while the Create Report screen is displayed, and then press F9 (Filter). If you are working with another type of report, just press F9 from the Create Report screen. The Filter Report Transactions screen appears, as shown in Figure 15.7.

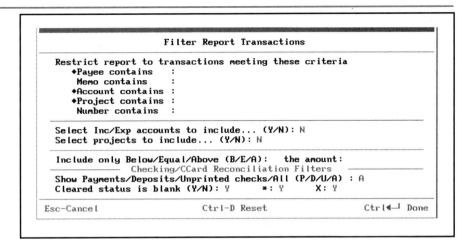

Criteria for filtering reports

SELECTING TRANSACTIONS TO INCLUDE

You can use the entries in the Payee, Memo, Account, Project, and Number fields to select the transactions you want included in the report. If you enter selection criteria for more than one field, the transaction must match each set of criteria for it to be included. Use the following five means of selecting transactions:

◆ If you leave the field blank, the transaction will be considered for inclusion, regardless of the data found in that field.

◆ If you want to include only transactions that contain specific data in a field, enter the exact characters you want to match; for example, *Birthday*.

◆ To locate a string of characters regardless of where they appear in the field, precede and follow the characters with two dots. For example if you search for *..mas..*, the program will find: *mas*ter, christ*mas*, and un*mas*k.

◆ To exclude a transaction that contains certain data in a field, place a tilde (~) in front of the keyword, or in front of the matching characters; for example, *~..mas..*, or *~Birthday*.

◆ To see a list of possible entries for a field preceded by a diamond, press Ctrl-L in that field.

DEFINING OTHER SELECTION CRITERIA

NOTE *You can press Ctrl-D to clear all the selection criteria and begin again.*

The five other prompts on the Filter Report Transactions Screen allow you to filter the report further.

All Income and Expense accounts are normally included. To restrict the report to certain accounts, respond Y to the prompt

Select Inc/Exp accounts to include

After you complete the fields on the Filter Report Transaction screen, the list of accounts will appear. Use the spacebar as a toggle to mark the accounts to include or exclude. Press Ctrl-↵ to exit the list.

All projects are normally included. To restrict the report to a few projects, respond Y to the prompt

Select projects to include

When you finish entering selection criteria, the list of projects will appear. Again, use the spacebar as a toggle to mark the ones to include or exclude. Press Ctrl-↵ to exit the list.

All amounts are normally included. You can restrict the report to transactions whose amounts meet certain selection criteria by entering a description and an amount at the prompt

Include only Below/Equal/Above   the amount

Enter B for below, E for equal to, or A for above, followed by the amount. For example, you can include amounts that are below $100, equal to $30, or above $1,500.

You can choose to show only payments, deposits, or unprinted checks by responding to the prompt

Show Payments/Deposits/Unprinted checks/All

Enter P for payments, D for deposits, U for unprinted checks or A to include all three types of transactions.

NOTE *See Chapter 12 for information about clearing transactions.*

You can specify the cleared status of the transactions by completing the final prompt

Cleared status is blank: :* :   X:

Enter a Y in the appropriate field as follows:

◆ Beside blank if you want to include transactions that have nothing in the Cleared field of the register.

◆ Beside the asterisk (*) if you want to include transactions that are waiting for final clearance.

◆ Beside the X if you want to include transactions that have been cleared.

SETTING REPORT OPTIONS

A *report option* is a means of controlling the presentation of the selected data on a report. To set report options press F8 (Options) while the Create Report screen is displayed. In some cases, you will need to press F8 (Customize), and then press F8 again to access the options. Depending on the type of report you are producing, you may see the following prompts.

If you want to round amounts to whole dollars, enter Y at the prompt

Round amounts to nearest dollar

When you include all transfers, the report shows both the originating and offsetting transactions. You can select to exclude transfers, thereby eliminating both the originating and offsetting transactions involved in a transfer, by responding to the prompt

Transfers to include:
1. Include all transfers 2. Exclude all transfers

You can select the amount of detail that will appear on the report by your response to the prompt

Detail level: None/Transactions/Splits

Enter N if you want a summary report that prints only totals, without showing supporting detail. Enter T to include transaction detail as well as totals on the report. Enter S to show the amount charged to each account in a split transaction.

You can print a column for memos or for accounts. At the prompt

Show Memo/Account/Both (M/A/B)

enter M for memos only, A for accounts only, or B to show both on the report.

SAVING AND REUSING REPORT FORMATS

After you customize a report, you can memorize it for future use. Report formats you have saved can be processed, renamed, or deleted.

MEMORIZING REPORTS

To memorize a report, enter a report title to appear as a heading on the report, and set up the filter and the report options, as explained in this chapter. You can press Ctrl-M to memorize a report either from the Create Report screen after you finish defining the report, or while the report appears on the screen. You can establish various formats with their own selection parameters for the same report and have QuickBooks memorize each different format.

When you select to memorize a report, QuickBooks displays the Memorize Report window. In the Title field, enter a name to identify the report format in the Memorized Report List. You should use a name that will differentiate this report format from others you might memorize. All parameters, except the date range, are saved. The program returns to the Create Report screen.

RECALLING MEMORIZED REPORTS

You can print, rename, or delete memorized reports. To work with a memorized report, select Memorized Reports from the Reports submenu. QuickBooks displays the Memorized Report List. Move the cursor to the report and take one of the following actions:

◆ To print the report, press Ctrl-↵. You can change the filter and options for this printing, and the memorized report format will not be affected.

◆ To delete a report format, press Ctrl-Del. This does not delete the actual report, only the report format that you created, with its specific parameters.

◆ To rename a memorized report, press Ctrl-E. Then press Ctrl-Backspace to erase the existing name and enter the new name, or just type over the existing name.

PRINTING OTHER DOCUMENTS

Reports are not the only information you might want to print. QuickBooks provides copies of other documents and listings of data from your records.

USING PULL-DOWN MENU OPTIONS

While the check-writing screen, the invoice-entry screen, or a balance sheet account register is displayed, QuickBooks provides related printing options. Press F2 (File/Print) and select what you want to print. Your choices include the following:

◆ Customer invoices

◆ Customer mailing labels

◆ Customer statements

◆ Vendor mailing labels

◆ Supplies order form

◆ Register listing

We have already printed customer invoices, statements, and mailing labels (in Chapters 9 and 11). Prior to reconciling our checking account, we printed the Check register (in Chapter 12).

Printing the Supply Order Form

The Intuit order form tells you how to contact the company to order checks and invoices to use with QuickBooks. The form lists prices, styles, and printer specifications.

To print the order form, press F2, select Print Supplies Order Form from the menu, and indicate the printer. Complete the form by hand and mail or fax it to Intuit.

Printing Vendor Labels

QuickBooks will print vendor labels, which you can use for mailings (notifications of your new shipping address, or to address 1099 forms, for example) and for reference in the warehouse (put them on index cards). Each label includes the information from the Pay To field of the vendor record, typically the vendor name, address, city, state, and zip code. As with customer labels, you can sort them by zip code or alphabetically. You can restrict them to a particular vendor type or zip code area. The information fits on a 1-inch label.

To print labels, while the Accounts Payable register is displayed, press F2 and select Print Mailing Labels. Then specify the sorting and selection criteria. If you are printing labels for a bulk mailing, sort by zip code. If they are for reference, sort them alphabetically. Load the labels, press F10, and select the printer to use. You can press F9 to print an alignment test. press When you are ready to print the labels, press ↵.

PRINTING COMPANY LISTS

When you display a company list, such as the list of customer types, vendors, or items/parts/services, you can print it. Press F7 (Actions) and select Print. A shortcut is to press Ctrl-P when the list is displayed.

The printed Customer List and Vendor List include transaction history.

In this chapter, you learned how to generate the reports provided by QuickBooks. Many of these reports are useful tools that can help you to analyze your business. You also learned how to customize and filter reports and select report options. The other QuickBooks items you can print include registers and company lists.

In the next chapter, you will learn how to set up QuickBooks for your own company. You can apply all that you learned from working with our sample company to your own business.

Preparing Your Data for QuickBooks

The hardest part of any new project is starting it. Fortunately, QuickBooks has half the work already done for you. It supplies the record format for your information. All you have to do is enter basic information, and then you're ready to go. You just have to fill in the blanks, so to speak.

Realistically, the development of any bookkeeping system takes some time and effort. Those of you who have been using a structured method of keeping books up to this point have an advantage, but everyone will catch up soon.

BOOKKEEPING METHODS

Check with your account- ant to determine if, under current tax law, you can operate on a cash basis.

QuickBooks allows you to process your books using either of two methods:

♦ A *cash-basis method*, in which you record income when you receive money and expenses when you write a check. In a cash-based business, you don't keep individual records for each customer and vendor.

♦ An *accrual method*, in which you record income when you make the sale, regardless of when you will be paid, and record an expense when you obligate yourself, regardless of when you will tender payment. You keep a record for each customer who owes you money and every vendor to whom you owe money.

CONVERTING FROM YOUR OLD RECORD KEEPING SYSTEM

These in- structions are for people who have not been using Quicken. If you are converting from Quicken, refer instead to Appendix D.

Before you convert to a new system, you should get your current system in order. Generally, you should complete certain tasks to begin the transition to QuickBooks (some of the points may not apply to your present bookkeep- ing system):

1. Record all activity to date.
2. List your unpaid customer invoices.
3. List your unpaid vendor invoices.
4. Note the balance owed on all your loans.
5. List and value your assets.
6. Count and value your inventory.

The following sections guide you through each task, whether you already have a formal set of books or keep your records in a shoebox. If you are tread- ing on unfamiliar territory, or just need to refresh your memory, refer to Ap- pendix E for basic accounting information and terms used in the QuickBooks application.

If you have been using a structured set of books, you or your accountant should also perform the following tasks:

1. Do a *trial balance* to determine the balance in each asset, liability, equity, expense, and income account.

2. Adjust the appropriate general ledger accounts. For example, reduce the balance in your inventory account by the value of missing or damaged pieces, record the dollar value of depreciation in your fixed asset account to reduce its balance, and record the consumption of advance payments (prepaid expenses) to reduce that asset.

3. Generate an income statement and balance sheet. If your books are in balance, the assets minus the liabilities should equal the equity.

4. Balance your accounts. Fix errors in your records so that the trial balance balances.

5. Close your present books. Make entries to bring the balances in your profit and loss accounts to zero and record the difference (the profit or loss from your income statement) in an equity account.

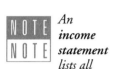 *An income statement lists all your income and expense accounts with their balances and determines the difference between them. That difference is your profit or loss. A balance sheet lists assets, liabilities, and equity accounts with their balances.*

After you create the appropriate records and enter your data in QuickBooks, you should produce QuickBooks reports and compare their results with the figures your current system generates.

RECORDING ALL ACTIVITY

Record all activity for the current accounting period. This step applies mostly to users of a standard bookkeeping method. It means completing all paperwork for the month.

For shoeboxers, it simply means making sure that you've opened all your mail, written down all your sales, deposited all your payments, written all the checks, and paid all the bills you are going to this month. In other words, bring all your activities up to date.

TOTALING YOUR CUSTOMER ACCOUNTS

Balance each customer account and total the entire outstanding receivables amount. This means verifying that all the totals on your customer records add up to the total in your accounts receivable account. If they don't, find the reason for the discrepancy and correct it.

Shoeboxers should sort the unpaid invoices into piles for each customer. Check each invoice to be sure it is correct. Add all the invoices together for each customer. Then add all the customer totals together to get a grand total for your accounts receivable amount.

If you decide to use the cash-basis method of keeping books, you will record the unpaid invoices as they are paid, rather than recording them as outstanding amounts when you set up QuickBooks.

TOTALING YOUR VENDOR ACCOUNTS

Balance each vendor account and total the entire outstanding payables amount. This means verifying that all the totals on your vendor records add up to the total in your accounts payables account. If they don't, again, find the reason for the discrepancy and correct it.

Shoeboxers should sort the unpaid bills into piles for each vendor. Check each invoice for accuracy. Add together all the invoices from each vendor. Then add the vendor totals together to get the total of your accounts payable amount.

If you want to use the cash-basis bookkeeping method, you will record these invoices as you pay them, instead of recording them as outstanding amounts when you set up QuickBooks.

NOTE *Consult your accountant before deciding which inventory valuation method to use.*

COUNTING AND VALUING YOUR INVENTORY

If you buy and keep a supply of items ready to sell, you should take a physical inventory of your stock on hand. No matter how structured your record keeping has been, this procedure is the same. Make a list of everything you have available for sale, and then count how much you have of each item.

The way that you value your inventory is important because it affects profit and tax calculations. The following are three standard methods:

◆ The *last purchase price method*, in which you value the quantity on hand of each product at the last price you paid for it.

◆ The *standard cost method*, in which you value each item at an arbitrary cost you designate.

◆ The *average cost method*, in which you value the quantity on hand of each product at an average of the various prices you have paid over time for it.

Usually, valuing your inventory initially is fairly easy. Next to each inventory item, write down what you paid for it. If prices have fluctuated, use an average price. Multiply the purchase price times the number of items you have for a total for each item. Add all the totals together to place a value on your entire inventory.

A *book inventory* is your record of the value of what you have in stock at a given point in time, as opposed to the actual value of the items physically remaining on your shelves. You can enter and periodically adjust the value of this important asset.

QuickBooks doesn't keep track of the number of items you buy for resale. To maintain this information, you must manually note your beginning count, keep a record of how many items you purchase, and then subtract the units sold (refer to the QuickBooks Sales report for the total of units sold). When you physically count the merchandise on hand, compare the tally with your ending count to determine if any of your inventory items are missing. You record the value of the difference as an expense and reduction in the inventory account.

LISTING AND VALUING YOUR ASSETS

TIP ▼ *It's a good idea to consult an accountant about the various considerations involved in judging the value of your assets.*

Take a physical inventory of your fixed assets. Make a list of everything you own (or are buying on credit) and use in your business. Fixed assets include vehicles, machinery, office equipment, furniture, buildings, and property. If it is not immediately expendable in the course of business, it's a fixed asset. For example, your computer is a fixed asset; computer paper, however, is considered an expendable office supply.

If you have not been recording fixed-asset values, you will need to assign a value to each item. A rule of thumb is to determine what you would pay for the item today if you bought it in its present condition.

List and value your *current assets*, which include the cash you have (on hand and in the bank), your accounts receivable, notes receivable, inventory, and prepaid expenses.

RUNNING A TRIAL BALANCE

Run a trial balance on your current system to determine the balance in each asset, liability, equity, expense, and income account. All the balances added together should equal zero if your books are in balance. If you have been using a general ledger and preparing financial statements, this should be a familiar process.

ADJUSTING GENERAL LEDGER ACCOUNTS

 *If you do not have a structured set of books, you can skip this step.*

If you have a conventional system in place, make the necessary adjustments to your book inventory, assets, and prepaid expenses. The purpose of this step is to arrive at a true value in each of your accounts.

Bring each account up to date from a bookkeeping standpoint. Record depreciation, inventory losses, transfers from prepaid expenses, reserve for bad debts, accrued expenses, and so forth. Your accountant may do this for you.

BALANCING AND CLOSING YOUR BOOKS

Balancing your books in a conventional system means being sure your assets minus your liabilities equal your equity account. QuickBooks makes balancing easy; it takes care of making entries in the appropriate accounts when you record a transaction.

Closing your books in a conventional system means making an entry in each income and expense account to bring the account balance to zero. The difference between the income and expense balances is your gross profit. This difference is posted to your retained earnings account as the offsetting entry to the ones that closed your income and expense accounts.

In QuickBooks you do not "close" a period. You can determine the activity in your income and expense accounts by printing a report that restricts the data to the time frame you want to review. At year-end, however, your accountant may give you some figures to record changes that are not evident from daily operations, such as depreciation, transfer of profit or loss to your owner's equity account, or reduction in deposits for prepaid expenses.

PLANNING YOUR CHART OF ACCOUNTS

Everyone needs a chart of accounts. You enter opening balances in the general ledger accounts only once, during setup, for activity that occurred before you converted to the QuickBooks system. Thereafter, QuickBooks updates this information automatically during routine processing.

The chart of accounts is the foundation of your bookkeeping system. Everything that happens in your business should eventually find its way to a pigeonhole called a general ledger account. These accounts, which form your chart of accounts, summarize all your financial transactions. Your *financial statements*—the Balance Sheet, Profit and Loss Statement, and Cash Flow Forecast reports—are based on the information stored in the general ledger accounts.

A *balance sheet* lists your assets, your liabilities, and the resulting equity. If you do not have an established set of books, create this report from data on hand. It will form the basis for the current balances in your general ledger accounts.

The listing of income, expense, and profit for a period is called an *income statement* (or a *profit and loss statement*). QuickBooks will help you keep track of what it costs you to be in business and the profit you are making.

If you don't already have a general ledger, you can make five major lists (assets, liabilities, income, expenses, and equity) and break them down into categories and yet smaller subcategories, using the following procedure:

1. List your assets and group them into categories labeled Bank Accounts, Current Assets, and Fixed Assets (categorize your assets as described in the previous section). Sort each category into subcategories, such as Checking, Savings, Petty Cash, Receivables, Inventory, Equipment, and Vehicles.

2. List your liabilities and group them into categories labeled Credit Cards, Accounts Payable, Current (Short-Term) Liabilities, and Long-Term Liabilities. Accounts Payable are vendor accounts. Current Liabilities are short-term notes payable and the taxes you

owe, such as income tax and payroll taxes. QuickBooks provides a special Sales Tax Liability account. Long-Term Liabilities include mortgages and long-standing notes payable.

3. List your income and your expenses. The difference between income and expense amounts becomes the profit or loss that is reflected in the Current Earnings notation on the QuickBooks Balance Sheet report. Periodically, you will distribute these earnings to the owners or to a Retained Earnings account.

4. List your equity, which is the difference between what you have (*assets*) and what you owe (*liabilities*). Basically, it is what the business owners have left for themselves. Equity can take the form of an owner's capital account, stock, and retained earnings.

Look at the charts of accounts supplied with QuickBooks to get an idea of what to put on your list. You can use or edit one of them, or create your own from scratch. Also, your accountant can help. He or she may even have a chart of accounts already set up for you.

Selecting Account Identifiers

In QuickBooks, account identifiers can be either alphabetic or numeric. The standard scheme, 1000 to 5999, is described in Chapter 3. If your company has only a few accounts, you can use numbers 100 to 599. Even if you select to use alphabetical abbreviations to identify your accounts, the accounts should follow a hierarchy similar to that shown in Chapter 3.

Companies that sell products often use a slightly different structure so they can separate sales income and related expenses from other forms of income and other operating expenses. However, QuickBooks does not provide an efficient structure for detailed inventory tracking.

A simple chart of accounts could include the accounts listed in Table 16.1. A product-based business would add a Returns and Allowances account under Sales Income, and a Cost of Goods account in the Expense section.

Reviewing Predefined Account Listings

QuickBooks provides sample charts of accounts for several types of businesses. Most contain account identifiers that are simply abbreviations of the account description. Two samples contain numbers for the account identifier. Abbreviations may be easier for a novice to work with. Most accounting books, however, use numeric identifiers for the accounts in the chart of accounts. If you expect your business to grow, you may want to begin with

TABLE 16.1:
A Sample Chart of Accounts

ACCOUNT CATEGORY	ACCOUNTS
Assets	Checking Account
	Cash on Hand
	Accounts Receivable
	Fixed Assets
	Inventory
Liabilities	Accounts Payable
	Credit Card Liability
	Taxes Payable
	Notes Payable
Equity	Capital
	Drawing
	Retained Earnings
Income	Sales
	Other Income
Expenses	Advertising
	Auto/Truck
	Freight
	Interest Paid
	Legal & Professional Fee
	Office Supplies
	Rent

ACCOUNT CATEGORY	ACCOUNTS
	Repairs and Maintenance
	Taxes
	Business
	Payroll
	Travel and Lodging
	Meals
	Wages & Commissions

numeric listings to make your transition to a more sophisticated accounting program easier.

QuickBooks provides a sample chart of accounts for the following types of businesses:

NOTE *Although you can add accounts during data entry after your books are established, you should set up the accounts for your real company in advance rather than as you go.*

Accounting/Bookkeeping	Manufacturing
Agriculture/Farm	Medical/Dental
Canadian	Non-Profit Organization
Construction/Contractor	Numeric-Product
Consulting	Numeric-Service
Engineering	Real Estate/Property Management
General Business	Religious Organization
Government	Retail
Graphic Design	Service Business
Insurance	Wholesale
Law	

If you plan to use one of the predefined chart of accounts, you should review the lists of accounts so you can decide which one best suits your company. You cannot view the samples unless you start to add a new company. However, you can *begin* to add a company, view the lists, and then *cancel* the procedure without adding any records.

You can review the listings without adding your company by following these instructions carefully:

1. From the Main menu, select Set Up/Customize, and then choose Add a New Company from the submenu.

2. In the Add New Company window, enter a temporary company name.

3. Press Ctrl-L at the prompt

   Preset income/expense accounts to use

4. When the list of business types to choose from appears, press F1 to display Help text about the preset account lists.

5. In the Help window, press PgDn to display the business types.

6. Press Tab to move the cursor to the business you want to review, and then press ↵ to see the chart of accounts provided for that type of business.

7. Press Backspace to return to the list of businesses (within the Help text).

8. Select another set of accounts to review, or press Esc to return to the list of business types to use for responding to the prompt.

9. Press Esc twice to leave the option without adding a company.

DECIDING HOW TO SET UP YOUR FILES

You will need to set up your files to take full advantage of the features of QuickBooks. The time you put into setting everything up right in the beginning is worth the effort. You will save time, avoid frustration, and gain the capability to make good management decisions to ensure the health of your business.

If you operate under a cash system (entering a sale when you receive payment and a bill when you pay it), you do not need to define customers or vendors. However, if you operate under the accrual method (which reflects what is owed to you and what you owe), you should enter a definition for each vendor and customer for whom you have unpaid invoices, as well as their outstanding invoices. Then you can start processing your daily work, adding inactive vendors and customers as you deal with them.

The other QuickBooks lists are designed to facilitate your operations and daily processing. Examples of such files are billing item codes, invoice message codes, customer and vendor types, sales tax rates, payment methods, and customer payment terms. Some lists, such as those for customer terms, customer types, and vendor types, relate to an accrual style of bookkeeping and are not necessary if you are using the cash-basis method.

CREATING CODES

QuickBooks, unlike most computerized accounting systems, does not require you to identify all your vendors and customers by code. However, you can reserve the first line of the name and address field in the record for a code if you already have one in place.

Products and services are identified by code. Because QuickBooks allows both letters and numbers in codes, you can keep the coding system you now have. If you are creating a coding system for the first time, try to assign codes that are easy to remember, so that you can enter or look them up quickly. You should also consider how your codes will be sorted (arranged in lists), as explained in the next section.

PLANNING FOR SORTING

QuickBooks uses a specific hierarchy to sort codes, names, and descriptions. When you are setting up your records, you should consider how the items will be arranged on your lists.

Sorting Codes

QuickBooks uses the following rules for sorting codes:

- Blanks, then symbols come first.
- Numbers come before letters.
- Numbers are sorted from left to right, not in ascending or descending order.
- Letters are sorted alphabetically.

Here is an example of the result of sorting codes that contain blanks, symbols, numbers, and letters:

4 87

4-56

4019

423

Bell

Da Silva

Daley

Lange

M321

M94

Smith

Sorting Customers, Vendors, Employees, and Items

QuickBooks uses the following sorting rules for your customer, vendor, and item records:

◆ Customers are sorted by the first line in the five-line name and address field.

◆ Vendors are sorted by their company name.

◆ Employees are sorted by their initials.

◆ Items are sorted by code within item type.

◆ Other items, such as payment methods, are sorted by their description.

If you want to be able to sort customer names alphabetically, enter last names first, as in *Kachrenko, Anna*. The disadvantage to this method is that the address on invoices, statements, and labels will print the last name first, which is not the most acceptable format for an address.

Names of customers and vendors and descriptions of products and services can be in uppercase or initial capitals followed by lowercase. For example, a name could be entered as *EMMA SILVA* or *Emma Silva*. QuickBooks treats uppercase and lowercase letters the same when sorting.

When deciding which convention to use, consider that readability tests prove initial capital and lowercase combinations are easier to read. Whatever convention you select, the cardinal rule is: Be consistent.

PREPARING FOR SETUP

After your accounts are in order, you must define each record in detail. The process will go smoothly if you take one record type (such as accounts, customers, billing item codes, or vendors) at a time.

Although you can set up records as you go, it is easier if you prepare worksheets for each record before you begin entering any data into Quick-Books. The rest of this chapter details the information you need for these worksheets, which are provided in Appendix B. Put a record with its field name on a sheet of paper, leaving room to write in the information exactly as you will enter it in each field. Make copies of your original worksheets and fill out a worksheet for each record. When you finally sit in front of the computer, worksheets in hand, data entry will be a breeze.

Before you enter any other information into QuickBooks you should define your company. A company is an entity with a federal tax identification number for reporting profit and losses.

SETTING UP YOUR CHART OF ACCOUNTS

To convert your general ledger to QuickBooks, you will need a hierarchical list of your accounts with their current balances. Sort your accounts into assets, liabilities, equity, income, and expense categories. Then categorize them according to the QuickBooks account types and determine their opening balance, as described in Table 16.2.

Choose a date to begin using QuickBooks (preferably the first of the month). Complete and record all your business activities that occurred before that date. Then determine the balance for every activity. These are the balances you enter when you define your accounts.

ACCOUNT TYPE	OPENING BALANCE
Checking Account	Enter the balance in your checkbook as of the date you are establishing your records.
Accounts Receivable	You do not enter a balance amount. QuickBooks calculates the balance from the customer invoices you enter.
Current Asset	Enter the amount of cash you have on site or the value of other assets as of the date you are establishing your records.
Fixed Asset	Enter the present value of the asset.
Accounts Payable	You do not enter a balance amount. QuickBooks calculates the balance from the vendor invoices you enter.
Credit Card	Enter the total of all unpaid charges as of the date you are establishing your records. You can also record your credit limit.
Current Liability	Enter the amount you owe as of the date you are establishing your records.
Long-Term Liability	Enter the balance due as of the date you are establishing your records.
Equity	Enter the amount of retained earnings available as of the date you are establishing your records.
Income	You do not enter a balance amount. QuickBooks calculates the balance from the transactions you enter through the Invoicing option.
Expense	You do not enter a balance amount. QuickBooks calculates the balance from the transactions you enter through the Checkbook and Accounts Payable options.
Subaccount	You do not enter a balance amount. QuickBooks calculates the balance from the transactions you record when you begin keeping books in QuickBooks.

DEFINING YOUR ASSET ACCOUNTS

You can press the Tab key to skip from one account type to the next in the chart of accounts.

Business assets are typically cash, in the bank or on hand; receivables; inventory you keep on hand for resale; your equipment; and possibly real estate.

The QuickBooks asset account types include Checking, Accounts Receivable, Fixed Asset, and Current Asset. The assets you should include in each of these classifications are described in Chapter 3. Your treatment of your Accounts Receivable and Fixed Asset accounts depends on whether you are using a cash-basis or accrual system of bookkeeping.

Accounts Receivable Accounts

Money your customers owe you is a unique type of asset, called *accounts receivable.* If your customers do not pay for their purchases when they make them, you are keeping your books under an accrual system. Thus, you must use an account called Accounts Receivable in addition to a record for each customer. The total of what every customer owes you equals the balance in the Accounts Receivable account. QuickBooks creates an Accounts Receivable account for you when you add a new company. You can add other Accounts Receivable accounts as necessary. When you have more than one Accounts Receivable account, invoices and receipts must be initiated from the register of the specific account you want to use.

A cash system does not have any true receivables. In QuickBooks, you can keep your books on a cash basis without an Accounts Receivable account in the general ledger, and still maintain customer records with transaction history.

Fixed Asset Accounts

If you want to keep track of certain assets individually, such as pieces of equipment or real estate, you should set up a Fixed Asset account for each one.

If you use an accrual system, or your accountant makes adjustments to report on a modified accrual basis, you should have an *Accumulated Depreciation* account to show the reduction of the value of your fixed assets from wear and tear. Accumulated Depreciation is a *contra asset.* It is listed in the asset section of your chart of accounts, but it actually reduces the amount of your assets. During setup, when you enter a balance that reduces the total for the account type, precede the balance amount with a minus sign.

SETTING UP YOUR LIABILITY ACCOUNTS

Liabilities are what you owe, and they reduce your equity or ownership in the business. QuickBooks helps you stay on top of these obligations. You will manage minor debts in your Credit Card and Accounts Payable accounts. Larger indebtedness is handled in Current or Long-Term Liability accounts.

To keep accrual books in QuickBooks, you create a liability account for each debt you want to maintain separately, and then enter the full amount you owe as an increase to that account.

A cash system does not have any true liabilities. When you pay a bill, you simply charge it to the appropriate Expense account. If you operate on a cash basis, QuickBooks will not record transaction history, even if you create vendor records.

Current and Long-Term Liability Accounts

The debts you incur for a business are typically loans you've received to start the business or buy equipment, and money owed for items you did not pay for right away. Large amounts you owe over a long period are set up in QuickBooks as Long-Term Liability accounts. Lesser debts, such as notes payable that will be paid off soon, are set up as Current Liability accounts.

Accounts Payable Account

Smaller, revolving amounts you owe to vendors, are totaled together in one Accounts Payable account. The Accounts Payable account is the summary of what you owe all your vendors, and its balance is calculated by the program as you enter outstanding vendor invoices. Each vendor record has one balance due to that vendor.

QuickBooks creates an Accounts Payable account for you when you add a new company. You can add other accounts of this type if necessary. When you have more than one Accounts Payable account, bills and payments must be initiated from the register of the specific account you want to use.

DEFINING EQUITY ACCOUNTS

You should have a capital account and drawing account for each partner. A Retained Earnings account shows how much of the profits you are keeping in the business and have not distributed to the partners.

Seek the advice of your accountant regarding equity accounts, especially if you are incorporated.

If you have a corporation instead of a sole proprietorship or a partnership, your Equity account keeps track of the shareholders' investments. It is usually titled Capital Stock.

SETTING UP INCOME AND EXPENSE ACCOUNTS

You probably want to separate the various ways money comes into your company and why it goes out. This allows you to analyze where you generate the most profit and where you are spending the most money. You can use this information to determine where to expend the most energy.

Note that Income and Expense accounts don't show a balance in the general ledger in QuickBooks. You must run a report to see how much you have earned or spent in each account.

Summary versus Detailed Income Accounts

A single account, Sales, would be sufficient to record income. However, accounts titled Labor Revenue, Parts Revenue, Rental Revenue, and Interest Earned are more specific.

You must decide how much detail you want in the general ledger. Each item you defined through the QuickBooks Company Lists function can be recorded in a specific general ledger sales account, or you can use the same general ledger account for all the items. If you decide to use the same sales account for all your items, you can still see the detail in the Sales report, which breaks down units sold and dollars charged for sales of each item.

Summary versus Detailed Expense Accounts

You could have a single account called Cost of Sales, but you would get a better picture if you had accounts titled Labor Costs, Parts Costs, and Rental Costs. You could even divide your Expense accounts for parts into specific items, such as Tires, Oil, and Air Filters. You could then compare these Expense accounts with the related Income accounts. By subtracting what goes out against what comes in, you can determine the profit on each thing you do.

Subaccounts

You create subaccounts by highlighting the primary Income or Expense account on the accounts list and pressing Ctrl-Ins. Then enter a name and description of the subaccount.

Only Income and Expense accounts can have subaccounts under the primary account. A primary account can total the amounts from the more detailed subaccounts below it. Account numbers usually follow an outline format with the primary account on top, supported by subaccounts. For example, your primary account 5200 (Repairs) might have three subaccounts: 5201 (Auto Repair), 5202 (Truck Repair), and 5303 (Office Equipment Repair).

You can add three more levels of subaccounts beneath any subaccount. However, doing so would be quite unusual and would create an unnecessarily complex chart of accounts.

Budgets

As explained in Chapter 15, you can create budgets for your Income and Expense accounts. You can enter budget amounts at any time for past and future months in the year. To prepare a budget worksheet, list the months down the side of the page, list the numbers of the accounts you want to budget across the top of the page, and enter an amount for each month.

SETTING UP YOUR OTHER RECORDS

After you set up your chart of accounts, you are ready to enter your other data into QuickBooks. If you are using an accrual bookkeeping method, you will create records for your customers and vendors. With either bookkeeping method, you may need records for your employees, products, and services, as well as for the other items related to your business.

DEFINING CUSTOMER AND VENDOR TYPES

Types make it possible for you to group your customers and vendors for reporting. QuickBooks provides four predefined customer types: Dealer, Distributor, Manufacturer, and Wholesaler. The predefined vendor types are Design, Materials, Supplies, and Tax Collector.

You can delete types or add new ones. Customer and vendor types can be as long as 15 characters.

IDENTIFYING PAYMENT TERMS

Quick-Books allows only one set of predefined vendor terms, which are defined under Company Options, as explained in Chapter 2.

Terms define when an invoice is due, when a discount can be taken, and the discount amount. In QuickBooks you can define these parameters for customer invoices by number of days from the invoice date, number of days an early payment discount is available, and amount of the discount.

QuickBooks provides the following predefined payment terms:

◆ 1% 10, Net 30

◆ Due on Receipt

◆ Net 10

◆ 2% 10, Net 30

◆ Prepaid

◆ Net 30

You can delete and add terms codes as necessary. After you define terms codes, you can assign the terms to customers.

SETTING UP YOUR EMPLOYEES

Appendix C provides information about using QuickBooks for payroll.

You might want to set up your employees in QuickBooks for several reasons:

◆ To assign salespeople to service specific customers.

◆ To have the employee name and address appear on the paycheck automatically (if you will be using QuickBooks for payroll).

◆ To determine how much each salesperson has sold for commission computations (by printing the Sales report by employee).

SETTING UP YOUR CUSTOMERS

Initially, you might want to set up only the customers who have an outstanding balance. You can add records for returning customers as they become active again. Basically, you will need lists of all your customers, the balance they still owe you, each outstanding invoice's number and total amount, and the terms you allow each customer. If you don't have a record of each invoice, you can enter one invoice for the entire amount due.

Your list of outstanding invoices should include the following fields:

◆ Invoice Number

◆ Invoice Date

◆ Amount Due

SETTING UP YOUR VENDORS

Initially, you might want to enter only the vendors to whom you still owe money. Basically, you will need lists of all your vendors; the balance you still owe them; and each outstanding invoice's number, total amount, and due date. If you don't have a record of each unpaid invoice, you can enter just one invoice for the balance that you owe.

Your list of outstanding vendor invoices should include the following fields:

◆ Invoice Number

◆ Invoice Date

◆ Due Date

◆ Invoice Amount

DEFINING SHIPPING METHODS

Shipping methods are ways you deliver merchandise to your customers. This information is useful if you have a product-based business and choose to use the QuickBooks product format invoice.

QuickBooks provides the following predefined shipping methods:

◆ Airborne

◆ DHL

◆ Emery

◆ Federal Express

◆ UPS-Blue

◆ UPS-Ground

- ◆ UPS-Red
- ◆ U.S. Mail

You can delete the methods you don't use and add other methods.

DEFINING PAYMENT METHODS

Payment methods indicate how a customer paid your bill. You can group deposits by payment type. QuickBooks provides the following predefined methods:

- ◆ American Express
- ◆ Cash
- ◆ Check
- ◆ Diner's Club
- ◆ MasterCard
- ◆ VISA

You can delete the types of payment you don't accept and add other types. The name you use for a payment method field can be as long as 10 characters.

CREATING INVOICE MEMOS

Invoice memos are messages you can select to print on invoices without having to retype the message whenever you want to use it. Defining invoice memos in QuickBooks is described in detail in Chapter 4. Refer to that chapter for the list of predefined messages.

You can delete and add messages, as well as edit the predefined ones. Your messages can be up to two lines of 30 characters each (50 characters each on Professional invoices).

IDENTIFYING PRODUCTS, SERVICES, AND OTHER CHARGES

To set up your product and service file, you need a list of all the products (called *parts* in QuickBooks), services, and other charges, with their sales prices and unique codes to identify each item. Other charges are incidental fees, such as shipping insurance or returned check charges, and how much you bill the customer for them. You must also identify the general ledger Income accounts where you want to record each sale and charge when it is recorded on an invoice.

Item Codes

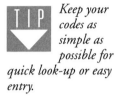

Keep your codes as simple as possible for quick look-up or easy entry.

Code fields are 10 characters—not quite long enough for 14 character UPC (uniform product code) numbers, but possibly long enough for your own SKU (stockkeeping unit) number. As described in Chapter 2, through the Company Options function, you can choose to require an item code for every sale so that QuickBooks can keep track of the units sold.

Item Prices

QuickBooks requires that you specify the price for each item. *Each* can be either the most common quantity or the smallest quantity in which you sell the product or service. Examples include *one* sandwich, a *dozen* eggs, a *can* of soda, a *gallon* of paint, a *case* of oil, a *day* of gardening, an *hour* of therapy, a *week* of child care, or a *month* of dance lessons.

When you sell an item, QuickBooks multiplies the quantity sold by the Price Each amount in the product record. When you sell *whole units*, enter whole numbers in the Quantity field of the invoice. If you sell *portions of units*, enter the portion as a decimal.

To simplify invoice entry, price the majority of items at what you charge for the smallest quantity you sell.

For example, if you price jelly beans by the pound but will sell a portion of a pound, you would enter the quantity sold as .25 when you sold one-fourth of a pound. Perhaps you price roses at $36 a dozen but will sell less than 12 roses at a time. When you sell only six roses, or one-half dozen, enter .5 in the Quantity field. QuickBooks will compute the charge as $18. If you price sodas by the six pack, but will sell each can individually, enter .17 (or one-sixth) when you sell just one can.

DEFINING OTHER INVOICE-RELATED ITEMS

In addition to what you sell, other items often appear on invoices. You should set up records for the invoice-related items described in the following sections.

Price Discounts

You may offer a price reduction when a customer buys a large quantity, when an item is "on sale," or for other reasons. QuickBooks will supply the amount of the discount when you enter a discount code on the invoice.

Early payment discounts are a part of the Payment Terms definition described earlier in the chapter. The discount you define here covers other circumstances.

Sales Tax

When you set up sales tax item codes, QuickBooks creates a sales tax rate table containing the rates. Then, when you enter one of these codes on an invoice, QuickBooks calculates the sales tax amount.

Each sales tax item code represents a specific taxing district. You should set up a separate vendor for each taxing district. When you use the tax code on an invoice, QuickBooks records the liability in the vendor record. The program assigns a due date for paying the taxes according to whether you chose monthly, quarterly, or annual payments for sales tax when you set company options (see Chapter 2).

NOTE NOTE *The Sales Tax report shows only what is collected, not what is owed or has been paid. You can print the vendor history to view sales tax activity.*

When you select to pay bills (through the Accounts Payable submenu), the balance due each district will appear on the list when it is due. Select to pay the tax bills as you do other vendor invoices.

Refunds

If you give refunds instead of issuing a credit for returned merchandise, set up refund codes. Then, when you enter a refund code on the invoice, Quick-Books will automatically write a check for the amount of the refund.

Subtotals

A subtotal sums the amounts on previous invoice lines up through the last subtotal line. You must create a subtotal code definition if you want to subtotal the entries on an invoice.

You can use subtotal codes to obtain a subtotal of products for calculating sales tax. Also, you might want to subtotal all the items that are on sale to obtain a figure for calculating the price discount.

SETTING UP PROJECTS

NOTE NOTE *To use projects, turn on project tracking through the Company Options function, as described in Chapter 2.*

A *project* is a means of tracking income and expenses for a specific enterprise. For example, if you assign transactions to projects, you can determine which department brought in the most money, which apartment complex incurred carpeting expense, or which phase of a construction job cost the most.

Projects are QuickBooks' method of traditional cost accounting. They are used in addition to the accounts in your general ledger.

To add a project, select Company Lists from the Main menu, then Projects from the submenu. Press Ctrl-Ins to add a project. Enter a project description that will be used in report headings.

You can also create *subprojects*, which further define a project. Setting up and using subprojects is similar to creating and using subaccounts. To add a subproject to a primary project, highlight the primary project, and then press Ctrl-Ins.

You can display and select from the Project List by pressing Ctrl-L when the cursor rests in the Project field in a transaction. Projects are listed in alphabetical order. You can edit or delete projects in the same way that you change items on other QuickBooks lists.

The following are examples of QuickBooks entries that involve projects:

◆ **Rental Income account, Cody project:** Records a transaction in your Rental Income account, and keeps track of the income for the duplex on Cody Way.

◆ **Rental Income account, Rodgers project:** Records rent collected from the apartments on Rodgers Street.

◆ **Appliance Repair Expense account, Cody project:** Records repair of a refrigerator in the duplex on Cody Way.

◆ **Appliance Repair Expense account, Rodgers project:** Records maintenance on the washing machine in the utility room at the apartments on Rodgers Street.

The Rental Income account will show how much revenue was generated by all rentals. The Appliance Repair account will show how much it cost to maintain the appliances for all your properties. The Cody project will show how much income and expense occurred as a result of that duplex. The Rodgers project will show the profit or loss resulting from those apartments.

DETERMINING DOCUMENT NUMBERS

Documents are pieces of paper on which you do business. They include invoices, purchase orders, checks, and so on. Usually, each set of documents has its own numbering scheme.

QuickBooks assigns and keeps track of invoice and check numbers for you. You can designate the beginning number for the current printing. You can also manually enter the number for invoices or checks prepared outside of QuickBooks.

HANDLING ACCOUNTING PERIODS

You do not define accounting periods or fiscal years in QuickBooks. Traditional *accounting periods* commonly coincide with a calendar month. A *fiscal year* can coincide with the calendar year or with a company-defined year that is determined by taxing considerations or by when you opened your business.

Although QuickBooks doesn't use traditional accounting periods, you can run reports that present a view of the activity, profit or loss, or balance sheet account balances for a given period of time, such as a month. Controlling your finances is easier when you review activity in these smaller segments rather than waiting until year-end to see the whole picture.

Your accountant can guide you in using a fiscal year for tax returns and reporting periods appropriate to your situation. You can restrict access to previous periods by using passwords, as discussed in the next chapter.

AN OVERVIEW OF TRANSFERRING YOUR DATA TO QUICKBOOKS

Now that you have your accounts in order, you can complete the worksheets presented in Appendix B. Then you can set up your system and transfer your own data into QuickBooks. To accomplish the conversion, you must take the following steps:

1. Install the software and set up your printer in QuickBooks.
2. Customize QuickBooks to suit your working habits.

3. Add a company. This will become the repository for your real company's data, separate from the Training Company we set up for the examples in this book.

4. Select or enter your chart of accounts.

5. Add the current balance to your accounts.

6. Complete the company information, address, and tax identification.

7. Customize the company options to suit your preferences.

8. Enter customer and vendor types if desired.

9. Define customer payment terms.

10. Add active records to your customer file and enter outstanding invoices.

11. Add active records to your vendor file and enter outstanding invoices.

12. Add product and service records.

13. Define other items involved in invoice processing, such as subtotals, price discounts, and sales tax.

14. Print company lists in QuickBooks and verify them against your data-input sheets.

15. Print a balance sheet in QuickBooks and compare it with the one from your previous system.

16. Correct any errors you might have made during data entry and run a corrected set of reports to keep on file.

17. If desired, define passwords, as described in the next chapter.

 *If you've chosen to keep your books on a cash basis, skip steps 8 through 11 and continue with step 12.*

This chapter described how to get ready to use QuickBooks with your own company data. Fill out the worksheets (in Appendix B) and enter the information. Because you have gone through the steps of setting up a sample company, you should find it easy to set up your actual records.

The final chapter of this book explains how to manage your files in QuickBooks. You will learn how to use passwords to protect your files, work with multiple companies, back up your data, and use other QuickBooks utilities.

CHAPTER

17

Managing Your Files

uickBooks provides options for setting passwords, working with more than one company, and backing up and restoring your files. This chapter explains how to use these options.

ESTABLISHING PASSWORD PROTECTION

With QuickBooks, you can use passwords to protect your financial data. Passwords safeguard the integrity of your files by restricting users to certain areas of your accounting system. They also keep unauthorized people out entirely. After passwords are defined, users must enter the password needed to gain entry to protected levels.

QuickBooks offers two password levels: Owner and Bookkeeper. A user with an Owner password has access to all functions, including the Password Level Assignment screen. On this screen, you define which functions are restricted to the people with Owner passwords, which ones are restricted to those with Bookkeeper passwords, and which functions do not require passwords.

DEFINING PASSWORDS

You can define passwords at any time. Perhaps you and your spouse did the books. Then you hired someone to help, and you want to restrict his access by defining a Bookkeeper password for him. You can also use a password to "close a period" by restricting access to transactions dated earlier than the password allows.

To set up or change passwords, select Set Up/Customize from the Main menu, choose Customize Current Company from the submenu, and then select Passwords. The Set Passwords screen appears. You must enter the Owner password before identifying a Bookkeeper password. Type a password of up to 16 characters for one or both levels.

If you want to restrict transactions by date, enter the ending date of the time frame you want to protect. When you press Ctrl-↵ to record your entries, you must enter the Owner password a second time to confirm it. Then QuickBooks displays the Password Level Assignment screen, as shown in Figure 17.1.

FIGURE 17.1:

The Password Level Assignment screen

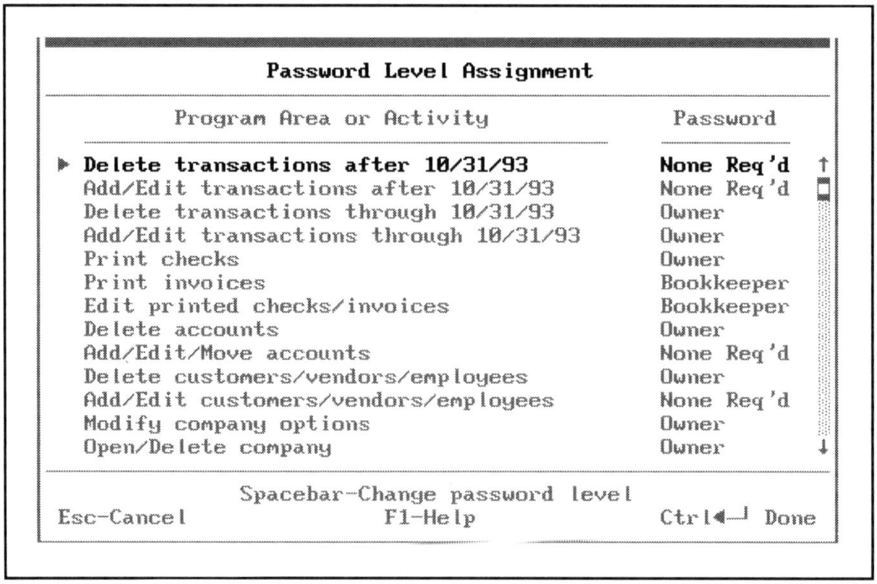

ASSIGNING PASSWORDS TO ACTIVITIES

On the Password Level Assignment screen, you indicate which password, if any, is necessary to access certain functions. When you first define the Owner password, QuickBooks presents the screen for completion.

When the Password Level Assignment screen appears, mark the activities as Owner, Bookkeeper, or None Req'd (no password required). To mark a function, highlight it and press the spacebar. The first four functions relate to the transaction-restriction date you entered with the password definition. If you want to protect transactions from previous periods, select Owner as the password required to delete, add, and edit transactions through the password date.

You can change the password assignments by selecting Customize Current Company from the Set Up/Customize menu, and then choosing Password Table. QuickBooks displays a table of your current assignments, which you can edit as necessary.

USING PASSWORDS

After you establish passwords, QuickBooks will require users to enter their password to access the program and to use any restricted options. If an option is not accessible to a user's password level, he or she will not be able to select it.

The password you type will not appear on the screen. As you type, QuickBooks blocks out the characters. This prevents people from leaning over your shoulder and learning the password.

WORKING IN MULTIPLE COMPANIES

You can use QuickBooks to maintain records for more than one company. After you add another company, you can choose the company in which you wish to work.

ADDING A SECOND COMPANY

To add your real company after completing the tutorial, follow the steps for adding a new company (in Chapter 2), but replace the examples with your own data. When you are defining the new company, QuickBooks sets the Data Directory field to the drive, directory, and subdirectory where the program is stored. You can designate a different path for the new company, as long as the directory and subdirectory already exist.

After you have added a company, the new company's Chart of Accounts screen, with the account list you elected to use, appears. All your entries affect the new company until you change to another company.

CHOOSING A COMPANY

When you you start QuickBooks, the company name appears in the lower-left corner of the screen. Be sure to check the name when you have more than one company to ensure your entries will be made to the correct files.

To change to another company, select Set Up/Customize from the Main menu, and then choose Select/Add a Company from the submenu. The list of companies includes the company name, file name, date created, current size of files, and when the next event is scheduled. Use the ↓ key to highlight the company you want, and then press ↵ to select it. You will see the Chart of Accounts screen for the company you chose. All your input will now be recorded in that company.

PROTECTING YOUR FILES

Computers can be temperamental. They are sensitive to power fluctuations, cigarette smoke, and magnets (and perhaps, to full moons as well). You should always take the precaution of backing up your files. This means making a duplicate copy of your work. If your files are damaged, you can use the backup files to restore your data. The amount of work that you will have to redo depends on how often you back up your files.

It is best to make backup copies of your work onto floppy disks and store the disks somewhere other than in your office. You can create a sub-directory on your hard disk (for example, one named BACKUP in the

QBOOKS directory) and back up your data files into it instead of using floppy disks. However, this is not recommended because if anything happens to your hard disk, both your original data and the backup data could be corrupted or lost.

If something happens to your hard disk and your QuickBooks program files are damaged, you can reinstall the program from your original installation disks. Follow the same instructions for installing QuickBooks as when you first loaded the program.

BACKING UP YOUR FILES

Follow these steps to back up your QuickBooks data files:

You can press Ctrl-B from the Main menu to go directly to the back-up procedure.

1. Format several blank disks. The number of blank disks you will need depends on the size of your data.

2. Place the first blank disk in drive A.

3. Select Set Up/Customize from the Main menu, and then choose Backup/Restore/Copy Company Files.

4. Choose Back Up Company Files from the submenu.

5. Select the company whose data you want to back up.

6. In the Backup Directory window, designate the drive to which you want to direct the backup, or accept the default A:\ (for drive A).

If you are backing up to your hard disk, you must designate both the drive and the directory in which you want to store the backup. QuickBooks allows you to keep 99 different backups on your hard disk. It numbers these backups incrementally with the extension S01, S02, and so on.

As the files are copied to the designated location, they are listed on the screen. If your data exceeds the space available on the first floppy disk, QuickBooks prompts you to remove the disk and replace it with a fresh disk.

From the Backup Directory window, you can press F9 to exit to DOS and use the FORMAT command to format floppy disks. Type EXIT to return to QuickBooks and continue with the back-up function.

7. Label each floppy disk as you remove it from drive A with the date and time of the backup routine and assign it a sequential number starting with #1. If you need to restore your data using backup disks, you must reenter the data in the order it was copied.

8. Press Esc to return to the Main menu when the backup is complete. Store the backup copies in a safe place.

RESTORING YOUR DATA FROM A BACKUP

If you back up your files regularly, losing data will not be a catastrophe. If you must resort to a backup, follow this procedure to restore the most recent copy of your work:

1. If your backup copy is on floppy disks, place the backup disk labeled #1 in drive A.

2. Select Set Up/Customize from the Main menu, and then choose Backup/Restore/Copy Company Files.

3. Choose Restore Company Files from the submenu.

4. In the Restore Directory window, press ↵ to accept A:\ (for drive A), or enter the drive, directory, and subdirectory from which you are restoring the data. All the data found on the disk in drive A (or in the backup subdirectory) will be loaded into the subdirectory where your current QuickBooks data is located.

5. If you are restoring from your hard disk, choose the company that you want to use from those listed in the Select a Restore File window.

 The data from the backup replaces the data currently in your files. Any entries since the last backup operation will be lost when you restore data.

If your data is stored on more than one disk, QuickBooks prompts you to remove the first disk and replace it with the second backup disk. Be sure to restore the backup disks in the order you made them. As the files are copied back into the QuickBooks subdirectory, their names are listed on the screen.

DELETING A COMPANY

After completing this book, you can either delete or retain the Training Company. If you delete it, other staff members can have hands-on experience recreating the Training Company and following the examples in this book. If you retain it, you can try new transactions or experiment with unfamiliar functions in the Training Company without risking the data in your real company.

Follow the steps below to remove the Training Company from your disk. You can use these steps to remove any company you no longer need. When a company is removed, all the data you recorded in that company is lost.

1. Select Set Up/Customize from the Main menu, and then choose Select/Add a Company.

2. Highlight the Training Company (or the company you want to delete).

3. Press Ctrl-Del to delete the company and all its records. Quick-Books displays the prompt

   CAUTION! Permanently removing this company's files.
   Are you sure?

4. Enter **Yes** to confirm that you want to delete the company.

USING OTHER QUICKBOOKS UTILITIES

QuickBooks offers several other options you might want to use after your company begins to grow and change:

◆ Copy/Shrink Company Files

◆ Merge Company Files

◆ Change Data Directory

After you copy or merge companies, you will probably want to delete the originating companies, as explained in the previous section.

COPYING A COMPANY

If you need to conserve space on your hard disk, use the Copy/Shrink Company Files option to make a copy of your files, and then delete the original files.

When you copy an existing company, QuickBooks creates a duplicate company. The program reduces the size of the files in the new company, making better use of the space on the hard disk.

To copy a company, begin working in the company you want to copy. Select Set Up/Customize from the Main menu, then Back Up/Restore/Copy Company Files from the submenu, then Copy/Shrink Company Files. Enter the name for the resulting company, and the file name for the resulting company. You can also enter a date range to indicate the transactions you want to include in the copied company.

You can use this option to create a second company with the same structure as an existing company. QuickBooks copies just the company lists and the chart of accounts if you enter a date prior to the date you began recording transactions in the company being copied.

You can also purge prior years' activity by restricting the date range. For example, if you want to keep only two years' history on your disk, and today is January 1, 1995, enter 1/1/93 through 1/1/95 for the date range. In the new company's files, QuickBooks will retain the transactions from the past two years, and delete transactions with a date prior to 1/1/93. You could then delete the original company.

MERGING COMPANIES

You can merge two companies into one. However, the companies you are merging cannot have accounts with the same name. Before merging two companies, compare their chart of accounts. If you find duplicate names, determine if the account data should be combined in the new company or reside separately. In either case, select one company and change the names of any duplicated accounts.

Print another chart of accounts and circle the accounts you changed. Make a note of which accounts in the new company they should be combined with, if any.

To merge companies, begin working in the first company you want to unite with a second existing company. Select Set Up/Customize from the Main menu, then Back Up/Restore/Copy Company Files, then Merge Company Files. Press Ctrl-L and select the company you want to combine with the current company from the Merge File and Company Names List. Enter the name for the resulting third company, the file name for the resulting company (or accept the name supplied by QuickBooks), and a date range.

If you need to combine accounts after merging companies, display the new chart of accounts and highlight the account you want to join with another account (the one you no longer need in your chart of accounts). Press F7 (Actions) and select Combine. Then highlight the account into which you want to add the data from the other account and press ↵. QuickBooks will add the transactions to the second account and delete the first one.

CHANGING A COMPANY'S DATA DIRECTORY

Changing the data directory simply *tells* QuickBooks that you have moved the company records to a different directory than the one you specified when you first added that company. It does not rename the existing directory, nor move the files to the new directory.

After you have moved your records to another directory, select Set Up/Customize from the Main menu, and then choose Change Data Directory. Enter the new location of your files.

This chapter provided the information you need to manage your QuickBooks files. You learned how to set passwords, add and delete companies, and protect your files.

Now that you have completed the book and understand how to use QuickBooks, you will be able to maintain your business records accurately and efficiently. The appendices that follow provide extra information you may need for reference and for special work within QuickBooks.

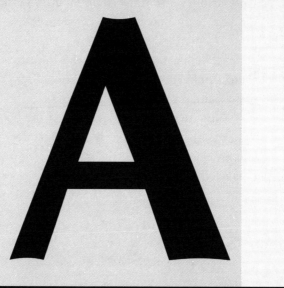

APPENDIX

A

Installing QuickBooks

Before you can use QuickBooks, you must first install the program. Follow the installation instructions that came with your software; you cannot simply copy the program disks to your hard disk. This appendix describes what you need to run QuickBooks and the procedure for installing the program.

COMPUTER SYSTEM REQUIREMENTS

Your computer system should have at least the following components to install QuickBooks:

Intuit recommends expanded memory.

- ◆ An IBM XT, AT, PS/2. or 100 percent compatible computer
- ◆ DOS 2.1 or later
- ◆ 640K random-access memory (RAM)
- ◆ One floppy disk drive (either 3½ or 5¼-inch)

◆ Hard disk with 3 megabytes available

◆ Monochrome or color monitor

◆ Dot-matrix or laser printer

Optionally, you can use a Microsoft or compatible mouse with the program.

PROTECTING YOUR DISKS

*Handle your computer disks with care. Always handle a disk by its jacket. Keep disks away from dust, smoke, heat, liquids, and magnets. Write on the label **before** sticking it on the disk.*

To protect your original disks, you should make copies of them, and then use the new working copies to install the program. In preparation, format either two blank 3½-inch disks or three 5¼-inch disks and label them to match the original QuickBooks disks. Place write-protect tabs over the notch on the original disks to safeguard their contents.

Place the original disk in drive A and the blank, formatted disk with the matching label in drive B. At the A: prompt, type **DISKCOPY A: B:** to copy the original disk (in the *source* drive) to the blank disk (in the *target* drive). If you have only one floppy disk drive, the source drive and the target drive in the command will be identical (DISKCOPY A: A:), and you will need to switch disks when prompted. Follow the instructions on the screen. After you copy them, store the original disks in a safe place.

INSTALLING QUICKBOOKS

The CONFIG.SYS file tells the computer how your system is configured. During installation, QuickBooks will either create or edit an existing CONFIG.SYS file to meet its minimum requirements of Files=12 and Buffers=16. The Files indicator shows how many files can be open at one time, and the Buffers indicator shows how many buffers you have available to store directory and file allocation table (FAT) information. If your CONFIG.SYS file is set higher, QuickBooks will not disturb your settings.

QuickBooks also creates a QB.BAT file in the root directory (renaming any existing file of the same name to QOLD.BAT). This file allows you to start the program from the root directory, rather than first changing to the directory where the QuickBooks files are stored.

Do not create a directory for QuickBooks, because one will be created during installation. If you have partitioned your hard disk, change to the drive where you want QuickBooks installed. Substitute its letter for C: in the instructions that follow, and enter it as part of the path name when you are prompted.

When you install QuickBooks, you can optionally install Bizminder, a QuickBooks program that reminds you when items you recorded in Quick-Books are due. Bizminder adds a line to your AUTOEXEC.BAT file so that the reminders appear when you turn on the computer. The program renames your old AUTOEXEC.BAT file to AUTOEXEC.B00.

At any time during the installation process, you can get on-line help with the procedure by pressing F1. You will see Help text provided by Quick-Books. If you want to go back one or more screens and change what you did, just press the Esc key.

Follow these steps to install QuickBooks:

In the instructions, **enter** *means to type the characters indicated, and then press ↵ to record the input. At any time during the installation, you can press the Esc key to cancel the process.*

1. Turn on your computer, monitor, and printer.

2. Place the disk labeled Install Disk 1 in drive A.

3. At the C: prompt, enter **A:** to change from drive C to drive A, where the QuickBooks disk is currently located.

4. At the A: prompt, enter **INSTALL**.

5. At the prompt

   Do you have a color monitor?

   enter 1 if the answer is Yes, or 2 if you do not have a color monitor.

6. At the prompt

   Drive from which to install:

   press ↵ to accept the drive entered by the program, or enter A, B or O (for other) to designate where you placed the floppy disk that contains the program.

If you install Bizminder, you can deactivate it later.

7. At the prompt

   Would you like to install Bizminder?

   enter 1 for Yes if you want to be reminded of bookkeeping tasks, or 2 for No.

8. At the next prompt

Enter QuickBooks Directory

accept the program-supplied path name, C:\QBOOKS, to have the program files copied to drive C into a directory named QBOOKS. If you want to give the directory another name, type over the QBOOKS. Be sure to leave the drive letter, semicolon, and back-slash (\). The program will create the directory you specify.

The QuickBooks Installation Summary screen appears after you specify the QuickBooks directory. It shows your responses to the previous questions: the drive from which you are installing, the drive and directory into which you are installing QuickBooks, and if you decided to install Bizminder.

9. Press ↵ to continue or Esc to back up and make corrections.

When you select to continue with the installation from the Installation Summary screen, you will see messages about the status of the installation. Quick-Books informs you as it is copying and decompressing files. You will eventually see the prompt

Waiting for new disk
Please insert the Install Disk 2 into drive A, then press ↵.

10. Remove Disk 1 from drive A and replace it with Disk 2, and then press ↵.

If you are installing from 5¼-inch disks, you will later be asked to remove Disk 2 and replace it with Disk 3. The installation process will continue, and you will be notified when it is complete.

11. If the installation is successful, when you see the message

Installation Complete

press ↵ to finish the process.

If the installation is not successful, you will see the message

An error occurred while installing; QuickBooks has not been installed correctly.

Press ↵ to acknowledge the message. You will return to the A: prompt. Review the hardware requirements to be certain your system is adequate, and then repeat the installation steps.

12. When you see the message

> To run QuickBooks type QB at the DOS prompt and press Enter

press ↵ to acknowledge it.

After successfully installing the program, remove the QuickBooks disk from the A: drive and store all your original disks in a safe place. You can now proceed to Chapter 1 of this book to learn how to use QuickBooks.

B

Preparing Worksheets for QuickBooks

his appendix contains worksheets in Tables B.1 through B.24 to help you set up your own data in QuickBooks. The worksheets list the fields as they appear on the screen and describe the entries you can make. You should put each record with its field names on a sheet of paper and leave space to write in the information exactly as you will enter it in the fields. Make copies of your field name lists and refer to the tables in this appendix as you fill out a worksheet for each record.

Worksheets are not provided for items that can simply be added to a predefined list:

- Customer types
- Vendor types
- Shipping methods

◆ Payment methods

◆ Invoice memos

See Chapter 16 for details about setting up these lists. See Chapter 3 for definitions of the QuickBooks account types.

TABLE B.1:

Company Information Worksheet

FIELD	DESCRIPTION
Company (name, then address)	The name and address you want to appear on your documents and report headings. You can enter up to five lines of 30 alphanumeric characters each.
Employer ID number (optional)	The tax identification number assigned to your business by the federal government for reporting your income, payroll taxes withheld, and payments to employees.
Usual FOB (ship from) location	The location from which your product-based business most often charges customers for shipping merchandise to them. The FOB (free on board) location appears automatically on product invoices. You can enter up to 13 characters.
Usual shipping method	The carrier on your Shipping Method List that your product-based business uses most often to send merchandise to customers. You can enter up to 8 alphanumeric characters.

TABLE B.2:

Checking Account Worksheet

FIELD	DESCRIPTION
Name for this account	An identifier for the general ledger account for this bank account. Identify your accounts with the standard numeric accounting scheme, or use abbreviated alphabet character names. You can enter up to 15 alphanumeric characters.
Account balance	The balance in the account. You can enter an amount of up to 9,999,999.99.
As of	The date the amount in the Account balance field was correct. Use the *MM/DD/YY* format.

TABLE B.2:
*Checking
Account Worksheet
(continued)*

FIELD	DESCRIPTION
Description	The name of the bank account to appear on the chart of accounts. You can enter up to 21 alphanumeric characters.
Notes/Account number	The number assigned to your account at the bank. You can enter up to 30 alphanumeric characters.

TABLE B.3:
*Accounts Receivable
Account Worksheet*

FIELD	DESCRIPTION
Name for this account	An identifier for this receivables account in your general ledger. (This account is in addition to the one QuickBooks automatically creates.) You can enter up to 15 alphanumeric characters.
Description (optional)	A description to appear in your chart of accounts.

TABLE B.4:
*Fixed Asset Account
Worksheet*

FIELD	DESCRIPTION
Name for this account	An identifier for this general ledger account. You can enter up to 15 alphanumeric characters.
Account balance	If you have reported depreciation, use the original value of the asset. Otherwise, use its current value.
As of	The date the amount in the Account balance field was correct. Use a *MM/DD/YY* format.
Description	A description to appear in your chart of accounts. You can enter up to 21 alphanumeric characters.
Notes/Account number	A notation of what this account represents, or any other notation that further identifies this account. You can enter up to 30 alphanumeric characters.

TABLE B.5:

*Current Asset Account
Worksheet*

FIELD	DESCRIPTION
Name for this account	An identifier for this general ledger account. You can enter up to 15 alphanumeric characters.
Account balance	The present value of this asset.
As of	The date the amount in the Account balance field was correct. Use a *MM/DD/YY* format.
Description	The name to appear in your chart of accounts. You can enter up to 21 alphanumeric characters.
Notes/Account number	A notation to differentiate this account from other current assets. You can enter up to 30 alphanumeric characters.

TABLE B.6:

Current Liability Account and Long-Term Liability Account Worksheet

FIELD	DESCRIPTION
Name for this account	An identifier that is consistent with your numbering/naming convention for general ledger accounts. You can enter up to 15 alphanumeric characters.
Account balance	The unpaid balance for this account.
As of	The date the amount in the Account balance field was correct. Use a *MM/DD/YY* format.
Description	The name to appear in your chart of accounts. You can enter up to 21 alphanumeric characters.
Notes/Account number	The number assigned to you by the creditor, or any other notation that further identifies the account. You can enter up to 30 alphanumeric characters.

TABLE B.7:

Accounts Payable Account Worksheet

FIELD	DESCRIPTION
Name for this account	An identifier for this payables account that is consistent with your numbering/naming convention for general ledger accounts. (This account is in addition to the one that QuickBooks automatically creates.) You can enter up to 15 alphanumeric characters.
Description (optional)	A more detailed description of the account. You can enter up to 21 alphanumeric characters.

TABLE B.8:

Credit Card Account Worksheet

FIELD	DESCRIPTION
Name for this account	An identifier that is consistent with your numbering/naming convention for general ledger accounts. You can enter up to 15 alphanumeric characters.
Account balance	The unpaid changes on your credit card statement.
As of	The date the amount in the Account balance field was correct. Use a *MM/DD/YY* format.
Description	The name of the credit card company. You can enter up to 21 alphanumeric characters.
Credit limit	The greatest unpaid balance you are allowed by this credit card company. You can enter an amount of up to 999,999.99. QuickBooks uses your credit limit entry to calculate your available credit (which is displayed in the register) from your charges and payments to this account.
Notes/Account number	The number on your credit card (usually an abbreviated version because of the restricted length of the field). You can enter up to 30 alphanumeric characters.
Vendor	The name you want to appear on the check when you make a payment to the credit card company. Select from the Vendor List.

TABLE B.9:
*Equity Account
Worksheet*

FIELD	DESCRIPTION
Name for this account	An identifier that is consistent with your numbering/naming convention for general ledger accounts. You can enter up to 15 alphanumeric characters.
Account balance	The balance in the account. If this account keeps track of an owner's withdrawals, it is a contra account, which requires a negative entry.
As of	The date the amount in the Account balance field was correct. Use a *MM/DD/YY* format.
Description	A description of the account. You can enter up to 21 alphanumeric characters.
Notes/Account number	The name of the person or stockholders represented by this account. You can enter up to 30 alphanumeric characters.

TABLE B.10:
*Income Account
and Expense Account
Worksheet*

FIELD	DESCRIPTION
Name	An identifier for the Income or Expense account. You can enter up to 15 alphanumeric characters.
Description	The description of the account. You can enter up to 25 alphanumeric characters.

TABLE B.11:
Budget Worksheet

FIELD	DESCRIPTION
Budget Amount	The amount you want to place in every calendar month's budget field.
Jan - Dec	Enter a specific budget amount for each month
Varies by Month	QuickBooks enters Yes in this field if you enter a separate amount for each month..

TABLE B.12:
Customer Payment Terms Worksheet

FIELD	DESCRIPTION
Terms	An abbreviation of the conditions on the payment terms you offer customers. You can enter up to 12 alphanumeric characters.
Net due in how many days?	The number of days from the invoice date in which the invoice must be paid. You can enter up to 2 numeric characters.
Discount percentage (%)	The discount allowed off the total invoice if it is paid early. You can enter up to 2 numeric characters.
Discount if paid within how many days?	The number of days from the invoice date the bill must be paid to allow the customer to subtract the early payment discount from the invoice total. You can enter up to 2 numeric characters.

FIELD	DESCRIPTION
Initials	The initials of the employee. If two employees have the same three initials, add a number as a suffix; for example, DEY1 and DEY2. You can enter up to 4 alphanumeric characters.
Employee (name, then address)	The employee's name and address. If you use QuickBooks to write payroll checks, the program will supply the address on the check. You can enter up to five lines of 30 alphanumeric characters each.

FIELD	DESCRIPTION
Bill To (name, then address)	The customer's name and address as it is to appear on invoices, reports, and labels. You can enter up to five lines of 30 alphanumeric characters each.
Ship To	The name and address where the customer's merchandise is to be sent. This information appears on Product invoices only. You can enter up to five lines of 30 alphanumeric characters each.
Customer Type	One of the customer classifications included on the Customer Type List. You can use this field to filter reports.
Contact	The person who handles this customer's account. You can enter up to 25 alphanumeric characters.
Tel	The contact person's area code, phone number, and an extension of up to 4 characters.
Contact	The name of a second contact for this customer.
Tel	The area code, phone number, and extension of the second contact person. You can also use this field to record the customer's fax number.
Representative/ Salesperson's initials	The initials of one of the salespeople included on the Employee List (the one who handles this account). This information can be used to filter reports.

TABLE B.14:
Customer Worksheets
(continued)

FIELD	DESCRIPTION
Payment Terms	One of the codes included on the Terms List. It indicates when the invoice is due and if the customer is allowed an early payment discount.
Credit (blank if no lmt)	The highest unpaid balance you allow this customer. If the customer exceeds this limit, QuickBooks will notify you when you enter an invoice for the customer. If you do not place a limit on the amount the customer can charge, leave the field blank. The maximum amount you can enter is 9,999,999.99.

TABLE B.15:
Vendor Worksheet

FIELD	DESCRIPTION
Pay To (name, then address)	The name and address that is to appear on checks you write to this vendor, as well as on reports and labels. You can enter up to five lines of 30 alphanumeric characters each.
Vendor Type	One of the vendor classifications included on the Vendor Type List. You can use this information for reporting purposes.
Account Number/notes	The number assigned to your account by the vendor. It prints on the memo line on checks. You can enter up to 20 alphanumeric characters.
Taxpayer ID Number	The identification assigned to the vendor by the federal government under which the vendor reports income. It appears on the QuickBooks 1099 report.
Contact	The name of the person at the vendor's office who manages your account. You can enter up to 25 alphanumeric characters.
Tel	The contact person's area code, phone number, and an extension of up to 4 characters.

TABLE B.16:

Part Worksheet

FIELD	DESCRIPTION
Code	A code to identify this product. It prints on Product invoices and the Sales report. You can enter up to 10 alphanumeric characters.
Account	The Income account in your chart of accounts in which you want to record sales of this item.
Price each	The amount you charge for one of these products. You can enter an amount up to 999,999.999 (three decimal places are allowed). The price is multiplied times the quantity and rounded to arrive at a two decimal place dollar amount on the invoice.
Description to show on invoice	The description of the product, which prints on the customer's invoice. You can enter up to three lines of 44 alphanumeric characters each for Service invoices, 33 for Product invoices, or 60 for Professional invoices. Only the first 25 characters appear on the Item List, but the entire description prints on the invoice.

TABLE B.17:

Service Worksheet

FIELD	DESCRIPTION
Code	A code to identify this service. It is listed in the Sales report. The code prints only on Product invoices. You can enter up to 10 alphanumeric characters.
Account	The Income account in your chart of accounts in which you want to record sales of this service.
Price each	The amount you charge for this service. You can enter an amount up to 999,999.999 (three decimal places are allowed). The price is multiplied times the quantity and rounded to arrive at a two decimal place dollar amount on the invoice.

TABLE B.17:
Service Worksheet
(continued)

FIELD	DESCRIPTION
Description to show on invoice	The description of the product, which prints on the customer's invoice. You can enter up to three lines of 44 alphanumeric characters each for Service invoices, 30 for Product invoices, or 60 for Professional invoices. Only the first 25 characters appear on the Item List, but the entire description prints on the invoice.

TABLE B.18:
Other Charges
Worksheet

FIELD	DESCRIPTION
Code	An abbreviated identification of this charge. You can enter up to 10 alphanumeric characters.
Account	The general ledger account in your chart of accounts in which you keep track of income from this item. Often, you will need an Expense account that parallels this Income account, because you are billing the customer for something you already had to pay for, such as freight or insurance.
Price each	The amount you charge for this item. You can enter an amount up to 999,999.999 (three decimal places are allowed). Leave this field blank if the amount fluctuates.
Description to show on invoice	A description of the item, which prints on the customer's invoice. You can enter up to three lines of 44 alphanumeric characters each for Service invoices, 33 for Product invoices, or 60 for Professional invoices. Only the first 25 characters appear on the Item List, but the entire description prints on the invoice.

FIELD	DESCRIPTION
Code	An abbreviated description of this discount; for example, 10%Disc. You can enter up to 10 alphanumeric characters.
Account	The Expense account in your chart of accounts in which you keep track of pricing discounts.
Price each	The amount of the discount. If it is a dollar amount, enter the amount. If the discount is a percentage, follow the amount by the % sign. The discount will show as a negative amount in the Price field on the Item List, and the calulated amount will be subtracted from the invoice amount. You can enter an amount up to 999,999.999 (three decimal places are allowed).
Description to show on invoice	A description of the discount, which prints on the customer's invoice; for example, *Reduction for Items on Sale.* You can enter up to three lines of 44 alphanumeric characters each for Service invoices, 33 for Product invoices, or 60 for Professional invoices. Only the first 25 characters appear on the Item List, but the entire description prints on the invoice.

TABLE B.20:

Sales Tax Worksheet

FIELD	DESCRIPTION
Code	A code to identify the rate or district for this sales tax record; for example, *875* or *OHIO*. You can enter up to 10 alphanumeric characters.
Tax rate (%)	The rate charged in this tax district. The percent sign is supplied by the program. QuickBooks converts the amount to a four decimal place figure in calculations; for example, 8.75% becomes .0875. This is multiplied by the amount on the preceding line of the invoice (usually a subtotal line) to determine the sales tax to be charged. You can enter an amount up to 999,999.999 (three decimal places are allowed), although 100.000 is probably the largest amount you would use.
Tax district name	The district for whom you are collecting the tax. You can enter up to 30 alphanumeric characters.
Vendor	The government agency for whom you collect the tax (one of the vendors included on your Vendor List).
Description to show on invoice	A description to identify the tax charged on the customer's purchases, which prints on the invoice. You can enter one line of up to 44 alphanumeric characters for Service invoices, 33 for Product invoices, or 60 for Professional invoices. Only the first 25 characters appear on the Item List, but the entire description prints on the invoice.

TABLE B.21:
Refund Codes Worksheet

FIELD	DESCRIPTION
Code	A code to identify this refund. You can enter up to 10 alphanumeric characters.
Account	The checking account in your chart of accounts against which the refund check will be drawn.
Refund Amt	The amount of the refund. If the amount fluctuates, leave this field blank. If it is to be a percentage of the preceding line on the invoice rather than a dollar amount, enter the % sign after the numbers. You might, for example, refund 95% on returned merchandise, keeping 5% for restocking charges. You can enter an amount up to 999,999.999 (three decimal places are allowed).
Description to show on invoice	A description of the refund, which prints on the customer's invoice; for example, *Refund for returned merchandise, less restocking fee.* You can enter up to three lines of 44 alphanumeric characters for Service invoices, 33 for Product invoices, or 60 for Professional invoices. Only the first 25 characters appear on the Item List, but the entire description prints on the invoice.

TABLE B.22:
Item Subtotal Worksheet

FIELD	DESCRIPTION
Code	A notation to identify this subtotal. You can enter up to 10 alphanumeric characters.
Description to show on invoice	A description of the subtotal, which prints on the customer's invoice; for example, *Taxable Item Subtotal* or *Subtotal of Discounted Items.* You can enter one line of up to 44 alphanumeric characters for Service invoices, 33 for Product invoices, or 60 for Professional invoices. Only the first 25 characters appear on the Item List, but the entire description prints on the invoice.

TABLE B.23:

Project Worksheet

FIELD	DESCRIPTION
Name	A name that identifies this project. You can enter up to 15 alphanumeric characters.
Description (optional)	A more detailed description of the project. This information can be used in report headings. You can enter up to 25 alphanumeric characters.

TABLE B.24:

Password Worksheet

FIELD	DESCRIPTION
Owner (high-security) password	The password to be used by the person who has access to all the QuickBooks functions. You can enter up to 16 alphanumeric characters, with spaces. Passwords are not case-sensitive.
Bookkeeper (low-security) password	The password to be used by office staff to process daily work. You can enter up to 9 alphanumeric characters.
Date through which books are closed	The date as of which you want to prevent changes to previous transactions. Users will not be able to edit transactions dated before this date.

C

Using QuickBooks for Payroll

This appendix describes handling payroll in QuickBooks. The information presented here is a brief overview. Not only do payroll regulations change, they vary from state to state. You should obtain a copy of labor and payroll regulations from both federal government and state agencies and adhere to those regulations. Also, have your accountant review your setup and reporting practices.

If you have several employees, you should consider using QuickPay, a separate Intuit program, instead of QuickBooks for your payroll.

The optimum time to start keeping track of payroll transactions is at the beginning of a calendar year. The next best time to begin is at the start of a new quarter. At any other time, you must enter data from your old system into the new system. Each employee's year-to-date wages and the total taxes withheld in each tax category, for example, must be included in records begun midyear.

PAYROLL TERMINOLOGY

You should understand four payroll terms:

- ◆ *Gross wages* : The total amount the employee earned.
- ◆ *Net wages* : The amount the employee receives on the paycheck after deductions.
- ◆ *Deductions* : Amounts that you take out of the employee's gross earnings.
- ◆ *Contributions*: Amounts you, the employer, must pay in addition to anything the employee has withheld.

For example, Federal Withholding Tax is a deduction. The employee is the only one who pays it. If the company, not the employee, pays for health insurance, that is a contribution. Deductions are a liability only. Contributions are first an expense, but also a liability because you owe money to some other entity.

Gross wages are an expense, because they are the amount it cost you to have the employee work for you. Income tax deductions are *not* expenses. However, the portion of FICA that you, the employer, must pay *is* an expense. It is over and above the portion you withhold from the employee's wages.

ADDING SPECIAL ACCOUNTS

In order to handle payroll with QuickBooks, you must set up several special accounts to meet your requirements. You need to manage the gross amount the employee earns. From that amount, you must subtract taxes, and maybe union dues or insurance premiums. The amounts you withhold from an employee must be paid to someone else. You are just the temporary custodian of those funds. These amounts are recorded as liabilities. When you pay the taxes to the government, the dues to the union, or the premiums to the insurance company, you reduce your debts to those organizations.

To record payroll activity, you need Expense accounts and Liability accounts. QuickBooks requires that you begin the name of each payroll-related account with the word *Payroll*. This prefix is how QuickBooks selects transactions for the Payroll report, described later in this appendix.

You will need an Expense account for each of the following items:

◆ Gross Wages

◆ FICA (employer's portion)

◆ Medicare (employer's portion)

You may need an Expense account for other payroll expenses. If you, the employer, must pay all or a portion of something, over and above what is deducted from your employees' gross wages, set up an account for that item. The following are other Expense accounts you may need:

◆ State Disability

◆ Workers Compensation

◆ Federal Unemployment

◆ State Unemployment

◆ Retirement Fund Contributions

◆ Health Insurance Premiums

You will need a Liability account for each of the following items:

◆ Money withheld for Federal Income Tax

◆ Amounts withheld for State Income Tax

◆ The amounts withheld from the employee and contributed by the employee for FICA

◆ The amounts withheld from the employee and contributed by the employee for Medicare

Additionally, you must set up a Liability account for any other monies you withhold or must pay directly, such as the following:

◆ Union dues

◆ 401K

- 125P Cafeteria Plans
- Insurance Premiums
- State Disability
- Workers Compensation
- Federal Unemployment
- State Unemployment
- Retirement Fund Contributions

These lists are not comprehensive. Payroll is a very complex application, and you should consult your accountant and refer to government regulations regarding payroll setup.

WRITING A PAYROLL CHECK

NOTE *Chapter 8 of this book describes how to distribute transactions among several accounts.*

When you write a payroll check, the entry is a payment with the employee as the payee. The payment amount is the net wage, after deductions. You should distribute the paycheck amount among your Expense and Liability accounts:

- Charge the full amount of the gross amount earned by the employee to the Gross Payroll Expense account.
- Charge the Federal Withholding amount, as a negative entry, to the Federal Income Tax Liability account.
- Charge the State Withholding amount, as a negative amount, to the State Income Tax Liability account.
- Charge the amount withheld for FICA for the *employee's* portion, as a negative entry, to the FICA Tax Liability account.
- Charge the *employer's* portion of FICA, as a positive amount, to the FICA Expense account.
- Charge the *employer's* portion of FICA, as a negative entry (for the same amount as above), to the FICA Tax Liability account.
- Charge the amount withheld for Medicare for the *employee's* portion, as a negative entry, to the Medicare Liability account.

◆ Charge the *employer's* portion of Medicare, as a positive amount, to the Medicare Expense account.

◆ Charge the *employer's* portion of Medicare, as a negative entry (for the same amount as above), to the Medicare Liability account.

Continue to distribute the paycheck amount among all other deductions and contributions. Remember, contributions require both a positive entry to an Expense account and a negative entry to a Liability account. Deductions from the employee's gross wages are just negative entries to a Liability account.

You can memorize the paycheck for recall in the next pay period. If the gross wages change each pay period, create a check and enter the accounts for the distribution, but leave the amount fields blank. When you recall the "blank" check, fill it in with the amounts appropriate to that employee for that pay period. If your employee payments remain constant, memorize each check with the amounts completed. You will find it easier to process paychecks if you put all the memorized checks in a transaction group.

 *Chapter 13 describes the use of memorized transactions and transaction groups.*

HANDLING PAYROLL TAXES

If you are an employer, the government requires you to withhold and submit payment for payroll taxes. At some point, you also must send the government reports on your payroll activity. You can use QuickBooks to make the payments and accumulate the information for payroll reports.

PAYING TAXES

To send your quarterly tax payments to the government, write a check, and, in the Account field, enter the name of the Tax Liability account. QuickBooks will make a transfer entry that reduces that liability.

Also write the checks for amounts you pay to any other facility and charge them to the appropriate Liablity account. For example, enter the payment to the union or the insurance company, and charge it to the Union Dues or Insurance Premium Liability account.

PRODUCING PAYROLL REPORTS

The Payroll report subtotals amounts by payee (employee). It includes transactions for only the accounts whose name is preceded by the word *Payroll.* To generate the report, choose Reports from the Main menu, and then select Payroll Report.

Use the information on the Payroll report to complete such forms as the W-2 Wage and Tax Statement, 940 Employer's FUTA Tax Return, and 941 Employer's Quarterly Tax Return. You may be required to complete other forms for the government or labor union.

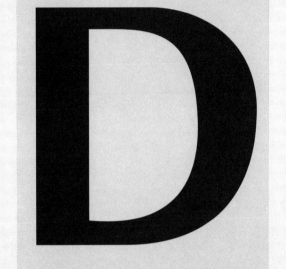

APPENDIX

D

Converting Data
from Quicken

If you have been using Quicken and want to bring your data into QuickBooks, you can convert your Quicken files. QuickBooks will accept data from Quicken 3 or later or from Quicken for Windows. If you have Quicken 1 or 2, you can get a free update from Intuit, convert your files to the later Quicken version, and then bring them into QuickBooks.

When you convert to QuickBooks, your original Quicken data is not affected. You can continue using Quicken and take advantage of some of the Quicken options that are not in QuickBooks, such as investment tracking.

The instructions in this appendix assume that you are familiar with the QuickBooks program and know how to select options from menus, move the cursor around on the screen, and so on. This information is given in Chapter 1 of this book.

CREATING A COMPANY FROM QUICKEN DATA

To convert your Quicken data into a new QuickBooks company, start QuickBooks, and then follow these steps:

1. From the Main menu, select Set Up/Customize, and then choose Add Company Using Data from Quicken from the submenu.

2. In the Specify Quicken Data Directory window, which shows the location of your Quicken data, press ↵ to accept the location supplied by QuickBooks, or enter the drive, directory, and subdirectory of the Quicken data you want to convert. If your data is on a floppy disk that you have placed in drive A, type **A:**.

3. If you have more than one account group in Quicken, the Select a Quicken File window appears. Highlight the file you want to use to create the new QuickBooks company and press ↵. If you have only one group, you will not see this window and can skip this step.

4. At the prompt

   Your Company's name

   enter the name you want to use for the new company in Quick-Books. You can type up to 30 characters, including spaces.

5. In the Creating Company Files window, QuickBooks displays the file name it created from the company name you entered. Press ↵ to accept that file name, or enter a different name in acceptable DOS format.

6. QuickBooks displays the name of the data directory in which it will store your company data. You can press ↵ to accept that directory or enter another drive, directory, and subdirectory (in *drive:\directory\subdirectory* format).

QuickBooks begins to convert your Quicken files. During the conversion process, it displays messages as it copies the header, creates accounts, copies records, and so on. You will be notified when the conversion is completed.

7. Press ↵ to display the chart of accounts (your old Category and Transfer List) for the new company.

WHAT'S DIFFERENT

QuickBooks changes your Quicken categories and subcategories into accounts and subaccounts, respectively. It also adds the following accounts:

- ◆ Accounts Receivable
- ◆ Accounts Payable
- ◆ Sales Tax
- ◆ Open Balance Equity

If you had accounts by these names in Quicken, they will be retained with their own balances, but their names will be changed as follows:

- ◆ Quicken A/R
- ◆ Quicken A/P
- ◆ QSales Tax A/P

The difference between your balance sheet accounts is recorded in the Open Balance Equity account. Your accounts retain the transaction history from your activity in Quicken. You might want to shrink the new company, eliminating transactions from some time ago (see Chapter 17).

The account types you had in Quicken are converted to the following account types in QuickBooks:

QUICKEN ACCOUNT	QUICKBOOKS ACCOUNT
Bank	Checking
Credit Card	Credit Card
Cash	Current Asset
Other Asset	Current Asset
Investment	Current Asset
Other Liability	Current Liability

Your Quicken classes are converted into projects and placed on the Projects List (see Chapter 16). Memorized transactions are placed on the Memorized Transaction List with the name, address, memo, and general ledger accounts they had when they were memorized. They can be recalled for use when appropriate, or deleted from the list if you no longer need them. Your Quicken transaction groups are placed on the Standard Transaction Group List. (See Chapter 13 for information about recalling and grouping transactions.)

QuickBooks does not copy your Quicken memorized reports nor the passwords you set up in Quicken. You can customize and memorize Quick-Books reports (see Chapter 15) and define new passwords for the program (see Chapter 17).

Refer to the inside covers of this book for a complete list of QuickBooks Ctrl-key shortcuts.

Some of the quick keys you are accustomed to using in Quicken have been changed in QuickBooks. Most notably, Ctrl-L is used to look up entries on any list. You use Ctrl-Del to delete items or transactions; Ctrl-D deletes only single lines in a transaction.

UPDATING YOUR NEW COMPANY

Complete the company information to define your company in QuickBooks (it has only the company name you entered during the conversion). Enter the address, federal tax indentification number, and shipping information (see Chapter 2).

QuickBooks creates new Accounts Receivable, Accounts Payable, and Sales Tax accounts for you. All new activity should be recorded in these new accounts. You will phase out the three accounts that you used in Quicken: the Other Asset account for receivables, the Other Liability account for payables, and the Other Liability account for sales tax.

In the account converted from the Other Asset account for customer invoices, record payments that were outstanding when you converted to QuickBooks. When you pay vendor bills that were outstanding when you converted to QuickBooks, make the payments from the account that was converted from the Other Liability account for payables. Pay the outstanding sales tax from the account that was converted from the Other Liability sales tax account, but record tax on new invoices in the sales tax account provided by QuickBooks.

You cannot delete an account that has transfers to other accounts.

When the balance in your old Quicken receivables, payables, or sales tax account reaches zero, stop using the account. Delete any memorized transactions involving these accounts.

You should remove any accounts that pertain to your personal transactions. Business and personal transactions should not be mixed in a QuickBooks company.

Your Quicken investment accounts have been reclassified as Current Asset account. If the account is truly an investment that you want to show as a *business* asset, leave it in QuickBooks. Otherwise, delete the investment account from your business records. Increase or decrease the value of the business investment periodically in QuickBooks, just as you increase or decrease the value of your inventory account. You will need an Expense account in which to record losses and an Income account in which to record gains whenever you update the investment account.

You can continue to record all investments in Quicken.

APPENDIX

E

Glossary of QuickBooks and Accounting Terms

Account: A unit used to store the accounting data of a business. In Quick-Books, it is a means of classifying transactions for grouping on reports (equivalent to a *category* in Quicken).

Account balance: The net result of all transactions affecting a general ledger account.

Account type: A category to classify general ledger accounts. Standard account types are asset, liability, equity, revenue, income, and expense. Quick-Books defines 12 account types: Checking, Accounts Receivable, Current Asset, Fixed Asset, Accounts Payable, Credit Card, Current Liability, Long-Term Liability, Equity, Income, Expense, and Subaccount.

Accounts payable: Debts owed by a business for purchases of goods or services.

Accounts Payable account: A QuickBooks account type that keeps track of small purchases from vendors, including invoices and payments.

Accounts receivable: Monies owed to a business by its customers.

Accounts Receivable account: A QuickBooks account type that keeps track of the amounts owed to a business.

Accrual: An amount that accumulates over time, such as the liability for wages owed to employees for the current, incomplete pay period.

Accrual bookkeeping: An accounting method in which income is recorded when goods or services are delivered, and expenses are recorded when they are incurred.

Accrued assets or liabilities: Unrecorded assets or liabilities that exist at the end of an accounting period.

Accrued revenue: Money a business has earned, but not yet received, such as interest on an investment that accumulates but is not paid until the investment matures.

Accumulated depreciation: A contra asset account that records the depreciation claimed on the related asset.

Adjusting entries: General ledger entries that update accounts for changes in financial status that are not reflected in routine transactions, such as depreciation or a prepayment.

Aging period: A time frame that determines the age of an invoice based on its due date.

Aging report: A listing of invoices, their balances, and the age of the balance (determined by how many days from the current date the due date falls).

Applied: Payments or adjustments made against a specific invoice.

Asset: An item of value owned by a business, such as property or money owed to you.

Average cost: A method of valuing resale merchandise in which the cost for all items purchased is divided by the number of units purchased.

Bad debt: An amount due that is not collectible.

Balance forward: In QuickBooks, a method of automatically applying a payment to the oldest invoices. Also, in standard accounting, a statement type that shows only the current period in detail and carries forward amounts due from previous periods in the form of an accumulated balance.

Balance sheet: The assets, liabilities, and owner's equity in the business, presented in a formal report.

Beginning balance: In QuickBooks, the balance in an account or on a statement before all the transactions appearing on it have been accounted for.

Bizminder: In QuickBooks, a reminder that pops up automatically when you start your computer if you have postdated checks to print, vendor invoices that are almost due or past due, or a transaction group scheduled for processing.

Budget: In QuickBooks, a preset amount a business expects to receive or spend per month for a specific income or expense account.

Capital account: A general ledger account in which an owner's investment in the business and percentage of the company's earnings are recorded.

Cash-basis bookkeeping: An accounting method in which income is recorded when payment is received, and expenses are recorded when they are paid.

Chart of accounts: A listing, usually numeric, of all the accounts in the general ledger.

Checking account: A QuickBooks account type that keeps track of transactions in a bank account, such as a checking, savings, or money market account.

Closing the books: Transferring the balances from all income and expense accounts into the Retained Earnings account. Although this is not required in QuickBooks, your accountant might recommend that you do so.

Contra account: An account whose balance is subtracted from an associated account on the balance sheet.

Contractor: Someone who agrees to do work for a business under contract, usually with no income taxes or other items deducted from the payment.

Contributions: Payroll-related amounts paid solely by the company, such as Federal Unemployment Tax.

Cost: The amount paid to obtain assets or resale merchandise.

Cost of goods sold: An expense denoting the cost of goods purchased then resold to customers.

Credit: An entry to a general ledger account that decreases an asset or expense account and increases a liability, equity, or income account.

Credit Card account: A QuickBooks account type that is a liability and keeps track of transactions charged to a credit card.

Credit memo: A form issued by a business to reduce the liability of a customer.

Current asset: Cash and other assets that can be converted to cash quickly (usually within one year). In QuickBooks, funds in a checking account are separate from the Current Asset account type, although in standard accounting, this cash is included as part of the definition.

Current Asset account: A QuickBooks account type that keeps track of assets that can be converted to cash quickly.

Current balance: In QuickBooks, the balance in an account as of the current system date. It does not include transactions recorded with a future date.

Current liability: A debt that is due within a year or less (also known as a short-term liability). In QuickBooks, monies owed to vendors and on credit cards are separate from the Current Liability account type, although in standard accounting, they would be included as part of the definition.

Current Liability account: A QuickBooks account type that keeps track of amounts a business must pay within a short period of time.

Custom report: In QuickBooks, a report that allows selection of specific records in your database.

Customer: A person, company, or organization who purchases merchandise or services from a business.

Customer balance: The net result of all charges and payments in a customer's record.

Customer type: In QuickBooks, a means of classifying customers for grouping on reports.

Debit: An entry to a general ledger account that increases an asset or expense account and decreases a liability, equity, or income account.

Debit memo: A form issued by a business to increase the liability of a customer.

Deductions: Amounts taken out of an employee's gross wages, such as income taxes or union dues.

Depreciation: A portion of the cost of an asset posted periodically to an expense account. It represents a reduction in the value of an asset.

Discount: An amount deducted from the invoice amount if the invoice is paid within a specified time period, or a reduction of the price of the item. In QuickBooks, early payment discounts are handled through your customer payment terms, and price discounts are recorded on an invoice through discount codes.

Discount date: The last day on which a company or customer can take an early payment discount on what is owed on an invoice.

Discount percent: The percentage a company or customer is allowed to deduct from an invoice when taking a discount.

Drawing account: An account to record withdrawals by a partner or proprietor in a business.

Early payment discount: The discount a customer is allowed to take when paying an invoice early.

Effective date: The date transactions are reflected in the general ledger or on a customer or vendor record.

Ending balance: In QuickBooks, the balance in an account after all recorded transactions have been considered.

Equity: The combination of capital invested in a business and earnings retained in the business.

Equity account: A QuickBooks account type that keeps track of the worth of business ownership.

Expense: A cost related to conducting business, such as postage expense.

Expense account: A QuickBooks account type that keeps track of business-operating costs.

Filter: In QuickBooks, a method of excluding database records that do not meet your selection criteria from a report.

Finance charges: A penalty assessed for not paying an invoice in the specified time period.

Financial statements: Records of the financial status of a business, including a balance sheet and income (profit and loss) statement and, often, a statement of changes in financial condition.

Fiscal year: A company's normal business cycle. It may or may not coincide with a calendar year, but it is of the same duration.

Fixed asset: An asset not readily convertible to cash nor acquired for resale, such as property or machinery that is used in the operation of a business.

Fixed Asset account: A QuickBooks account type that keeps track of the decreasing or increasing value of fixed assets.

Forecast: A prediction or estimate of future business transactions.

General ledger: A ledger containing the financial statement accounts of a business.

Income: Money or value received as a result of doing business.

Income account: A QuickBooks account type that keeps track of each type of revenue generated by a business.

Inventory, physical: The count of merchandise actually on hand and available for sale.

Inventory, value: The value recorded in the general ledger asset account, Inventory, for merchandise held for resale.

Invoice: An itemization of goods or services purchased and the amount charged for them (a bill).

Invoice memo: In QuickBooks, a predefined message that can be printed on an invoice.

Item code: In QuickBooks, a user-defined code placed on invoices to charge the customer for parts, services, miscellaneous items, and sales tax; to give a discount or refund; to enter a payment; or to create a subtotal.

Late charge: An amount added to a past-due invoice as a penalty for nonpayment.

Liability: A debt owed by a business.

Long-term liability: An amount owed on large items or money borrowed for a long period of time.

Long-Term Liability account: A QuickBooks account type that keeps track of long-standing debts.

Memo: A notation on a check or transaction that can appear on the printed check or be used as selection criteria for a report.

Memorized report: In QuickBooks, a report format that you saved by having the program memorize it.

Memorized transaction: In QuickBooks, a recurring transaction that you saved by having the program memorize it.

Net profit: The amount by which income exceeds expenses.

Net sales: The amount of sales after deducting sales returns, freight charges, and discounts allowed.

Normal balance: The typical balance (debit or credit) of a given type of account. For example, asset accounts typically have a debit balance.

Notepad: In QuickBooks, a place in each vendor and customer record where you can make notations.

Notes payable or receivable: Long-term debts or receivables evidenced by a note, which are recorded separately from ongoing accounts payable or receivable.

Offsetting entry: An entry that counterbalances (equals) another in a transaction.

Open item: In QuickBooks, a method of applying a payment to specific invoices. Also, in standard accounting, a statement type that includes all open transactions, regardless of the period in which they occurred.

Open payables or receivables: Invoices from vendors or on customer accounts that have not yet been paid.

Open period: A period in which you can still record transactions; one that has not been closed. In QuickBooks, you restrict prior periods by a date in the password definition.

Opening balance: In QuickBooks, the balance of a balance sheet account when you first set up your data in the program.

Packing slip: A copy of information on an invoice, without the prices or amount due, that usually is enclosed with the merchandise.

Pay date: In QuickBooks, the date a vendor's invoice is due.

Payee: The person or company to whom a check is written.

Period: A division of an accounting year. In QuickBooks, you do not set up periods. Instead, you restrict reports by dates to reflect the period.

Posting: Applying transactions to customer, vendor, and general ledger accounts. In QuickBooks, the program does the posting for you when you record a transaction.

Prepaid expense: An expense that has been paid for in advance. It is recorded as an asset and reduced as the actual expense is incurred.

Primary account: In QuickBooks, an account that accumulates the total of all transactions posted to lower-level subaccounts.

Product costing: The means of valuing inventory: by average cost, standard cost, or last purchase price.

Profit and loss statement: A financial statement showing the net profit or loss in a business for a specific time period (also known as an income statement).

Project: In QuickBooks, a means of separating your transactions by very specific definitions beyond general ledger accounts (equivalent to a *class* in Quicken).

Purchase discount: The discount a business takes when paying a vendor early for goods or services purchased.

Purchase order: A form used to place an order for products or services.

Purchase return: Merchandise returned to a vendor for credit.

Purchase tax: A tax a business pays when making a purchase, usually of a non-resale item.

Quarter-end: In payroll processing, the end of a three-month period when wages and taxes must be reported on IRS Form 941.

QuickTrainer: In QuickBooks, Help text that pops up automatically when you begin to use the program. It can be turned off through the Options selection on the Customize QuickBooks submenu of the Set Up/Customize menu.

Recurring transaction: A transaction that is recorded repeatedly and can be memorized and recalled as needed.

Register: In QuickBooks, a listing of the transactions that have affected a given account, including the resulting balance.

Resale item: An item purchased (usually without paying sales tax) for resale to a customer.

Retained earnings: The accumulated net earnings of a business, less distributions to owners or stockholders.

Revenue: An amount earned, for example, interest or money from a sale.

Reversing entry: A general ledger entry on the first of the month to reverse adjusting entries made at the end of the preceding month; for example, for accrued salary expense.

Sales return: Merchandise returned by a customer for a refund or credit.

Sales tax: The tax a customer pays when purchasing from a business.

Split transaction: In QuickBooks, a transaction whose amount is recorded in more than one account.

Standard cost: A nonfluctuating estimate of what an intentory item will cost.

Subaccount: An account subordinate to a primary account. In QuickBooks, only income and expense accounts can have subaccounts.

Subproject: In QuickBooks, a classification that further defines a project.

Taxes payable: Taxes that must be paid by a business to the appropriate taxing agency, such as income taxes withheld from an employee's gross wages and the employee's related liability, or sales tax collected.

Taxpayer ID: The federal tax identification number for a vendor, used on IRS Form 1099 to report payments made to that vendor.

Terms: Conditions under which a sale is made or a debt incurred; they outline how and when payment is expected.

Transaction: Recordable event that affect the general ledger accounts of a business.

Transaction group: In QuickBooks, several memorized transactions that you place in a group and recall for processing all at one time.

Transfer: A movement of monies between balance sheet accounts.

Trial balance: A complete listing of the accounts in the general ledger, with the debit and credit balances totaled to determine if they are equal. It is used to verify the accuracy of posted transactions.

Vendor: A person or company who sells goods or services.

Vendor balance: The net result of all charges and payments in a vendor's record.

Vendor type: In QuickBooks, a means of classifying vendors for grouping on reports.

Year-end: The end of a fiscal or calendar year when a business closes the income and expense accounts and calculates its retained earnings.

INDEX

This index differentiates between mentions of items, listed in regular type, and explanations of items, listed as **bold** page numbers. *Italic* page numbers refer to figures.

B

S

About the Author

Darleen Hartley Yourzek has been a bookkeeper, manager, and owner in a variety of business settings, and has written training materials for several software development companies. Her other books include *Mastering DacEasy Accounting, Mastering Peachtree Complete III, Up & Running with Quicken 4, and Learn Quicken for Windows Fast!*, all from SYBEX.

SYBEX

FREE BROCHURE!

Complete this form today, and we'll send you a full-color brochure of Sybex bestsellers.

Please supply the name of the Sybex book purchased.

_____

How would you rate it?

_____ Excellent   _____ Very Good   _____ Average   _____ Poor

Why did you select this particular book?

_____ Recommended to me by a friend
_____ Recommended to me by store personnel
_____ Saw an advertisement in _____
_____ Author's reputation
_____ Saw in Sybex catalog
_____ Required textbook
_____ Sybex reputation
_____ Read book review in _____
_____ In-store display
_____ Other _____

Where did you buy it?

_____ Bookstore
_____ Computer Store or Software Store
_____ Catalog (name: _____)
_____ Direct from Sybex
_____ Other: _____

Did you buy this book with your personal funds?

_____ Yes   _____ No

About how many computer books do you buy each year?

_____ 1-3   _____ 3-5   _____ 5-7   _____ 7-9   _____ 10+

About how many Sybex books do you own?

_____ 1-3   _____ 3-5   _____ 5-7   _____ 7-9   _____ 10+

Please indicate your level of experience with the software covered in this book:

_____ Beginner   _____ Intermediate   _____ Advanced

Which types of software packages do you use regularly?

_____ Accounting	_____ Databases	_____ Networks
_____ Amiga	_____ Desktop Publishing	_____ Operating Systems
_____ Apple/Mac	_____ File Utilities	_____ Spreadsheets
_____ CAD	_____ Money Management	_____ Word Processing
_____ Communications	_____ Languages	_____ Other _____

(please specify)

Which of the following best describes your job title?

_____ Administrative/Secretarial   _____ President/CEO

_____ Director   _____ Manager/Supervisor

_____ Engineer/Technician   _____ Other _____
                                                        (please specify)

Comments on the weaknesses/strengths of this book: _____

_____

_____

_____

_____

Name _____

Street _____

City/State/Zip _____

Phone _____

PLEASE FOLD, SEAL, AND MAIL TO SYBEX

SYBEX, INC.
Department M
2021 CHALLENGER DR.
ALAMEDA, CALIFORNIA USA
94501

SYBEX

SEAL

QUICKBOOKS CTRL-KEY SHORTCUTS

Key Combination	Function
Ctrl-↑	Finds the previous occurrence of the transaction meeting your search criteria (after using Ctrl-F)
Ctrl-↓	Finds the next occurrence of the transaction meeting your search criteria (after using Ctrl-F)
Ctrl-A	Displays the chart of accounts
Ctrl-B	Backs up your file (from the Main menu)
Ctrl-C	Displays the Calculator
Ctrl-D	Deletes a line on an invoice, a check, or an account distribution (from an invoice-entry or check-writing screen); resets the default settings (from a Print Report window)
Ctrl-Del	Deletes the highlighted item or transaction
Ctrl-E	Displays a window for editing the highlighted item or transaction
Ctrl-F	Finds a transaction
Ctrl-F1	Displays the Help Index
Ctrl-G	Selects a file (from the Main menu)
Ctrl-H	Displays the highlighted transaction's history
Ctrl-Ins	Adds an item to a list
Ctrl-J	Displays the Transaction Group List
Ctrl-L	Displays the related list (from a field marked by a diamond)
Ctrl-M	Memorizes a check, invoice, transaction, or report